Angela

This bod

Mums Cousin Priscilla's cousin, who like her fled the invasion of Malaya.

Priscilla Snelling (married name Syme). now lives in Perth.

WAITING FOR THE DURIAN

A Child's Life as a Prisoner of War

Susan J. McCabe

Order this book online at www.trafford.com
or email orders@trafford.com

Most Trafford titles are also available at major online book retailers.

© Copyright 2010 Susan J. McCabe.
All rights reserved. No part of this publication may be reproduced, stored
in a retrieval system, or transmitted, in any form or by any means, electronic,
mechanical, photocopying, recording, or otherwise, without
the written prior permission of the author.

Note for Librarians: A cataloguing record for this book is available from Library
and Archives Canada at www.collectionscanada.ca/amicus/index-e.html

Printed in Victoria, BC, Canada.

ISBN: 978-1-4251-3942-1 (sc)

Trafford rev. 03/24/2010

www.trafford.com

North America & international
toll-free: 1 888 232 4444 (USA & Canada)
phone: 250 383 6864 fax: 812 355 4082

Dedication

*This book is dedicated to the children
who lost their youth in the prison camps
of Indonesia during World War II.*

Acknowledgements

Many individuals participated in the realization of this book. I'd like to thank the 'Gelare' group of friends who have provided valuable suggestions and insight. They are Francine Giguere, Janeen Bradley, Hazel Nicholl, Joanna Foreman, and Marlene Rattigan. Special thanks also to Michele Druart for the many hours and skills she provided teaching me to produce a full body of writing for publication.

No amount of thanks is enough for my special friend, journalist and author Carole Jerome, who gave constant encouragement and many helpful suggestions during the writing, and made invaluable contributions to the final rewrite and copy edit of the manuscript. She has believed as deeply as I that Des Woodford's story had to be told.

Much appreciation also goes to my husband Robert Forbes and our children, Jacqueline, Justine and Brendan for their words of encouragement as well as for the sacrifices they made while their mother devoted much of her time to this very important project.

Finally, I want to express my deep and enduring gratitude to Des Woodford for opening his heart and childhood and for his many letters detailing his painful memories.

Contents

Forward xiii

Chapter 1. Singapore 1
Chapter 2. Waiting for the Enemy 8
Chapter 3. Upheaval 16
Chapter 4. Invasion 25
Chapter 5. The Giang Bee 31
Chapter 6. Refugees at Sea 38
Chapter 7. Attacked Again 47
Chapter 8. Survival at Sea 56
Chapter 9. The Island 64
Chapter 10. The Tappah 69
Chapter 11. Captured 75
Chapter 12. Separation 83
Chapter 13. The Women's Camp 88
Chapter 14. The Men and the Dog 99
Chapter 15. The Sword 107
Chapter 16. Uprooted Again 113
Chapter 17. Ozaki 120
Chapter 18. Life and Death in Prison Camp 130
Chapter 19. Taken from Rosie 138
Chapter 20. The Boys' Voyage 146
Chapter 21. Muntok Jail 154
Chapter 22. The Banker 161

Chapter 23. Work at the Tinwinning 169
Chapter 24. Fighting Back 174
Chapter 25. School 182
Chapter 26. Waiting for the Durian 186
Chapter 27. The Durian Falls 191
Chapter 28. Koefer and Bluey 194
Chapter 29. Training the Chicks 205
Chapter 30. Saving Sonny 212
Chapter 31. Sacrifice by a Young Man 216
Chapter 31. Moving from Muntok 224
Chapter 32. On the Move Again 229
Chapter 33. Leeches and Lovebirds 240
Chapter 34. Coffins for the Resistance 245
Chapter 35. Foraging for Life 249
Chapter 36. The Wrath of the Earth 255
Chapter 37. The Doorway to Death 263
Chapter 38. Bagby 268
Chapter 39. The Hero 277
Chapter 40. The Hospital 281
Chapter 41. Japan Surrenders 288
Chapter 42. Waiting for Rosie 296
Chapter 43. A Surprise Threat 302
Chapter 44. Liberation 311
Chapter 45. Freedom 317

Epilogue: After the War 323

The durian

The durian tree is a lofty bearer of a large spiny fruit that some say looks menacing, smells awful, and tastes even worse. Others say that once the gatherer accepts the pungent smell, it is a gift of nature's bounty, with a taste of nectar. To those who love it the fruit of the durian tree is like Heaven; to those who loathe it the durian is like Hell. Like life, it is a paradox, hiding its treasure in layers of difficult disguise, to be discovered by some, and remain hidden from others.

Forward

Perth, Australia has the most beautiful blue sky I have ever seen. The southern sun displays itself in glory with little haze, cloud or pollution in the atmosphere to mar its striking force. The Canning River waters glint in crystal shards, cutting through the city. It is the Swan River's pretty younger sister, a youngling who grew up to capture the notice of those who dared to settle in such an isolated pocket of the world. Black swans glide gracefully along its current, while kookaburras cackle and mock the parrots overhead. The charm of Perth lives in its naivety and its individuality, borne of isolation.

It is within this idyllic landscape that I first met Des Woodford. He was introduced to me by his wife Jill, with whom I had been friends for the three and a half years I had been living in Australia. What started as a polite enquiry into each other's interests soon drew out a story that both Des and I knew we wanted to recount for readers now and in the future, a story far from our tranquil existence in Perth.

It is difficult to imagine that this calm serene gentleman, a father and husband, well-spoken, and educated at one of Perth's most prestigious boys' schools, spent his most formative years as a prisoner of the Japanese during the Second World War. His ordeal began at the age of ten, when the Japanese invaded Singapore in 1942. As Japanese planes pulverized the city Des and his parents escaped on a refugee ship, only to be cast adrift in a lifeboat when the ship was sunk. Those in the lifeboats were taken prisoner after a failed rescue. Their ordeal had barely begun: almost four years in the torment of prison camps.

Many of these survivors have told of their unspeakable experiences at the hands of their Japanese captors. Their stories have left an indelible impression on the post-war psyche of nations on both sides.

Des Woodford's story is especially poignant because it tells of life as a prisoner, and a survivor, from a child's point of view. Many children lost their innocence within the internment camps of Malaysia and Indonesia, and thousands lost their lives.

I was particularly moved by Des Woodford's story because I had a previous experience dedicated to prisoners in these same camps. For many years I have been singing with The Oriana Women's Choir in Toronto, and in 2002 we performed the music written in Bangka prison camp for women by Margaret Dryburgh, a British prisoner of war who eventually died in captivity in Belelau women's camp. She wrote from memory *a cappella* four-part harmonies of classic works of Beethoven, Handel, and Mozart, and others, as well as popular songs, and taught them to a group of her fellow prisoners. Her story was immortalized in the book *Song of Survival,* by Helen Colijn, another former inmate. It was a deeply moving experience to learn their story and to sing the music these brave women created and performed in captivity to keep their spirits alive. Rosie Woodford was in the same prison camp as the choir for a long period of time, but she was not a singer.

We have generally used only first names, and in some cases have changed names, out of respect for the privacy of some individuals and families who prefer to leave these experiences in the past. In order to make this a vivid, flowing and readable account, I have in places elaborated Des's accounts to me with details and conversations that he may not have remembered literally, but I have stayed true to his memories of events. In some cases, he has remembered the very words spoken, especially with his parents.

I have used the geographical names current at the time, such as Malaya, rather than the present day Malaysia. To avoid confusion, I have called the Japanese heads of the prison camps the Commandant, and the prisoners' own leaders, their Commanders, though they used the title Commandant.

Although Des came close to death on several occasions, his powerful will to live, even as a young boy, prevailed. Now we have finally put into words the story of that child-prisoner. Most of his fellow internees have passed away and the years have dimmed the image of the Japanese sun banner over Singapore. But Des's memory remains as clear as ever, a lingering tribute to the sacrifices of so many who shared his experience.

Perth, 2010

1. SINGAPORE

Bonzo's paws clicked across the wooden floor, then were muffled for a second as he made his way over the mat beside Des's bed. The boy stirred and opened his eyes when the big sturdy dog heaved a human-sounding sigh into his face and tenuously licked at Des's mouth, his whiskers tickling the boy's chin. Des gently batted the dog's snout out of the way, and clambered out of bed from his afternoon nap, Bonzo happily following him, wagging his big tail.

Ah Mah, the tiny Chinese woman who was both nursemaid and housekeeper for his family, entered and stood quietly in front of the door, waiting for Des to notice her. She was about thirty, and a bit plain and serious looking, but Des knew she had a heart of gold, and he adored her, even though he knew part of her job was to report his behaviour to his parents in the evenings.

She spoke rarely, but was aware of everything going on around her.

"Bonzo has a message for you," she said in her quiet way. "Ah Wah waits for you outside. You go out and play now."

Des hopped out of bed. He needed no coaxing from Ah Mah to leave the house and play with her impish daughter Ah Wah, who was eleven, just a year older than he was. He never understood the adults' desire to waste the best part of the day with sweaty sleep. He preferred the unrelenting sun of a Singapore afternoon to tossing and turning in a hot bed.

He went outside with the ever-loyal Bonzo, who loved to gallop around joining in games of tag or hide and seek. At night the devoted dog slept outside, under Des' bedroom window, and would woof when he sensed the boy stirring. After breakfast he would follow Des to school, then go back in the afternoon to get him with one of the servants. Everyone on the street recognized the scruffy brown dog with the dark brown patches on his sides.

Stopping on the porch to put on his shoes, Des set out down the steps to find Ah Wah. The late afternoon had cooled some of the relentless heat that suffocated the midday. Bonzo took off around the corner, returning in a few seconds with the little girl, her shiny black hair flying, the dog panting with delight at his accomplishment.

Very fair-skinned for her race, and with eyes that sparkled with life and mischief, Ah Wah was already growing taller than her tiny mother. For Des, she was like a sister, and his parents treated her like their own child.

She grinned at Des, rubbing her eyes, still puffy from her afternoon nap.

"Bonzo always finds me," she chirped, ruffling the fur on his head.

"Hold him for a minute. Let's see how good he is."

Des dashed behind the house from where Ah Wah had just emerged. Ah Wah held Bonzo in her grasp.

"Find Des! Go get Des! Good boy."

Bonzo's legs found a gallop while he was still held in Ah Wah's arms, kicking wildly at the dirt until she let go. Bonzo raced around the house and barked happily at Des in his hiding place behind the storage shed.

"Hold him for me now!" Ah Wah called as she ran out to the front and onto the property of the empty house next door.

Des held Bonzo, releasing him after a minute or so when he was certain Ah Wah was well hidden. But Bonzo ran off in the other direction, around the side of their own house. Ah Wah stepped out of her hiding place.

"Why's he going down there? I'm over here. Dumb dog," Ah Wah complained.

"He is not dumb," Des retorted, "he just doesn't like you."

Des dashed around to the neighbour's garage, stopping to peer around a corner. While his back was turned, a cat flew into his legs, scaring him, and tripping him into a stumble. Bonzo's bark sounded immediately as he chased the cat across the yard, finally stopping when the cat took cover under the garden hedge. Des was fuming, his heart racing.

"We have to get that darn cat," he panted to Ah Wah.

"What cat?" Ah Wah asked.

"I don't know. I've never seen it before; looks like a stray."

Des had scurried over to Bonzo and grabbed his collar. "Stay away from that flea-bitten thing Bonzo. You don't know where it's been."

The following weekend, Des was out again by himself, scouting around the back of the neighbour's house. On the property a short distance from the house was a deep well, left over from earlier days before most of the houses in the neighbourhood were connected to the city's reservoir. Des looked across the yard and angrily noted the same stray cat, perched on the bricked edge of the well, basking in the sunlight. Its back was to him and it did not move as Des crept closer. The cat's tortoise-shell coat gleamed in the sun's rays, softening its scraggy look. As Des continued to inch closer to the cat, he could see its ears twitch against the onslaught of a hungry fly. Des's foot rustled in the dirt. He froze. The cat's ears came forward in a show of alertness. Des did not move as the cat's senses relaxed, apparently satisfied that there was no threat. When Des was almost upon it, he sprang forward and pushed the cat over the rim and into the well. In triumphant jubilation, he ran back home, pleased with himself for his revenge.

At dinner, Des started to feel uneasy, as he listened to his father Sonny talk about the Japanese advances through China.

"I think you're upsetting Des," his mother Rosie said meaningfully, raising her eyebrows in a sign to her husband to change the subject.

Des was indeed upset but said nothing to his parents about why, content to allow them to believe that talk of the Japanese advances across the Moore Causeway were the reason for his mood. The truth was he was full of remorse and worry for the cat. He had always loved animals, and his bad-tempered action was completely out of character. He remembered one time when he tried to teach the neighbour's cat to swim, thinking it would be a treat. Instead, he got badly scratched on both arms, and learned his first lesson in respecting the habits and feelings of animals. Now maybe he had killed one.

That night Des was unable to sleep.

In the morning, he told Ah Wah about it and the two of them snuck over to the neighbour's backyard to look into the well. When they peered over the side, they discovered the worst. Des half-sobbed as he saw the bloated body floating on the surface while several flies buzzed around it. Des swore Ah Wah to secrecy as they both walked back into their own house, feeling utterly despondent.

As the Japanese advanced, rumours abounded that they intended to poison the reservoirs on their way into Singapore. Des's father gathered the family and servants into the salon.

Sonny Woodford was respected by his family, friends, and staff as a calm, reliable leader. Des adored him. In his mid-thirties, he was almost six feet tall, with a solid build, light olive skin and already thinning brown hair. His eyes showed a disposition that was intense, but kind. Des sat quietly off to one side of the room, trying to keep his distress about the cat from showing on his face.

"You have undoubtedly heard talk of the Japanese movements and their intention to poison Singapore's water supply," Sonny said gravely. "I want you all to rest assured that we will not be affected if this happens as we have a plentiful supply of fresh water from the well next door."

Everyone heaved a sigh of relief, except for Des and Ah Wah who looked at each other long enough to catch the reflection of each other's misery. Another sleepless night ensued and in the morning, both children pledged to dig another well. They would enlist the help of Sami the gardener, who was Des' trusted friend and confidante.

Sami, who looked after the garden and the cars, was in his early twenties, of medium height, very slim, and extremely dark with very white teeth, which were constantly displayed in his happy almost permanent smile. Des loved the way his smile shone in his dark face. Before Sami was born, his parents had come from Madras, in southern India, to work in the rubber plantations in Southern Malaysia, where Sami and his younger brother were eventually educated in a Government English-speaking school.

For Des and Ah Wah, Sami was like a protective big brother. When they showed him the dead cat down the well, he groaned in sympathy.

"It will take a month to dig down to the underground water supply," he said. "It's twenty feet at least."

Des felt sick to his stomach. He had doomed them all to a painfully slow poisoning from water tainted by the cat's rotting corpse.

"Don't worry about it," Sammy offered. "The reservoir will be quite safe, even if I am unable to fish the cat out of the well. Besides," he boasted, "the Indian army is here. They will drive back the Japanese before they have a chance to poison anything!"

Des and Ah Wah slept a little better that night.

2. WAITING FOR THE ENEMY

Des Woodford had been born to his British parents Sonny and Rosie in 1931 in Ipoh, a major tin mining town in Malaysia where his father Sonny worked as a bookkeeper with a stationery company. Like most of their class, they had a big comfortable home and several servants, including Ah Mah. It was the time of the Great Depression, though, and it hit even the relatively insulated life of the colonials. With unemployment rampant, and people willing to work for next to nothing, Des' father had to do two jobs for the wage of one and considered himself lucky, able to provide for his small family.

When Des was four years old, the economy was recovering, and his father surprised him with a Shetland pony, who happily settled in with the family dog they had at the time. Des was delighted as he and the pony and dog played catch and fetch and raced around the huge grounds surrounding the house.

Then it all changed, the first ripple of the dramatic, traumatic changes to come in his young life. When Des was five, Sonny was offered a managerial position with a large English department store in Singapore. For the little boy, it was devastating to be uprooted, and he wailed as he had to leave behind his beloved pets with neighbours and friends. Rosie and Ah Mah tried to keep him busy with all the excitement and distractions of the big bustling city, but it took him a long time to get over the upheaval.

The new Woodford house in Singapore was one of the two-story homes that lined Florence Street, in a quiet neighbourhood of the city. Built solidly from local wood earlier in the twentieth century, it sported a separate garage and the usual servants' quarters – still a normal luxury even for average families in that part of the world - in the back gardens

Inside the home though, it was British through and through. Rosie Woodford saw to that. Linens and crewel work graced the side tables nestled against upholstered armchairs. It was a comfortable homey refuge, warm and inviting, not imposing like the opulent mansions of the wealthier English ex-patriots. Both his parents made it a loving home for their growing boy.

Des thrived, becoming a solidly built child with blonde wavy hair and candid hazel eyes, strong and full of energy. When he wasn't in school, he would spend hours tinkering with anything he could hijack from around the premises.

His father Sonny was happy and jovial with his family, enjoying good food, and a scotch and soda on the verandah at sunset. Des sometimes resented his strict discipline, but deep inside he knew he himself was a bit of a mischief-maker - like the time he got a carpentry set for Christmas and decided to try it out by shortening the legs of the dining room chairs. That earned him a few swipes of the cane from his Dad. (Ah Wah was more upset than Des because she blamed her eagle-eyed mother Ah Mah who had told on him.) Even so, Des knew his Dad was always fair, and tolerated a lot more of his antics than some fathers might. In the evenings, Sonny taught his son a love of reading, and encouraged his curiosity about life. The bond Des felt for his father was deep and strong.

A wooden shim propped open the front door of the house, where Des stood idly as the sun-darkened labourers brought in the never-ending line of crates for their belongings. The terrible shadow of the Japanese advance now loomed over their placid lives, and preparations were under way for another departure, this time under this awful threat. Ten-year-old Des could feel the tension and fear, without fully understanding what it all meant.

Rosie whizzed back and forth with lamps and figurines, packing them, hardly stopping to notice her son as he swung on the timeworn doorknob. Des contemplated his beautiful mother. Rosie Woodford was tall, slim and fair, with curly hair that shone like dark burnished gold in the sun, strong handsome features and deep-set expressive eyes. While Sonny was English, Rosie brought the fire of her Welsh blood to the family, and she sparkled with energy. For Des she was the prettiest mother anyone had. Loving and protective of her son, she was happy and contented with her life. Always well organized, she managed the household servants with discipline, but even the young Des understood her respect for their cultures.

In addition to Ah Mah and Sami, they also had a cook, logically called Cookie, who was remarkably tall for a Chinese, around five foot ten, with devastating good looks and a ready smile. Des regarded this dignified figure with awe.

Rosie had worked professionally as a nurse, and was obsessively particular with her son's diet, since he had a delicate stomach. Though Rosie herself was talented in the kitchen, and her meals were a special treat, Cookie took care of marketing and almost all meals, and was only allowed to make Des basic English fare, no spicy Malaysian or Chinese dishes.

Eighteen months after Des' arrival, while they were still in Ipoh, a baby sister had been born, to the delight of both parents. But their joy was short-lived. After only three months of life, the little girl became seriously ill and died. Des had missed her deep in his small two-year-old heart, feeling an aching hole where he had cradled his love for her.

Rosie lapsed into a nervous breakdown and nearly died of grief, and a nurse cared for her until she eventually recovered, but a shadow of sadness remained. Almost a year later, Des' parents promised him they would have a sister for him in time. Des thought maybe that was why they treated Ah Wah like a pampered daughter. He knew how much they wanted a little girl of their own.

But now he was jerked back to the present.

"You'd better get ready for school," Rosie admonished him mildly

"I don't understand why I have to go to school if we're moving anyway," Des ventured.

His mother wheeled around, a stack of folded linen in her arms.

"Because we don't know exactly when we are leaving, or if we're going at all. They still say the Japanese will never penetrate the British defences over the Causeway. Your father hasn't received his discharge from the Civil Defence department. I have no clue when it will come in. It could be weeks."

She turned to walk away. Instead, Ah Mah took the bedsheets from her and carried them off into the next room. Rosie glanced back at him.

"Go and tell Sami to make sure the De Soto is ready. And tell him Cookie needs his help. Then off you go to school."

"But most of the teachers have left," he argued. "There won't be anything to do."

"Who told you that?" Rosie's eyebrows raised in surprise.

She often had difficulty seeing Des as the strapping ten-year-old he now was. Sometimes he understood far more than she wanted him to. The daughter of a Welshman, Rosie had inherited her own father's stern sense of responsibility, not to mention his occasional flash of temper when met with an injustice or any other obstacle to fairness. She hated the thought of fleeing. She tried to shield Des from the harsher realities of the approaching war, but the futility of this was becoming more apparent with each passing week.

"No one told me. I heard Grannie talking to Auntie Flo."

"Some of them will still be there—and cheeky boys need to go to school."

Rosie turned on her heel and walked to the back of the house and into the kitchen. Des followed her to a doorway that led out to the back garden and servants' quarters and made his way out the back to find Sami, who was in the children's garden picking rambutan fruit. Sami had placed a basket on the ground and was gently laying the rambutans on top of a couple of papayas and a small pile of limes. The limes weren't quite in season but Sami had managed to find a few almost ripe ones near the top of the tree where the sun's power was at its keenest.

"Mum wants to know if the car is clean and ready. Cookie will need your help inside later."

He picked up a papaya from the basket at Sami's feet and started to peel away its leathery skin.

"Please take one from the ground. I have promised these to Cookie," Sami said, taking the fruit and placing it back into the basket. As he did so, Des reached past him and snatched another papaya, running with it back to the kitchen door. Sami's forehead creased in a ridged line but only for an instant. Des smiled back impishly as he peeled the fruit and bit into its sweet aromatic flesh. He could always count on Sami to keep his acts of mischief between the two of them. Their alliance was unshakable and on more than one occasion, this friend had saved Des from a well-earned spanking. Sami walked over to the paw-paw tree and rattled one of the limbs, shaking off another piece of fruit. He picked up the basket and held it out.

"Here, Baba, you can take this to Cookie and come back out to help me."

In a flash Des was in and out of the house again. Now Sami was gathering a few of the garden things into a pile. Des handed him a hoe that was leaning against the fence.

"Here Sami, you'll need this when we get to India."

The stooped figure stopped his work to stare at Des. Sami's expression had lost its usual softness. Instead, the corners of his eyes flinched and he hardened his jaw. He sighed.

"Baba, we are friends, are we not?"

"Yes Sami. Surely, we are the best of friends."

"And you will always remember me."

"Of course, you belong to me. I belong to you." Des dropped his own smile, puzzled at the unaccustomed seriousness.

"And when we are no longer together, you will think of me often. You will keep your memory of me as sharp as it is today."

"But Sami, we will always be together," Des countered. "When I grow up you will come and live with me. We will travel around the world, to England, Australia, America and back to Singapore when the war is over."

"Little Baba, you will grow up, just as you say. You will have adventures just as you say. You will see all of those places and more. But I cannot go with you."

"Why not?" Des's face now matched Sami's expression.

"You will go to India soon, or maybe Australia."

"Yes. And you will come too, of course."

"No, Des, my place is here. My family is here. They need me."

"But I thought we were your family!" Des threw his half-eaten papaya on the ground, ignoring it as it bounced across the yard, stopping against the fence that marked the boundary of the compound. "You belong in India with us, if we go there. You are Indian. You should be happy there."

"My parents were born in Ceylon, but they are Malay now. There is no life for me in India, or anywhere else. I belong here."

"What about the evacuation order? I heard my father and mother talking about it. We must all go."

Sami turned away from Des and wiped his brow with his shirt sleeve. He motioned his young master away. "Please run and get me the old newspapers."

Des was undeterred. He repeated his question, this time with an edge to his voice that caused Sami to turn about to face him directly.

"No Baba. Only you and your family must go—and others like you. When the Indian army arrives, I will stay and fight with them. We will push back the Japanese. We will defend Singapore and liberate Malaya. I will never leave the place where I belong."

Des stared unblinkingly at the man who apart from his father meant more to him than any other man. He then turned abruptly and ran across the yard, past the rear windows of his house. He ran failing to notice the face of Ah Mah rigidly staring out, her eyes fixed on a spot beyond the fence that marked the perimeter of the Woodford's compound. She stared out into the grey horizon of the Singapore sky.

3. UPHEAVAL

Sonny Woodford stepped across the threshold of his front doorway. Des looked up from where he sat on the floor stroking Bonzo's fur, sneaking treats to him. Rosie Woodford heard her husband pad into the lounge and slump into an easy chair. His wife stayed silent, waiting, while he mopped his brow with a handkerchief. The summer sun was hot outside, and without the kindness of any wind to intervene, it released its unhindered force without mercy. At last, Sonny sat up straight, resuming his normal quiet dignity.

"They are on their way now," he said.

He had just put a group of relatives on board the Felix Rousell, one of almost four dozen ships carrying fleeing citizenry and military personnel from Singapore. The Japanese were unstoppable.

Des's mother shook her head, folding her hands in front of her. "How tragic to leave everything behind without as much as a backward glance," she said quietly.

"They may yet see this as the most fortunate day of their lives," Sonny corrected her. "There were many others trying to board the ship too. The officers were turning them all away unless they had the proper documents."

His wife turned her head, concealing the perpetual worry that set her jaw into a firm stance. Her Welsh pride would not permit her to show despair.

"I wish you and Des had gone to," Sonny added, looking at her with anxiety. "If the Japanese make it over the Causeway…" He did not finish his sentence.

"But they say the Japs won't get this far," Rosie countered. "The British will never let them in. And when the Dutch fleet gets here, and the troops from British India, this will all be over."

Sonny sighed. His face wore the outward signs of the burden he carried. His usually upbeat expression had of late given way to a sombre countenance. At thirty-seven years, he was still in his prime, but concerns over war had etched his face. He now appeared careworn and tired.

Sonny's position as air-raid warden put him in touch with some of the junior British officers. The grapevine provided a wealth of information, some authorized and some not, but most of it reliable.

"Perhaps it will be over quickly," he humoured his wife. "But we'll want to be away during the fight. There's no sense sitting right in the middle of the battlefield."

"Please Sonny, I thought we had agreed. We won't go until we can all go together."

Sonny looked toward Des, who still sat with Bonzo, seemingly ignoring his parents' conversation. Both parents remained silent for a moment.

Des buried his face in the ruff on Bonzo's back. He hummed a tune, yawned, did all he could think of to make his parents resume their conversation in front of him. Opportunities to eavesdrop were rare. Finally, Sonny looked back at his wife.

"It will be soon," he said, "very soon."

Later that day, Des invited Ah Wah into his room where the two children began a serious conference. Ah Wah agreed to be custodian of Des's most treasured toys, his stamp albums, and most importantly, Bonzo. Des had her raise her hand and pledge to protect them with her life. Ah Wah nodded her head gravely, her wide dark eyes reflecting the seriousness of her undertaking. Her small hand shook slightly as she made her vow.

"You've made an unbreakable promise," he cautioned. "You have a solemn duty now. Do you understand?"

Ah Wah nodded deeply, bowing her head until Des could only see the shiny top of her black hair. She then gathered up the items and walked from the room. He heard her steps quicken outside his bedroom door as she dashed with his things out of the house and into the privacy of her family's living quarters, where she could get a better look at them.

The next morning, Des woke to find that Bonzo was sick. He had contracted a dangerous infection. For Des, everything else faded in the face of this emergency. Cradling the panting dog in his arms, as he curled up beside him on the floor, Des pleaded with Bonzo to be strong and get better. A vet was called, but in the end, it was too late.

"No! No! Not Bonzo!" Des was inconsolable. At that moment the looming enemy invasion was a distant shadow; losing Bonzo was a sharp and immediate pain, and Des mourned with all his soul. He and Ah Wah cried together, and sat in the garden together, sharing the heartbreak. Sami tried to comfort them, saying Bonzo had had a happy life.

"They just don't live as long as we do," he said, "and it's always hard to say goodbye."

Sonny and Rosie gave him what comfort they could, but they were focused on the serious business at hand. A few days later, Des was at breakfast in the dining room. His mother and Ah Mah were in the kitchen, sorting food items to be added to the provisions they were stashing well away from looters, in the fields of bushland behind the house. Around the table were crates filled carefully by Cookie with silverware and china and heavier glass objects. Des's father entered the room dressed in his light beige summer suit. Although it was early, Sonny already showed signs of discomfort from the day's warmth. His forehead glistened with small beads of moisture that he dabbed with a handkerchief.

"Good morning Des,' he greeted his son, "you're up early."

"I want to get to school early. We have a game to finish. My side is winning."

Still bereaved, Des was trying to carry on his normal life. It was hard to pretend it was normal, without Bonzo trailing happily along with him to school. He had always liked the walk, even with the casuarina trees that lined some of the roads. He'd always disliked them, as their leaves and branches made an eerie whispering sound in the breeze, but he had felt safe with Bonzo. Still, he was determined to finish the game with his friends. It might be their last chance.

"No school today," was the reply, "I have some other tasks for you."

"What tasks?" Des asked.

"I want you to go the storage room and take out the small suitcase, the one you usually use when we go away. You must pack it lightly, with only the most essential items, nothing more. We need to be ready to leave Singapore at a moment's notice.

Des nodded. "Now?" he asked, getting up from the table. He stood still, waiting for his father's word.

"Yes, now. There's a good lad."

Des ran off to the storeroom and returned a short while later dragging the case with him into the dining room. Sonny was just finishing his breakfast. He raised his eyebrows as Des entered the room.

"That was fast. You're very efficient."

"You said to pack lightly. I only have the important things I need."

"Did Ah Mah help you?" his father asked.

"No," Des replied proudly, "I did it myself."

"We'd better see what you have there. Open it up."

Des unlatched the case and pulled back its top. Inside, were a few shorts and shirts, but mostly, the suitcase was crammed with Des's favourite toys, including his football, his precious stamp album, and a small carved wooden top that Sami had made for him.

Sonny Woodford took his son's things and dumped them onto the floor. He handed the empty suitcase to his wife, who was now seated at the table, sipping her tea. She rose and took the case from her husband

"I think he needs some help with his packing," he said, not unkindly. "Put these things back," he said to Des.

He rose from the table and left, leaving Des standing in the dining room beside the jumble of discarded items from his suitcase.

"Don't worry," his mother said, "I know just what you'll need. She picked up the small toy top from the floor and carried it out of the room along with the suitcase. "I'll pack what's important."

After dinner, Des's father gathered all of the servants into the kitchen for the last time. They waited in silence for him to speak. Cookie still wore his apron, covered with stains from the day's meals. Sami had changed into a cleaner shirt, chosen from the meagre selection he possessed. Ah Mah stood next to Rosie Woodford with little Ah Wah wedged in between the two women, her hands touching the skirts of both.

Sonny Woodford did not smile. His face was a chiseled mask, hardened by the disaster and the burden of hope. For weeks, the Japanese had advanced, circumventing The British, whose officers were trained to fight a more traditional enemy. Nothing in their experience had prepared them for the unfamiliar tactics of this enemy, and the terrain they met in Malaya. The Japanese were skilled in the art of war here, and knew well how to undermine the enemy. Sonny's belief that the advancing foe would never be able to cross the Moore Causeway had evaporated as the strafing and shelling of Singapore increased. Now they were at the doorstep and the few remaining British nationals had received their orders to get out. The Woodfords were lucky. They had somewhere to go. Those who were of mixed blood were cursed by the lightness of their skin. Without a tie to any other nation, they would be at the mercy of the Japanese.

The servants stood with sombre faces, respectful of their position amid the disintegration of a social order that some of them must have despised. But as humans, they were connected in their hearts to this family with whom they shared their existence. Not a crack appeared in the veneer of Sonny Woodford's countenance. He did not look directly at them, but seemed to stare at a spot beyond them. He began to speak.

"The time to leave you is nearly upon us. We don't know what will happen when the Japanese arrive. I assume there will be chaos for some time. I daresay you have heard stories of what has been done to the homes of those who have already left. I expect the looters will not make an exception for this house. If they arrive, you are not to defend any of the packing cases from them. The crystal, silver and wedding presents are not worth your lives. You may take whatever you wish from here when we are gone."

Des looked at Ah Wah, his eyes trying desperately to remind her of her sworn vow to defend his possessions with her life. He consoled himself that Bonzo was now safe from the coming storm. His father paused. His brow seemed to tremble and he closed his eyes briefly. When he opened them, they held fast to the faces of his household. He stood more rigidly at attention, bolstering himself,

"All of the food and supplies that have been concealed in the fields and in the roof are yours now. They should hold you for a while. After that, I don't know what will happen. From here on, you must do whatever is appropriate for your survival. Do not stay if it is not safe to do so. It may even be necessary to return to your own *kampongs,* your villages. Hardship is best endured when surrounded by family."

Rosie had moved off to the side of the room, away from the servants. She beckoned for Ah Wah who joined her at her side. Ah Mah smiled slightly as her daughter moved to stand beside their mistress. She gladly shared her only treasure with this woman who had so much. Ah Mah knew that all the china plates and crystal goblets in the world would never fill the gaping wound in Rosie Woodford's heart. Only Ah Wah could replace a fraction of the joy that had died along with the gentle soul of the baby girl that Ma'am had cherished and nurtured for nearly two years.

Sonny Woodford's voice continued. "I am leaving you each with six month's wages. Do not keep it with you. Find a safe place in the bushland and bury it. Make certain you are not seen." He then smiled slightly, retreating into irony tinged with faint hope. "This conflict may resolve itself in a few weeks. I may want an accounting when I get back."

Sami nodded, but stayed silent.

Sonny continued. "I want to say what a privilege it has been having all of you in our household. We shall endeavour to write when we are settled in our new home and the war is over. You will be in our prayers as you try to adjust to your times ahead under Japanese occupation.

We will think of you often and hope that you can overcome any hardships that come your way."

Des sat listening. He did not move as the servants left the room, but sat holding his position in the dining room on one of the chairs. The shells and gunfire in the distance did not move him from his posture. It was the guiding hand of Ah Mah that finally coaxed him away and into the bomb shelter with his parents and the other servants.

4. INVASION

The bomb shelter was eerily silent. No one huddled there made a sound. Outside, explosions of Japanese artillery pierced the air. Des felt as though the Japanese were banging on the door of their refuge. He plugged his ears against the thunderous noise. Des and Ah Wah huddled against the wall of the shelter while the grown-ups urgently discussed their plans for the next day. Each whistling scream of an artillery shell sliced the air heralding a spit second of silence before the deafening boom of an explosion.

The following morning brought no rest. Des's father left the shelter, venturing into the intermittent sounds that had kept their hearts pounding through the night. At three in the afternoon, Sonny Woodford returned with the news that he had finally received his clearance papers to evacuate. They were to leave immediately for the docks to board HMS Giang Bee.

The adults hurried to retrieve the family's suitcases from the house. Rosie hugged Ah Mah as both women burst into tears. The mood was infectious and soon everyone was crying and hugging one another. Ah Wah extended her arms toward Rosie. She held onto her waist in a death grip, refusing to let go when Ah Mah tried to coax her away. Rosie placed her arms around Ah Wah and buried her face in the little girl's black silken hair.

They gathered in the driveway. Sami and Sonny placed the bags into the boot of the car. Sami stood still, tears falling freely down his sun-darkened face, as Des stood before him as if rooted to his home, unable to tear himself away. Then without a word, Sami scooped Des into his arms and carried him to the car. Rosie and Sonny climbed into their DeSoto for the last time and the car's motor idled while the three Woodfords settled inside.

"I will accompany you to the docks," Sami offered. "You will need help to board the ship with your baggage."

Sonny's face strained with emotion as he waved Sami away. "No. You mustn't. It's too dangerous."

"But Sir," Sami argued, in uncharacteristic contradiction of his employer's advice, "I will be fine. They will not be after me and I know enough to find shelter if the shelling should begin again."

Des's father was adamant. "No, Sami," he said firmly, "I won't risk it. The British forces have set up too many roadblocks already. It may not be possible for you to return. We'll be fine."

The Woodford family sped off down Florence Street. Des took one long last look at his house and driveway, imprinting the last image of his home in Singapore into his memory. Ah Wah stood like a statue, growing smaller with distance. The tear-streaked faces of Ah Mah, Cookie, Ah Wah and Sami all stared out from the front yard of Des's house—his life, his history. The picture was etched on his mind forever. A single small suitcase and his memories were all Des would have from his childhood home.

Sonny Woodford drove at a reckless speed, going against his lifelong habit of rigidly obeying all laws and regulations. He was waved through at the roadblocks by guards who were aware of the pressing urgency for all British civilians to escape Singapore. All was chaos. Air raid sirens sounded frequently, followed by blasts of exploding shells. Des could see that his father was torn between habitual obedience to the directions of the air raid warnings and a compelling urge to press on for the docks. If they stopped, abandoning the car to take cover, their vehicle was a sitting target. Escape would be harder. If they continued to make a dash for it, they could find themselves driving straight into enemy fire. Des trembled, taut with anxiety.

Another siren screamed its warning. Sonny stopped the car and ordered Des and his mother out. But they sat frozen in their fear as several detonations pierced the smoky air. The normal musty sweetness of the Singapore streets was now replaced by the acrid odour of explosives and burning ruins. Japanese fighter planes continually flew in low, strafing their targets. Des clung to his mother in the back seat, cringing at the terrible percussive sounds that seemed to penetrate his quaking body. Changing gear, Sonny sped on, ignoring the wailing alarms.

The Japanese were masters of the sky now. Sonny's foot pressed heavily on the floor pedal, carrying his family to an uncertain safety. Rosie Woodford prayed that their ship, the Giang Bee, would still be floating when they arrived at the docks.

As they raced through the battered city towards the harbour, Des suddenly called out in a high-pitched shout, "I see the docks!"

His father gunned the motor and sped even faster down the artery that led to their salvation. The streets were heavier now with commotion as people fled for their lives. Ahead of them, a rumbling sound stirred in the sky, growing louder by the second. People in the streets scattered wildly, ducking into doorways and stalls. Des watched in horror as a Japanese plane swooped down towards them, head on. Sunny slammed on the brakes.

"Take cover in the ditch!" he screamed over the roaring motor of the enemy aircraft. Des and his mother rolled out of the car, into the long grasses of the muddy roadside. Des's knees scraped heavily against the ground sending a dim message of pain to his panicked brain. Adrenalin pounded his blood through his veins, pushing the pain away as he thought only of the docks ahead. The plane came in lower. Sonny Woodford sat frozen behind the wheel staring in awe as the attacker came closer and closer. He could make out the details of the propeller and the artistic markings painted on its hull. The plane was beautiful, sleek and graceful and Sonny knew it could perform its task with lethal precision. When the plane was upon them, it skimmed over the Woodford's car, its guns eerily silent as if boasting its power to display small mercies. The engine's roar receded as quickly as it had thundered upon them, leaving Rosie and Des lying crumpled and dirty in the ditch.

"What happened? Why didn't he...?" Rosie stammered.

Sonny, who had climbed out of the car to help his family, interrupted his wife, reminding her of Des's presence with his eyes.

"He must have been looking for another target; maybe he was out of ammunition. Hurry, we mustn't slow down now." He hurriedly ushered them back into the front seat.

Rosie's fine travel clothes were now dishevelled and dirty. Her legs and arms were covered with mud and her handbag's strap had torn, requiring her to carry it clutched in her hand. She held it tightly, as it was filled with the large sum of money she had stuffed inside. They rode the rest of the way in complete silence, shocked by their close call.

At last they arrived at the entrance to the docks. British troops guarded the main gate from the hundreds of desperate people of all races and nationalities trying to board the last of the ships stationed in the harbour. Only people with written authorization were permitted to enter. Des and his parents made their way to the front of the crowd and waited while an officer checked his father's evacuation papers. Sonny carried his wife's suitcase as well as his own, leaving her to cling with both hands to her bag, while its broken strap dangled jaggedly from one end. Rosie did her best to wipe off the drying mud streaks from their clothing. Her futile attempts to protect her dignity in the midst of a disintegrating order seemed hollow gestures now. Their rescue loomed a short distance away, in the form of HMS Giang Bee. It was a battered Chinese-owned coastal steamer, converted by the British for naval use. Reaching it now and sailing into safer waters was the only goal that mattered.

5. THE GIANG BEE

Smoke and sweat mingled together in a heady mix that clouded Des's senses. He squinted against the confusion and surveyed the chaos. Elegance and brutality danced side by side, tangoing in tandem. In the frantic scene of terrified people fleeing for their lives, beautiful expensive cars sat abandoned near the docks, some with doors still opened as if inviting anyone to step into their opulent interiors to another world. People milled about in their finery. Overhead, enemy planes still flew in to attack, dropping their payload on the stricken city.

Des took it all in. The faces of the evacuees showed plainly the fear and desperation he felt too, but tried not to express. Open suitcases spilling their contents were abandoned as passengers repacked their belongings into fewer bags in a frenzied rush. They had been ordered to take only one per family. Sonny put down their suitcases.

"We must repack as much as we can into this one," he said, indicating the larger one. "I'll carry it. Des you stay with your mother. Don't let go of her hand."

Within a minute, most of Des's clothes were removed from his small suitcase and rearranged in the larger bag. Rosie's favourite dresses lay where they were tossed, as well as several of Sonny's shirts and all of Des's small treasures. Out went the treasured wooden top that Sami had made for him, enhancing Des's panic. Rosie had included it, knowing its sentimental importance. But now it was no use protesting. Although nothing in his young life could have prepared him for a day such as this, something from deep inside Des told him that silent obedience was best.

The repacking was barely completed when a British naval officer summoned Sonny over. Together the family scrambled over to where he was standing, grateful to find a semblance of authority in all the chaos.

You must hurry! Get aboard the launch," the officer said, beckoning toward the water where several launches were floating among the other small vessels and junks belonging to the locals.

Obeying, the Woodfords went to the edge of the dock and gazed down a steep set of cement steps. The ocean had receded for low tide, displaying its sub-marine finery. Seaweed and shells clung to the sides of the exposed face of the wall. Small launches huddled low in the water at various stages of their journeys to and fro, ferrying the fleeing civilians to the ships. Further out was the the Giang Bee, waiting for those lucky enough to board her.

As he gazed down the dizzying steps, Des's heart pounded and he grew short of breath. Beneath him, the steps seemed to move of their own accord, waving and blurring in and out of focus. He had known this feeling before. Once, he had climbed onto the roof of a friend's house to see how far he could see. Together he and his friend, Luke, had moved close to the edge of the eaves. Des had faltered, but was goaded on by Luke. When he was perched at the edge, he had looked down onto the pavement below only to see it move and glide before his eyes. He had fought to retain his balance but was unable to clear his head of the roaring in his ears that increased with each second until he had stepped backward and sat down.

Now this familiar fear welled up inside him once more, threatening to betray the quiet calmness he so desperately tried to show. He was powerless against it and grabbed his father's hand tightly. Des could see that his mother was also very nervous of the long steep climb down to the launches, her nerves frayed by the ordeal. Any snag in the journey was another opportunity for panic.

Des clung to Sonny as they descended, step by step, until finally they reached the launch and climbed in with about thirty other passengers. He had made it. Rosie was shaking as she clambered in. As the boat set off toward the Giang Bee, Des watched as they passed the many small craft still anchored in the inner harbour. Once they were out past the breakwater, they all gazed back at the coast of Singapore.

The seemingly peaceful sight of the many harbour boats floating into their day's end settled in front of the Singapore skyline. Its many fruit trees, casuarinas and palms contrasted sharply with the smoky haze of the sky above, where enemy aircraft still scudded across the beleaguered city, dropping their deadly cargo. Explosions rocked the late afternoon, setting ablaze homes, offices and factories. Soon, as darkness fell, the sky would be alight with shining flames reaching their fiery fingers upward—Hell ascending to the gates of Heaven, emboldened by its triumph over Singapore.

Des's head filled with pictures. They paraded across the landscape of his mind like an album of memories, flooding him with despair. Back there in the smoking devastation of Singapore were his neighbours and friends. He shuddered as he thought of his extended family of servants, of his friend Ah Wah, all left to face the enemy. How could they survive? From what he had seen, the Japanese were intent on crushing all life out of the city. No one was safe.

The launch was nearly up to the side of the Giang Bee. The towering sides of her hull dwarfed the small craft below. They were close enough now to hear the waves of the sea lapping loudly against the ship. Des stared over the side of the launch at the deep, dark waters. He held tightly onto his father, wishing that he had learned to swim, trying to think clearly through the waves of his own fear.

Rosie, who had been silent for some time, raised her eyes up at the looming vessel. Her jaw slackened and opened slowly, displaying an expression of dread.

"Oh Heavens, Sonny, look at where we must go!" She gestured toward a frighteningly steep gangway. It was a set of narrow metal steps that clung to the side of the hull, bobbing and dipping with the waves. It's railing looked too fragile to give any support.

Des too, looked up. At that angle, right alongside, the ship seemed to reach up to the sky. Craning his neck, he could see the smoke stacks and a crowsnest high above him. The angle of their ascent was impossibly steep. Involuntarily, he shrank back.

"Come on," Sonny said, "I'll take your hand."

He stood up in the launch and reached for Des who cowered back, both hands secured behind his back away from his father's grasp.

"I can't," he said, "I'll fall off."

"Nonsense," His father answered, in a reassuring tone. "If you like, I'll carry you."

"No Daddy, please. I can't go up the steps. Not even if you carry me." Des's voice rose in panic.

"It's a cinch," his father countered, smiling. His voice was steady.

Des studied his father's eyes for any telltale sign of doubt. Sonny's gaze remained steady, betraying nothing. Des let his hands fall to his side from behind his back.

"Close your eyes," Sonny said. He lifted Des into his arms.

Rosie followed her husband and her son, clutching the slender railing with one hand, mustering enough strength to carry their only suitcase in the other, which for now held her purse with the money as well. When she reached the first step, she rested the bag for a moment and removed her shoes. As they progressed upward, Des held his eyes tightly shut. Sonny's constant stream of encouragement bolstered him.

"This is easy," Sonny said, "very safe."

"Are we at the top yet?" Des asked.

"Just keep your eyes closed," his father answered, "it won't be long now. You're doing well. There's a brave lad."

The mount seemed endless. "Are we close yet?"

"Almost."

"Tell me when we're close."

"I will. Just four more steps, maybe five."

Des could hear his mother's breath as she puffed under her heavy load. He opened his eyes to a mere slit. The vista before him swallowed up his fear, and as he opened his eyes fully, he was transfixed by the sight of a bustling deck of crewmen and sailors weaving busily among the hapless evacuees. Beyond them was the open sea, its slightly arced horizon dangling over it in resplendence. Behind, lay Singapore, made part of their past by one short boat ride. He saw his mother struggling behind them, harried and winded with the effort of carrying the suitcase. Her face held a frozen grimace of determination as she stumbled up, placing one stockinged foot in front of the other, her blond curls limp and dirty from all the smoke and sweat of the past moments. She glanced up and caught her son's eyes staring down at her from his father's arms. Like a flower, her face unfolded and spread itself into a smile—a mother's smile—reserved for no one else but her child. At that instant, Des thought her the greatest and bravest mother in the world.

Once on deck, the Woodfords were intercepted by a British officer, and asked to show their evacuation orders. Sonny retrieved them from his inside breast pocket and handed them over.

"This fellow will take you to your quarters," the officer grunted, motioning to a crewmember nearby. "He'll see you're issued lifejackets. Wear them at all times."

The Woodfords donned the cumbersome lifejackets and followed the crewman to a lower deck. Sonny now carried the family's suitcase as Rosie guided Des down the corridors of the ship. When they reached their quarters, Rosie was horrified to see that what she had hoped would be at least a small room with a couple of berths, was in fact a small area of bare floor space of wooden decking. This decking had been laid across the cargo hold to provide room for as many evacuees as possible. They made their way slowly through the dense crowd of people sitting on the floor, to find a spot to wedge themselves in. Suitcases were emptied of their contents to provide some softness against the hard surface of the floor. Des was struck by the expressionless faces of the other passengers. The silence around them all was almost total and they stared blankly into the dimness of the ship. Many had left their husbands and other close relatives behind. Des could not fathom why they seemed so calm, almost at peace. He settled on the floor with his parents. Within a few minutes, the Woodfords also were silent and calm. There was nothing else they could do. Their fate was now out of their hands.

6. REFUGEES AT SEA

Des felt a slight cramping as his folded legs cushioned the stiffness of the wooden boards beneath him. He changed his posture to find some comfort. Blank faces stared in every direction, their voices silenced by disbelief and trauma. Des looked up at his father, who now seemed preoccupied with scanning the crowd for a familiar form. After a moment he looked down, his eyes betraying no disappointment. Seconds later, the rumbling and clanking of chains, followed by an enormous shudder that shook Des to his heart's core, signaled the raising of the anchor.

The ship lurched. Sonny Woodford steadied his son with a firm hand, holding him close as they rolled slightly with the ship. Rosie sat quietly nestled against Des's other side, content with the warmth of her son's form against her body. Her mind was on everyone left behind - Ah Wah, Ah Mah, Sami, and Cookie. She allowed her thoughts to momentarily drift to her beloved possessions – the wedding gifts she and Ah Mah had worked so hard to polish and care for, and eventually to pack and crate. They would all be gone soon, seized by looters from the protective grasp of Sami and Cookie who had been instructed not to imperil themselves defending it all. She surprised herself at how little emotion she felt at their loss. Her handbag with its broken strap lay on her lap. In it was all the cash her husband could reserve after paying six months' wages to his household. Their only suitcase, filled with all they now owned, rested neatly in front of them. Although small, it loomed largely as a symbol of all that was material in their lives. They had nothing, really. Yet with her son and husband close beside her aboard the groaning planks of the Giang Bee's decking, she knew she had everything.

Sonny watched his wife's face. Her eyes were staring off distantly like the others. "The guns from the shore are quiet now," he stated. "Perhaps it would be a good idea to take Des up on deck and acquaint him with the ship."

Rosie nodded eagerly. "Yes," she said, even now able to take advantage of an opportunity to broaden her son's understanding of the world. "Who knows when we'll have a chance like this again—to see an armed navy boat up so close."

"I don't think this was always meant to be a navy ship. I believe it may have been pressed into service because of the war."

"You mean it can't protect us from the Japs?" Des interjected, worried.

"Not at all," his father countered. "I'm sure it's well equipped to do battle. Only it shouldn't be necessary.

We're out of range of the guns from the shore, and enemy planes wouldn't dare attack us from above while we're moving. The ship's guns would shoot them out of the sky before they ever got a proper bead on us. I'll show you now."

Sonny took Des by the hand and led him up on deck. They emerged into the early evening's glow at the stern of the ship and climbed to the top deck where several of the crew members were busily tending to their duties. Des noted the tension in their faces, but remained silent.

"Look at that," said Sonny, pointing upward at a single anti-aircraft gun. It was manned by a few crewmen in life jackets and tin hats. He pulled Des closer and guided his gaze up toward the men who were also looking upward at the skies.

"What are they looking at?" Des inquired, scanning the empty horizon for the object of their attention.

"Enemy planes. As long as they are on duty, they must always be looking up."

"Even at night?" Des asked.

"Yes, but the Japs won't come at night. With all of our ship's lights out, we'd spot them, or at least hear them first. They'd be shot out of the sky before they ever knew what hit them."

Des smiled, reassured. Rosie shuddered and grimaced at Sonny, knowing the defenses were utterly inadequate. They strolled around the ship as the sun ascended, casting incandescent warmth across the steely blue features of the Giang Bee.

"Perhaps we should eat something," mused Sonny out loud. "I'll find the galley and see what I can muster up for tea. You need to promise to wait here like a good boy. Do not leave your mother's side for any reason. I'll be back as soon as I can."

Sonny was back a short time later with a tray of sandwiches and a flask of Ovaltine. Des brightened at the sight of the Ovaltine, but somehow he did not feel hungry for anything else.

As if reading his mind, Rosie interjected, "Sonny, I don't think either of us feels much like eating at the moment. Perhaps later…"

"There may not be a chance later."

Des had not often heard his father speak so sternly.

"You must both eat. Force yourselves, if necessary. We can't be certain if any more food will be available later." He looked at Rosie and added, "under the circumstances."

Rosie looked back up at the crewmen and their solitary anti-aircraft gun. They continued their task, always looking upward, oblivious to the Woodfords below. She picked up a sandwich and handed it to her son.

"Come now, Des. You heard your father. I'll feel better knowing you have something in your stomach. So will you."

As he bit into the sandwich, Des heard a short volley of shots in the distance. Immediately, the crewmen above twisted their gun in search of a target.

Rosie stopped chewing her sandwich. Her face drained of colour.

"Sonny," she said, "I think I'd feel safer for all of us if we went to a lower deck."

Des squinted into the sun, wishing it downward, into the waters of the sea, wishing it into the darkness of night. Night would bring refuge from the worrying face of his mother. Neither would he see the fear masked in the reassuring stance of his father. The sun hung in space, an amber beacon keeping the perpetual day from its rest. He wanted to close his eyes, to sleep safely away from everything, his mother and father both at his side. But this day was interminable. Within it, his world had changed forever.

Sonny ushered Rosie and Des to the steep stairway where they proceeded down to the next lower deck. It was sheltered here. They walked along the roofed deck, sipping on their Ovaltine, as they watched the other evacuees milling about. For a moment, Des could almost forget his fear and imagine that he was on his way to some longed-for holiday retreat with his parents. His stomach was full and the noise of the Japanese shells had faded in his memory. Time and distance from the fighting allowed fatigue to creep upon him.

The silence of the early morning had given way to low slumberous voices rousing to the threats of a new day. Des got up and stretched his legs, and as usual eavesdropped on conversations around him. He heard one man telling his wife that the enemy bombers were buzzing overhead. Then he heard the menacing engines himself, and turned to cling to his parents.

In a desperate attempt to save his passengers, the captain ordered all military personnel to throw their weapons into the sea, and had the women and children stand on the deck, showing that this was a refugee ship, even though the Japanese had shown no sign of caring who they killed. The response was a bomber headed straight for them. The passengers scattered to the lower decks, then Des heard the shuddering boom of an explosion. His heart sank, and a trembling sickness spread over him. Some people screamed, but others addressed their fear by remaining quiet. Soon, word spread that the ship had not been hit. The planes returned again and again, but usually missed their target as their bombs dove into the surrounding waters. Finally one scored a direct hit that exploded against a derrick on the upper deck. The crew hurried to put out the fire.

With each attack, the Giang Bee's hull held fast. Occasionally, a plane would fly in low enough to strafe the surface of the deck, darting speedily out of the way in time to avoid the ship's lone gun. Minutes passed like hours. Des stayed close to his parents, afraid to leave their sight, lest they disappear forever. Rosie sat silent much of the time, jarred into visible fear with each explosion. The silences in between were fraught with sickening apprehension. Somehow, Sonny managed to scrounge up something to eat from the galley, grateful for the blessing that still held it in one piece. The small snack held Des through the afternoon. He passed the time stealing glimpses of the other passengers who milled about, drifting through one another in zigzagging paces to ward off their desperation.

He wasn't sure whether he knew just when he was jolted back into the stomach-churning reality of his circumstances. His father was pulling him close even before he was aware of the deafening explosion. The deck shook beneath his feet, sending a shudder up his legs and into his spine. He felt an electric shock course through his veins. A thunderous roar growled in his ears. The entire ship quaked. Water pipes overhead burst apart, gushing their crystal spray everywhere. Its force was painful, cutting into the bare skin of Des's legs. He cried out in pain. Others too, were running for cover as ear-crushing sounds cut through the air: the snapping of breaking wood, the shriek of torn metal, and the shattering of glass could be heard above the roar of the gushing water. Ahead, the Woodfords could hear shouting and screaming from the passengers. Rosie and Sonny held Des steady against the ship's wall, both of them soaked from the spray and the rapidly flooding floor. As Des watched the gushing pipes, he imagined the flow continuing until it flooded the deck. Soon the entire ship would fill with water. He began to panic.

"Daddy, there's too much water. Are we going to sink?"

His father looked blankly at him, not registering the question through his own shock. Des repeated his question. This time, Sonny smiled through his own concerns.

"What son? You mean because of all this spray?"

"Yes. Please can't they shut it off before the ship fills up?" Des's voice was shaking now.

"Yes Des, they can shut off the main valve I suppose, but even if they couldn't, there wouldn't possibly be enough water to sink the ship. It's all on board already, in the storage tanks. It's just spilling onto the floors now. It will stop in a moment, you'll see. Besides, these ships have bilge pumps, if they take water on, they can easily get rid of it."

Des's heart slowed its hammering inside his chest wall. The sandwich he had just finished a few minutes earlier no longer felt as if it was fighting its way back into his throat. Still, he felt it, like a leaden clump inside his stomach. The moment of tranquility he had almost felt earlier was forgotten. He had let his fear subside for an instant and danger had seized that very moment to reassert itself. He fought back tears.

"We would have been safer at home," Des complained to his mother.

Rosie said nothing in response, but stared ahead into the crowd. After awhile the noise subsided and the family made their way back to the deck where they had left their suitcase. As they rounded a corner, Des cried out.

"What's this on the floor, Mum? It looks like blood!"

"Someone has been injured," Sonny said as calmly as he could. "Try not to step in it."

Rosie had set her jaw firmly, her brow furrowed in an expression she had taken on since the explosion. As they neared the place where they had left their suitcase, they stopped in shock. The floor was gone. In its place was a gaping hole. The people who had been there had all vanished into the bottom of the ship, suitcases and other bundles falling with them. Des had a second to peer over the side before his mother pulled him back. She too had looked down into the hold at the jumble of bodies at the bottom. Rosie's gasp was cut off abruptly by her shock. Her face whitened and she began to shake. Seeing his mother so upset, Des fought back the urge to cry.

As crewmen and some refugees and soldiers frantically tried to find ways to rescue any survivors, he stood in a horrified daze. Des heard one man tell Sonny that if the ship could survive the daylight hours, they would probably be able to escape during the night and be out of the range of the Japanese bombers by morning.

Sonny turned to Rosie and Des. "Come with me, we need to find a safer spot," he said.

"If such a thing exists," added Rosie, forgetting to mince her words for Des's sake.

"We'll try the other side of the ship." Sonny circled his arm around his wife and led her along the corridors to another decked area similar to where they had been before. Des followed, sticking closely to his father's other side.

No one said a word as they finally found a space on the decking in an undamaged area. By now, the noise and commotion of the explosion had subsided. all was silent, except for the steady rolling of the engines, and the distant low moans of those few who were still alive after plummeting into the hold. Rescuers were still trying to save them. The people on board were either sitting, or meandering aimlessly, wordlessly, in the aftermath of the traumatic attack. As the sun cut into the horizon, Des settled into a hushed restiveness. Outside, night was casting its shading pall over the ship and her occupants, cloaking them from the perilous daylight. As he drifted off to sleep that night, Des heard the echo of the man's voice as it spoke to his father. *"…if we can survive the daylight."*

7. ATTACKED AGAIN

The morning failed to bring any relief to Des's fears. He had slept through the night, undisturbed by hunger, grateful for having been required to eat something the night before. His stomach was empty now, but the pains he felt were not those of a body in need of nourishment. They were due to the twisting grip of his desperate anxiety. He wiped the sleep from his eyes and stared out among the other passengers. He missed his own room. This was the time of day when Bonzo used to come to greet him, wagging his tail and smiling his familiar Bonzo grin with jaws open and tongue hanging lazily out of his mouth. Des's heart ached for all that was familiar. He had always been able to confide in Sami at such times, But Sami was gone too. Yesterday's bolstering touch of his parents was now insufficient to wipe away the flood of thoughts that poured through his mind in torrents of painful regrets.

Dusk was drifting into the light of day. "Can we go up on deck again?" Des asked, anxious to find some diversion.

"No," both parents sang out in unison.

A man sporting a bushy brown moustache was speaking. "It's mayhem up there. The Japs keep trying to hit us with those flimsy light aircraft. They aren't hitting much."

A second older Dutchman in a light grey suit joined in. "All they did was attract a couple of our Hudson airplanes. I was up on deck earlier and saw them. They shot at the bastards but couldn't get them—just made them madder. You just wait. The Japs will be back, only this time, you can be certain they'll get us."

The first man scoffed. "They can't carry anything much heavier than they've already been using. Their planes are too rickety."

"It isn't planes they'll be sending. It'll be a warship," quipped his companion, snuffing out a cigarette butt under his shoe.

Sonny, who had been silently listening to the others, glanced aside and noticed his son. Des caught his father's eye and tried to appear not to be listening by scanning the people milling on the lower deck, but it was too late. Sonny left the group and was joined by Rosie. The two of them guided him upstairs to the outside deck. It was now mid afternoon and time to think once more about how they were going to obtain their next meal. As they emerged into the daylight, Des saw several ships in the distance. His parents froze in their footsteps. They were Japanese destroyers.

Immediately, Des heard some commotion. Several men approached. He recognized two of them from their earlier conversation with his father.

"There's a cruiser on fire out there," one of them said.

"And four Japanese destroyers. We've been ordered to stop," another added.

Des immediately cocked his ear and pretended to occupy himself with something on the floor. The men took no notice of him.

"They've fired upon us. Just a shot. Maybe they mean us no harm. They could have sunk us, if they wanted," the same man added.

Des's father shook his head. "Perhaps they want to capture the ship intact."

Des felt as though his heart was beating in his throat. If this were true, then what was to happen to them? He remained silent, wanting to pester the men with a thousand questions, but wishing more to remain where they wouldn't notice him eavesdropping.

The group of men continued speculating for another moment, when a small thin man whom Des did not recognize joined them. He was breathless.

"I was just above. The Japs had two cruisers and four destroyers up there. They all left except for the one destroyer that tried to send one of its launches over to board us, maybe to negotiate a safe surrender. Then one of the Dutch planes dive bombed it and got in a couple of good shots."

"Thank heavens," Des whispered under his breath

"No, that Dutch plane did us no favours," said another passenger. "There will be no safe surrender now. That was our last chance."

"Bloody Dutch planes," Sonny said.

"But Dad, "Des corrected him, "don't you mean bloody Jap planes?"

"Shh," Rosie said, putting her arm around him, holding him close.

The bombers returned, and joined the destroyer in attacking the ship without mercy. With each explosion the Giang Bee listed further to her side. Fires broke out, and finally it was clear that the ship was doomed. They could see lights flashing as the Giang Bee exchanged signals with the enemy destroyer. Sonny looked at the time. It was after seven. A cracking of the loud speaker followed by the unwavering voice of a naval officer, gave a final order to the Giang Bee's passengers.

"We are under the control of the Japanese navy warship off port bow. All women and children are to take to the lifeboats immediately. All men are to remain on board with the exception of those family men who have been instructed to man the oars."

Rosie Woodford stared aghast at her husband, sick with the realization that Sonny had not been asked to man the oars.

"Let's get you two up to the lifeboats right away," Sonny ordered briskly. "There'll be a rush to get seats."

"What about you Dad?" Des howled. "Mum, where will Dad go?"

Both Rosie and Sonny tried to act calmly for their distraught son. "I expect the men will stay on board here to be escorted somewhere else," Rosie said distractedly, but trying to hide her panic from her son.

"I want him to come with us," Des wailed.

"I'll catch up with you and your mother later," Sonny reassured him. "You be a good lad and do what she tells you."

They approached the nearest lifeboat on the port side. Des could see the Japanese warship floating silent and ominous now on the still sea. It filled him with the dread of all the worst nightmares of his young life. He tried not to look at it as they made their way into the panicked crowd that huddled about the lifeboat in the smoke and chaos as the Giang Bee's metal body groaned and shrieked in its death throes. A ship's officer was standing by directing the women and children into the boat. He waved the Woodfords past.

"Go to the next boat," he ordered. "This one will hold no more."

They headed to another, and another, only to be told the same thing. With each refusal, their dash to the next boat became more urgent. The fourth and last lifeboat offered their only chance to leave the ship. Des eyed the craft in the fading light. It was completely full. Some of the ship's officers were pointing and telling people to move. Des and his mother waited numbly, as hope ran out for a seat on the last remaining lifeboat. Families embraced before being separated, a momentary attempt to hang onto futile hopes of staying together. At last, even though the boat's fifty-two person capacity was more than full, the ship's officer waved the two of them on board. Sonny helped his wife into the lifeboat first. They exchanged agonizing looks that spoke of immeasurable love and loss. Then she stretched out her hand to support Des, who scrambled in easily. Sonny Woodford leaned over the rail to give his son a last fierce embrace before the boat was to be lowered into the water, leaving him with the other men to face death on the Giang Bee. Even if by a miracle they survived, the Japanese, they knew, would have no mercy for any passengers. Des held on to his father's shoulders with desperation, locking Sonny in as tight a grip as his ten year old hands could manage. The deck hands were turning their attention to the ropes for lowering the boat. Des thought he felt his father's hold on him loosen in preparation for letting go.

"Dad!" he screamed. "Dad!"

The officer in charge scanned the people in the lifeboat, resting his eyes on Des's father as he leaned over his son from the deck.

"We need rowers," he said to no one in particular, but Des heard. Galvanized with hope, Des pulled his father into the boat and squeezed over to make space. Breathing heavily with the effort and flooded with relief, he nestled against his parents in the crowded lifeboat for a moment. Then Sonny moved to take his place at the oars. Des stared in a daze at his own bare knees, golden in the twilight, as the sun's aura darkened to pale orange. With a small jerk, the lifeboat descended.

The other lifeboats were also very full. As they hit the water, fountains of liquid came gushing up from the bottom and sides. To everyone's horror, they saw the hulls of several lifeboats, including the one carrying the Woodfords, had been strafed by machine gunfire from the attacking planes, an effort by the Japanese to make escape impossible. Des sat silently listening to the gasps of the women in his boat. Shocked screams could be heard from the other boats as the women and children aboard realized they would perish in the salty water. Another lifeboat, not fully lowered, was shot through one of its ropes, and the lifeboat tipped, spilling its human cargo into the sea. Even now, the Japanese were sporadically attacking.

The remaining lifeboats were rowing away from the ship while the passengers frantically stuffed the bullet holes with anything handy. Handkerchiefs, socks, shirts, anything on hand, was used to plug the holes and prevent the boats from taking on water faster than they could be bailed. There were frantic screams as some slowly sank into the sea, taking many of the refugees under the waves, leaving others thrashing in the water. Des watched in horror. His own boat now floated so low in the water it was in danger of sinking along with the others.

"Throw all weighted objects over the side!" a crewman on board bellowed. Every lifeboat had a few ship's crew on board to assist with the rowing and help the women and children. Handbags, wallets, keepsakes and jewelry went overboard. Des was told to remove his shoes as well. He pitched them over the side, sinking his feet into the water-filled bottom. The edges of the boat were perilously close to the water. Des heard some of the men speaking. Luckily for all aboard, two of the ship's engineers had been assigned to Des's boat, and they knew what to do. They called out to the others who were frantically bailing against the rising water level inside the boat.

"We have to go over and plug the holes from underneath. The others have sunk because they tried to plug the leaks from the top. The water pressure from below is too great. The plugs won't hold."

In a flash, the crewmen slipped over the gunwales. Rosie and the other passengers handed over everything they could think of to plug the leaks, all the while bailing from the inside. Des gave up his saturated socks to the men who dove down again and again to patch the hull. By now the sun was setting. The moon cast its reticent light onto Des and the others. The engineers had re-boarded the craft, satisfied now that they could keep the invading waters at bay for the time being.

The deafening booms of Japanese shells were followed at intervals by the Giang Bee's Beaufort gun as it fired back. For four days, Des had listened to the explosions in wonderment that the ship could survive the bombardment so long without sinking. Now he saw the Giang Bee's end crumble under a massive blast from the bow. The ship groaned and sank, sending the remaining men on board into the murky depths. Des plugged his ears against the pleading cries of the people in the water. He could hear their shouts to save them as the oarsmen rowed away.

"Help them," someone shouted.

"No. We mustn't or we'll all die," was the abrupt response of one of the men. "Any more and we sink."

Des saw his mother's stricken face, tears glistening on her cheeks as she watched helplessly. The lifeboat drifted along. The rest was up to God. Families prayed and soon, the night air was filled with their voices.

"Our Father, who art in heaven," Des prayed with his parents, mouthing the words he had spoken from his earliest days. "Hallowed be Thy name…"

Soon the cries of the dying faded with the growing distance as they rowed away from the empty waters where the Giang Bee had been.

They were about seventy people crammed into a lifeboat meant to hold about fifty. As he had been one of the last on, Des had been given a place near the side, towards one end. The sun's rays still clung onto enough of the Singapore day to cast some light into the space where Des now peered. He thought he saw some movement through the spaces between the floorboards and leaned closer to peer downward into the lifeboat's thin wooden hull below the loose floorboards. He gasped in shock. Expressionless faces stared back at him from underneath, their mouths unmoving. Only their eyes blinked, pleading for his silence. They were stowaways, cringing under the floorboards, in the hollow made by the curved hull. Des shook his head and put his finger to his lips, signaling his complicity.

The moon slid out of view as darkness blanketed their world, leaving them alone with the grinding of wood against the metal oarlocks and the rippling sound of the waves against the ever-moving blades of the oars. Sleep was impossible, as was movement. They were jammed in so tightly that Des's legs began to cramp. He had no room to stretch them out and began to fidget. His mother clasped his hand in hers.

"Please try to keep still," she whispered. "The Dutch fleet will be here soon and everything will be better."

Des stopped fidgeting. He believed her.

8. SURVIVAL AT SEA

The morning's aura finally interrupted the blackness of the seemingly endless night. Slowly, a pale streak of light emerged across the eastern horizon, spreading an ethereal glow. Des watched it in awe mixed with dread. Dawn was magnificent, but it tore away the protective cloak of night. The growing light turned to shades of red, orange and yellow, and at last was punctured by the first shocking sliver of sunlight. Des closed his eyes against the blinding flash, just as he had done against the blinding flashes of the Japanese bombs the previous few days on the Giang Bee. Each new morning had brought back the guns and bombs. Their arrival was unpredictable—two hours or forty minutes, five minutes or half a day. The British fighter pilots who had so briefly swept the skies had only fired up the tempers of the Japanese attackers, steeling their determination to succeed in their mission. Des now expected they would come back to finish their work. The sun continued to make its way up the sky. No Japanese returned, apparently having either lost interest in the survivors; or mistakenly believing there were none.

The crewmen from the ship assumed a leadership role on the lifeboat. There were several cans of water and a few boxes of biscuits, baked and dried to rock hardness in order to extend their storage period. They allocated the biscuits among the passengers. After some discussion, it was determined what the daily amount would be. Everyone would be required to drink from the same container to assure no person received a share greater than any other. One of the crew asked around for a suitable holder in which to pass around a small quantity of water. From somewhere, a Pond's jar was passed forward. Des did not see who had given it up.

"That jar will hold hardly enough to keep a mouse alive," a woman's voice complained.

"You won't be drinking from this jar," answered the officer.

"What then?" someone else shouted from the end of the boat.

The officer unscrewed the lid and placed the jar into the kit. Picking up one of the water containers, he opened it and poured a quantity into the jar's cover. He held it forward.

"This will be the daily water ration for each person.

Des could hear groans and gasps from all around the lifeboat.

Then his attention was drawn by tiny movements from below the floor of the boat. The stowaways were getting ready to emerge from their hiding spot. Tentatively, the first one unfolded himself and pushed the floorboard aside, squeezed himself through and climbed stiffly out. The other refugees were dumbfounded. Some gasped in shock, others began to shout angrily. With the huge leaky lifeboat already overcrowded with about seventy people, these newcomers, who turned out to be some of the kitchen staff from the Giang Bee, were not welcome. But there was nothing for it; they could hardly be thrown overboard. They huddled together defensively, their eyes begging for understanding; some of the others granted it, others glared at them in fury.

The survival kit on board that already contained far fewer survival supplies than were needed now had to be stretched even further.

As the day wore on, Des was given a hard biscuit to gnaw on. It was dry and bland but the amount of chewing required to swallow it gave some satisfaction. By nightfall, he was hungry again. The biscuit's dryness, along with the day's cloudless heat, fuelled his thirst. No more water would be available until the next day. Des looked over the side of the lifeboat at the rippling water and the crystal droplets cast into the air by the perpetual movement of the oars. If he could just rinse his mouth out…He dropped his hand out the side. The boat sat so low in the water, it wasn't much of a reach to easily scoop out a handful of cool liquid. It felt good on his hand as the lifeboat's forward movement pushed his hand backward against the water's refreshing resistance. He scooped up a small amount in the palm of his hand and brought it toward his face.

"No, you mustn't." His mother's hand grabbed his own, spilling the small bit of water onto Des' thighs. "It's salt water. It would make you much worse."

The tantalizing drops rolled sideways over his skin, evaporating within seconds.

The sun's light settled into the horizon for the second time, turning the daylight into a dazzling mixture of moon and starlight. A soft breeze swept in from the south bringing with it a small chill. Des and his parents were crammed in so tightly together that they scarcely felt the coldness. With nothing to support their backs, some people slept as they sat, perched on the rows of overcrowded benches. Soft snoring accompanied rowing noises as sleep blessed a few passengers. Des slept, leaning warmly against his mother's side, soothed by the familiar smell of her body's heat as it mingled with the salty, night mist.

In the morning another ration of water was allowed. Des took the green Pond's lid and tilted it to his mouth.

"Make it last. Take it in two or three sips," his father cautioned him. "It will have to get you through the day."

Des tried to do as his father urged but as the liquid touched his parched mouth, he was helpless to resist his instinct to take in all that he could. In an instant, he had downed his entire portion. His mouth woke up. His tongue moved freely again within his mouth. His mother allowed him to wash his face with sea water to lubricate his skin from the outside. After two bites of the same biscuits they had eaten the day before, Des felt almost comfortable. This comfort was short-lived, however, as his renewed strength began to signal the cramps in his legs to fire up anew.

The day wore on. Prayers and occasional groans of complaint gave way to silence, as the survivors tried to conserve their strength. Talking became impossible as the sun's heat drew the moisture from their bodies, aggravating their thirst. Des searched for signs of land in the distance. The overhead movement of birds told him an island might be nearby. But these were sea birds, capable of covering vast distances between the many islands around the Malayan Peninsula. The third day passed as Des sat and waited. Some of the women wept for their husbands left behind to perish with the Giang Bee. The kitchen employees who had stowed away underneath the floorboards were given their turn at the oars. Most of the other passengers were still resentful as they remembered their loved ones valiantly accepting the officers' orders to stay on the ship, only allowing the women and children to board the lifeboats.

They rowed, in silence mostly, heading for a destination that eluded them. During the afternoon, someone cried out. "Look, in the distance! Land!"

All turned to see a dark strip laid out across the horizon. Its blackness contrasted with the thin blue line that dissected Des's view, neatly dividing the pristine sky from the deeper blue of the sea. They rowed towards it with a quickened stroke, animated by their excitement at finally having a destination to approach. The tired rowers pressed on with renewed determination. At last, they would find refuge. After what seemed like ceaseless hours of rowing, this dark island began to raise itself in the hot February sky and they at last realized that their distant saviour on the horizon was merely a ghost—a flat rain cloud of illusory form. Despondency swept over the passengers. Des felt a sick pang in his stomach, which aggravated the hunger already tormenting him.

That night more people slept. Des had seen a girl his age, small and frail, staring blankly across the waves. She lay slumped against her mother as the sun dropped. Sleep favoured her with its mercy. The plugs in the bottom held the leaky craft afloat. No one rowed that night. Without any guide as to their direction, such movement for now was useless. It was better to save their energy and conserve precious body moisture. A small toddler's cries pierced the silence from time to time and woke up those who could sleep. His voice lifted in a screeching wail that pierced Des's battered sensibilities, evoking his resentment.

As daylight emerged, Des was offered the Pond's lid again. The sun continued to rise in the cloudless sky, offering no respite from its burning torment. Des's face, arms and legs turned red, his light skin offering no protection from the pounding rays. The odours on the boat sickened him. Body sweat and urine co-mingled with the murky sea aroma. Overshadowing these was the smoky stench of the burns of those whose flesh had not escaped the fallout from the exploding shells.

On the fourth morning, someone passed around the green Pond's lid for the last time. At about eleven o'clock, one of the crewmen called out, "Land Ho!" Everyone stared fixedly toward the point where the horizon was broken by a dark green line of trees. They were so debilitated they could do no more than gaze, but this time they had no doubts.

As they drew nearer, Des recognized the leafy casuarina trees that were so prevalent along the boulevards of Singapore. The small craft was guided into the shallows. Forgetting the thirst that had dogged them since they had left the Giang Bee, the survivors hopped into the refreshing waters, bathing themselves and soothing their burns. Several times on their floating sojourn, Des had seen Japanese planes buzzing overhead. Now, he heard talk of hiding the lifeboat.

"We had better pull her up into the trees. The Japs will spot the boat floating on the beach and come for us," someone suggested.

"We can't drag her. We don't have enough men. These boats are made from solid hardwood beams. They're not meant to be lifted by hand." One of the ship's engineers shook his head and rapped on the boat's stern.

Sonny Woodford spoke up. "Then we'll have to sink her. We can't risk it being seen by the Japanese air patrols."

"It would be seen anyway, the water's too clear. Something the size of this boat would be easy to see at these depths, even on the bottom. We'll have to dismantle her."

"No, no," several of the women gasped weakly, panic-stricken at the thought of destroying their only means of escape from the island.

Des struggled onto the shore, listening to the discussions of the adults. His advice would not be welcome, even if he had any to give. He stared up at the casuarinas. The tiny island stood before him displaying the trees he had always disliked. The wind rustled through their leaves, throwing off the haunting whisper that particularly characterized them. He had heard them before in the safety of his family compound, and on his way to school, and been eerily unsettled. Now, on this island, they took advantage of his vulnerabilities. His parents, thirsty, hungry and preoccupied with the onerous burden of survival, could not offer Des protection from a phantom of his own imagination. He pressed his hands to his ears against the mocking, sinister breath of the casuarinas and waited as small groups were dispatched in several directions to look for fresh water. Finally, Des was guided to a place where he could drink his fill. For the time being, the whispering casuarinas ceased their annoying disturbance.

With his thirst quenched, his legs now took in the firmness of the soil beneath his feet and several days of rocking gave way to an unaccustomed steadiness and he moved slowly and unsurely. He sat down within the island's infinite shade and looked wearily around him, watching impassively, too tired and hungry to feel, as the frightened stowaways from the lifeboat stole into the forest. He would never see them again.

9. THE ISLAND

They gathered in clusters of ten or twelve to a group, keeping to the back of the beach where they were hidden by trees and brush. Mothers queried crew members and servicemen about their fate. A few of the men forced their bodies to keep moving until they found a source of drinking water a short distance inland. Others sat on the ground under shady boughs, panting heavily with exhaustion and hunger. Some talked amongst themselves, making plans for a future they could only measure in hours or days. Des wanted to listen but was too tired. Their conversations sang like a lullaby in his ears, soothing the pain of his sunburned legs as his exhaustion carried him away. His mind wandered somewhere just underneath his own awareness, and he drifted from one thought to another, blending the external stimulation of sounds with dreamy visions.

A soft tingling swept over his arms and legs. It grew in intensity, stirring him to brush away the sensation with his hands. Soon, he was fully roused again as the tingling became a sharper snap against his skin. He swept at his legs, his neck and his forearms, realizing with rage that he was now under attack by an army of mosquitoes. He jumped up, slapping his hands against the onslaught, now bolstered by sand flies. He could hear similar slapping noises all around him as many of the others fought against the same siege.

The bites came relentlessly, each toxic sore hot and painful, hurting even more when he scratched. It was a torment. He heard the crying voice of the young baby he had seen earlier on the lifeboat. He listened to the voices of the complaining women around him as they too batted at the insects, wishing for the return of the men, who had left to find food. Many of the women lounged in the shade of the casuarinas, scratching only sporadically at their sores, which were not as numerous as Des's. He envied them the cover that their longer dresses afforded. His shoes and socks were gone, valiantly thrown overboard as a sacrifice for the greater good. His youthfulness, combined with the season, did not permit him long pants. Even his hair, cut in the shorter over-the-ear style of a proper Singapore schoolboy, left him vulnerable, in contrast to the longer tresses of the women.

Des whinged to his mother, who could offer no better consolation than to advise him not to scratch. He glowered at her.

"You don't want them to get worse do you?" she scolded.

Des was in too much discomfort to answer back.

"The last thing we need is for you to catch a fever," she added. "Get into the water. It will help you feel better."

Des did as he was told. The ocean provided a briny salve, cooling the angry soreness of his skin. He returned to the water at intervals, joined by the few other children on board the lifeboat. Their mothers also joined in the bathing, dressed as they were, some in their fine travel clothes, others in the house dresses they had been wearing before a hasty departure.

By midday, the men had returned with food they had managed to scrounge from the forest. Des was given some leaves that were said to be edible, but when he tasted them, he wondered if the men weren't mistaken. Pungent and gritty, they provided no satisfaction. There was some fruit that Des did not recognize, but was like ambrosia to his deprived palate. Later when the tide went out, it left behind some isolated pools in the sand that yielded up a meagre supply of trapped fish in its wake. These, as well as a few crabs were gathered and thrown onto a fire that also served to ward off the insects.

After days of starvation at sea, Des did not need very much to fill his stomach. The sun was setting upon his first day on the island. His muscles ached a little less than they had earlier, free now from their incessant immobility while adrift at sea. Fresh water from the island's interior had re-hydrated his withered flesh. His arms and legs, decimated from sunburn and sores, were cooling after a final sunset soak in the tropical waters of the ocean. He splashed in the twilight until he heard his father's voice calling him back up the beach to sit by a large fire. There would be no one searching from the skies for them in the darkness.

The men seemed confident, encouraged by the naval crewmen among them. They divided themselves into small groups, each with its own task to accomplish. The women helped when asked but left things mainly for the men to decide.

Shallow trenches were dug in the sand.

"This is where we will sleep," his father informed him. Wearing only his shirt and shorts, Des nestled himself in the trench. He peered out briefly in the dark. A few heads jutted up, silhouetted in the emerging starlight. Several fires cast their glow across the beach, with fingers of burning amber reaching up into the sky.

"Why do we need so many fires, when it isn't cold?" Des asked.

His voice was soft and quiet in the burgeoning stillness of the settling crowd. Sonny Woodford took his place in the trench with his son.

"They will keep the flies and mosquitoes away—and any wild animals too that may be around."

"Wild animals?" Des squeaked, wondering if there was no end to the countless perils that now played with his life.

"There's nothing to worry about," his father consoled him. "Nothing too dangerous. Besides, the fires are mainly to attract attention in case a rescue ship should come by."

"But what if the Japs see the fires first?"

"They aren't looking for us anymore," Sonny answered a little too lightly.

Des sensed something in his father's voice. It felt unfamiliar and worrisome. The voice he had always looked up to, whose word was final and undisputable, was now faltering in its own conviction. His mind coasted through memories of the last few days as his sense of security in the hands of his parents waned. From the first climb up the steps of the gangway enveloped in the assuring arms of his father, he had observed Sonny's confidence peel away. His father had been unable to stop the enemy from blasting apart the Giang Bee and leaving them to flounder in a sinking lifeboat. Now they faced an uncertain future without shelter or a reliable supply of food, at the mercy of the elements and possibly wild animals. Des's imagination conjured up formidable possibilities that he carried with him into the dreaded night before sleep finally came to him. In his dreams all these fears worked their mischief on his troubled mind.

10. THE TAPPAH

The next day Des awoke to the stinging bites of mosquitoes. They were a plague that tormented the survivors day and night. He brushed the pain away from his thoughts as he began to explore the area around where they were huddled.

"Stay close Des," his mother cautioned. "I don't want to lose you."

"Can I go in the water?" Des asked, certain of the answer.

"Of course, just don't go too far."

The water was cool against his reddened skin. It soothed his sores and eased the sting from his sunburned back. Some of the others joined him and soon, the shore waves were roiling with the splashes of adults and children alike as they sought out some relief from the bites of the marauding insects.

Food was not as easily found as the previous day. The men still divided themselves into groups for labour, but Des noticed they were a little slower in their movements. His father tried unsuccessfully to forage through the tide pools for crabs and fish. It seemed as if their initial success the day before had been a fluke. Discouraged by failure and too tired to keep up the effort, the men gave in to lethargy and their craving for rest after the ordeal at sea.

Des amused himself playing under the casuarinas until hunger depleted him and forced him to join his mother and the other women in the midday shade.

He stared at the vast expanse of ocean before him as he allowed the same lethargy to set in. His ennui was broken by the footsteps of his approaching father. Sonny Woodford sat down next to his wife.

"Some of the men want to take the lifeboat out to see if they can find the entrance to the Moesi River," he said. "The Giang Bee's engineers think that it might be some twenty miles or so due south—maybe thirty. We can't stay here. There's not enough food."

Rosie's face wore the worried look Des was now accustomed to seeing. She clutched Sonny's arm, squeezing it tightly.

"You're not going with them," she said, more as a question than a statement, her voice raised a tone.

"No, that wouldn't be right. A few of us are staying behind with the women. I would never leave you and Des here by yourselves. The others have no family here. Let them try. Maybe they can send help."

Rosie relaxed a little. "But the boat is full of holes."

"Yes, but it will be lighter too. And they have repaired it as best they could. It should stand up to a trip of that length. After all, it kept us all afloat until we reached safety, didn't it?"

Sonny's tone was jovial and Des thought he made perfect sense. They had put that lifeboat to the test, rowing it around God knew where in the seas around Indonesia and Malaysia. Day after day it had floated atop the water, its plugs held in place by the pressure of the water beneath them. Rosie shook her head slowly, raising her hand to her brow as she bowed her head into her palm.

"We haven't reached safety yet," she whispered, addressing no one in particular.

The sun was high in the sky when the survivors gathered around the shore to see the twelve men off. They had a supply of fresh water that had been located the day before, and some fruit and roots and leaves they had gathered as well. The rest of the group waved them off, hopeful that the men's departure would bring an imminent rescue. Des stood by his parents as the leaky craft made its way back into the ocean. He watched it grow smaller, its occupants rowing steadily until the movement of their oars was no longer discernable. Finally, it disappeared, swallowed up in the rippling horizon.

That night was as uncomfortable as the previous one had been. Again, they hunkered down within their trenches, slapping and swiping relentlessly at the incessant bites. The briny water had washed away the redness of some of their earlier sores, but now they were bothered by a fresh invasion. Des's mind once again tortured him with expectations of wild animal attacks. Every sound increased his foreboding. Each snap of a tree branch or rustle of leaves triggered a convulsive fear. The worst part was the casuarinas themselves. The wind wrapped itself around their leaves, creating a whispering moan that drove him mad with fear. As this fear grew, it gave way to anger and resentment at the very trees themselves. He hated them. He wished them gone. He wanted death for them—the same death he had witnessed just days earlier as human bodies floated like branches around his lifeboat. He pictured the casuarinas' branches, severed from their trunks and floating into oblivion. He let sleep overtake him, vaguely comforted by his image of the vanquished trees. Still, their moans persisted into his dreams.

Daylight brought with it at least the delight of an early morning dip in the ocean. Des hunted for crabs in the muddy ground of the receding tide and found some, along with a few small fish. These were cooked up along with bounty from the similar searches of the others. With fewer people to feed, Des was almost sated.

The women sat once again under the shady trees, talking amongst themselves, hopeful of an Allied rescue before they were discovered by the Japanese. The morning was still not fully developed when one of the women shouted.

"A ship! Look. It's a ship. They've come for us at last!"

Des looked up. He did not see a ship. He saw the horizon and its relentless rippling waters, like jagged bits of broken glass pulsing with a will of their own. For a moment, he saw a cluster of the despised casuarinas hovering in the water. They seemed to be moving of their own accord, slowing approaching in a sneak attack. Was he seeing things? Going crazy? These casuarinas did not whisper, though. Their leaves hung silently, drooping, while the trees stealthily moved closer to land—closer to Des. Now Des watched with a kind of detached curiosity, beyond any more sense of shock or fear. It would have to be something much worse than an impossible clump of menacing trees to stir his instincts to sound an alarm.

The trees neared the island, gliding on unseen roots. A perfect rhythm moved them in tandem with one another, as they held fast to their positions, fixed and stable in relation to one another. The left flank dipped as the right flank floated up, then fell again. *Yes. It was a ship - camouflaged with the foliage.*

"Shhh," someone said. "It may be the enemy."

"It's the enemy, all right—of the Japanese. That's an English ship!" bellowed another voice.

The heavily camouflaged vessel set anchor a short distance off shore and dispatched its lifeboats to pick up the survivors.

"Are we safe now," Des asked his father.

"We are safe now," Sonny answered, "but you shouldn't worry about that. We were safe here too."

Des thought back to his to wretched nights in the trench fearing wild animals and other terrors. He wanted to disagree with his father, but stayed silent.

"What is she called," he asked instead.

"Who," asked his father.

"The ship."

"They say she is the English warship, *Tappah*."

"What does that mean?"

"It means *ship that Des must board,*" Sonny answered, patting is son's back.

"Well I'm certainly not going to board her," someone said nearby.

"Nor I," said another voice.

"But you must," answered Sonny. "You can't stay here."

"Yes we can. They can leave us a boat and some provisions. We can go to another island. With so many islands around these parts, there's bound to be a village on one of them."

No amount of persuading could convince them to board the Tappah. Eventually, a group of about twenty, including Sonny, Rosie and Des bade a reluctant good bye to them and stepped into the lifeboats of the Tappah.

Once on board, the survivors of the Giang Bee were given a small amount of food and water. The Tappah stayed anchored several more hours and finally set off as the day was fading. As he sailed away, enfolded in the grasp of the floating forest of casuarina branches, Des glowered at their whispering sisters on the island, now silenced by the growing distance from the Tappah. Their land-bound leaves quivered in the fading sunlight, as if beckoning Des back. They shrank and faded, finally disappearing from his view.

11. CAPTURED

The Tappah bobbed in the night's dark cover, masquerading in the canopy of casuarina branches strategically placed over its decks. No more food was offered and scarcely any water, either. A fog settled in over Des's thoughts and he clung to his parents.

"Where will we go now?"

"Somewhere safe, I hope," his mother answered.

His father remained pensive. Des searched his face for a familiar sign—a reassuring nod, anything at all to show concurrence with Rosie's hope. This time, there were no kind words of hope, no comforting gestures to placate his fears. Waiting was all they had, their lives wrung dry and empty by days of thirst and near starvation. The Woodfords had gradually peeled off the layers of their belongings: the suitcases, now gone; Rosie's handbag with its broken strap; the contents of Sonny's pockets, and his jacket; even their shoes, all were discarded. They had rid themselves of everything that stood between them and life. Now, it was time to strip away all pretence. They had nothing left with which to cloak their situation. They had no mask to wear. Only the waiting was left to them.

Des took his parent's signs to heart and hid within his thoughts, riding them out on the Tappah until morning.

The day was calm and sunny, the sky blue, and sea tranquil. Then the illusion of peace was suddenly destroyed by the appearance of Japanese gunships. They stood off the starboard side of the Tappah, and rickety planes flew overhead. Des felt a chill of dread, waiting for the crack of the guns. He wasn't aware that the Captain, knowing that resistance or flight were both impossible, had obeyed a Japanese command to make for the nearest port.

Des had no idea what was happening, try as he might to eavesdrop on the adults' conversations. He drifted in the early morning hours, watching clouds above sail through their own deep blue sea, as the Tappah plowed through the seas, the gunships still in sight. As he sniffed the briny ocean air, Des' nose was suddenly grabbed by a new acrid smell of bitter smoke. Looking up, he saw land.

The Tappah moored at Muntok, at the tip of Bangka, a relatively small island just off the southeast coast of Sumatra, the largest of the islands of Indonesia. Their desperate journeys had taken them almost three hundred kilometers from Singapore, through the southern part of the Strait of Malacca, and the island-dotted South China Sea. But Des only knew that they had landed somewhere unknown to him, to be delivered into the hands of the Japanese.

When Des and his parents straggled off the boat, they and all the other exhausted escapees from Singapore saw the enemy face to face for the first time. These soldiers of the so-called Empire of the Sun were stony-faced, arrogant, and cruel. When their grim expressions did show feeling, it was to laugh at their victims, or to shout a strident command. Des stared at them as though they were figures from his nightmares come to life.

The prisoners were driven like cattle the length of the extremely long jetty, a ramshackle structure perched on poles set in the harbour seabed. It was wide enough for a rail line as well a road for trucks. It was a dreadful walk for the refugees, their shoeless feet burning and blistering as they trudged into the deserted town, where they were confined in an old movie theatre. Tired, hungry, thirsty and terrified, Des huddled next to Sonny and Rosie, listening to the murmurings of the others in the darkness of the musty place that once was full of happy filmgoers. Some rations of stale food and dirty water were brought to them before they finally fell into troubled sleep. The rations, awful as they were, meant that their captors meant to keep them alive, at least for now.

The next day, they were rounded up again, the guards yelling and barking orders at them in a mix of Japanese and pidgin English, and marched through the streets to a massive concrete structure that filled them with fear.

"The Muntok jail!" someone whispered in dread. "They can't put us there!"

Des looked at the monolithic prison building and shivered inside, overwhelmed by the grimness of the place. But there was a collective sigh of relief, replaced by new anxiety as they passed by the prison, and came instead to a huge barracks-like building next to it, where they were shoved roughly inside. Stragglers were beaten with batons.

"It looks like it was quarters for the tin workers," Sonny said.

Muntok had been the hub of the Dutch tin dredging industry in Indonesia, and was not really a community but a protected industrial enclave. The Dutch were gone now, dead in the invasion, or captives like themselves. Des looked about the place, half in relief, half in fear – relief that they were still alive and together, fear of what the next day might bring. Each family moved to claim bunks, listless, but with a spark of hope that this meant the Japanese really did plan to keep them alive. That night again, after more gritty rations, Des fell into a well of sleep, his stomach aching.

After languishing in the tin workers' quarters for a few days, they were suddenly roused by more strident yells from their captors. Des started in fear, snapped into the awful reality of the day from the deep sleep of utter weariness. As Rosie and Sonny rose and listlessly dusted themselves off, Des stayed as close to them as he could, terrified that this was the day they would be separated.

But this time, they were being shifted to what had once been a small neighbourhood of comfortable homes. From the outside, the residences appeared almost normal, a small community of dwellings, cosy and in harmony with the surrounding paths. Without their flowered gardens and trimming, they appeared stark and lifeless, but they had been homes where earlier families had dined and bonded with one another—where they argued too, and finally, where they were pushed out coldly into the hot night to fend for themselves or perish. Each property had been looted for anything of value: hardware had even been pulled from the cupboards.

The Woodford's shared one of these with their fellow prisoners. As they entered, Des clung as closely as possible to his parents. Once inside, it became clear that the original occupants had vacated these premises quickly. On the table sat a half-eaten breakfast, abandoned by its owners. Some of their group snatched the food, hungrily gobbling it up. Others quickly scoured the cupboards and pantry for other stores. The outside was inspected for herbs and fruit.

"These houses are Dutch; probably were occupied by plantation managers and their families," one woman said quietly.

"Where do you suppose they've gone?" asked one of the children.

Rosie turned and looked out the dusty window at a sky whitened by a haze of clouds made heavy with moisture. Des thought she must be thinking of her own hasty flight toward uncertainty and imagining the people here fleeing in a similar fashion.

Des walked through the house noting the ceiling fan still spinning overhead, and the cooking utensils on the table and bench tops, unwashed. He felt like an intruder. He pictured the family sitting down to breakfast. Perhaps the father would be preparing to go to his place of employment. The Dutch children would have been robust and blond, tanned golden by the rays of the Indonesian sun. He imagined the mother, at the beginning of her day, possibly giving instructions to her maid about the laundry which still sat soaking, warm and sudsy in the tub. He stumbled into the bedroom and noted a book, its pages parted, lying face down on the bedside table, never to be finished by its reader. On a chest of drawers he found a toy brass cannon, hesitated a moment, then decided he could take it. It reminded him of all the childhood treasures he had lost, and he held it tightly in his hand.

He looked around more. Clothes still hung in the cupboard, with no gaps or empty hangers to indicate that anyone had taken the time to pack. No one had had the time to do anything but run for their lives. But in all likelihood they were either captives somewhere, like Des and his parents, or they had perished.

He rejoined his parents, who had scrounged a bit of food. Sonny suggested they try to find some space in the garage as everyone seemed to be taking the main rooms of the house. Perhaps they could find a spot with some partial privacy. They left the others inside the house and ventured back out onto the veranda. No one was guarding them, or even watching them. No Japanese soldiers lurked behind the Dutch garden shrubs and no planes menaced overhead. Life seemed normal within the dusty streets of Muntok. An Indonesian villager cycled his way down the road. Des wondered if he was a local servant, or if perhaps he was even employed in one of the markets. As he neared the front of the house where the Woodfords stood, dishevelled and dirty from their ordeal, he noticed them. For an instant, he looked through them, beyond them, into the distance. Then, he faced them directly. He stopped his bicycle and got off completely. Holding the bicycle steady with one hand, he bent low from the waist, bowing to Des and his parents. Rosie and Sonny looked first at the Indonesian and then at each other, wondering what strange custom required this man to disembark from his ride and bow down before people like themselves. Des smiled and waved while his parents stood stunned, not knowing how to respond.

Rosie wondered aloud, "Why would anyone do such a thing? I'm certain he thinks we are the masters of this house, but how odd to actually stop in his tracks just to bow. It makes me wonder just what sort of people they are."

"It rather makes one wonder just what sort of masters the Dutch were," countered Sonny. "If this incident is any clue, the Dutch may be in for a tough time ahead. No wonder the Japs don't feel the need to keep us under guard. If we run, the locals will assume we are Dutch and probably turn us in."

They stood awhile longer on the veranda, until another local passed by, this time on foot, and again bowed upon seeing them. Des did not wave back. Instead, he followed his parents to the garage. Inside the cool enclosure, Des felt surrounded and penned in. He was in a prison with no guards, a toy of the Japanese caged within a European style dwelling. His surroundings were foreign to him but were better than anything his frightened imagination had conjured. For now, he was with his parents, he was fed, if only one meal, and he was alive. He breathed a small, shaky sigh of relief.

The respite was too brief. After a few days, the guards reappeared, as grim and vicious as ever. Barking orders in the harsh staccato Des had come to dread, the soldiers ordered them all out onto the dusty street again, snarling and laughing at their charges, their batons ready.

Des clutched his father, fearing he knew not what. Tired and hungry, his insides cramping with pain, he was now too battered and numb from trauma to even imagine what might lie ahead.

Once again, they were all forced back towards the Muntok port, their shoeless feet sometimes bleeding on the long, dreaded trek on the jetty to the wharf, where once again parents and children clung together in quiet anguish. They were all put on a dirty barge that took them on a long hot journey across the strait of waters that separated the island of Bangka from Sumatra. There, they continued up a muddy river that wound past lush greenery until they finally landed again.

Des didn't know it yet, but this was Palembang, on the main Indonesian island of Sumatra. Once again, they found themselves occupying the former homes of the vanquished Dutch, where a whole neighbourhood had been fenced off to act as a prison camp. Escape was impossible, as it was surrounded by dense jungle, where the few villages were full of people who resented their former Dutch masters.

Des and his parents were crowded into one of the homes with large numbers of their fellow prisoners, everyone trying to claim a corner somewhere that offered some sense of territory, a private space. They all settled as best they could, wondering what new ordeals were to come.

12. SEPARATION

In the early hours of the morning, if Des kept his eyes shut, he could imagine he was at home in his house on Florence Avenue. The muffled snores of the others in the house faded to the steady even breathing of dreamers. In the moments when sleep was receding, but he was not yet fully awake, Des could forget his empty stomach and the worry of an uncertain future. Birds sung their calls to awake just as they had done all his life in Singapore. Their cheery messages gave no signal that the world was at war. Instead, they boasted of gaiety as they called to one another with their songs. The magpies especially, gave Des a sense of ease. He was used to their sad caws that sounded like the commiserating moans of a sympathetic friend. In contrast to other birds, they did not seem to pursue the morning in a frantic rush. Often, this sensation was over before he could fully appreciate it. Other times, Des languished within it trying to make it last.

The sound of many tramping feet ruptured his peace. Faint at first, it grew louder until Des could hear them marching up the stairs of the main house. A door banged open. Shouts and commands flew through the air, making everyone in the house jump up and frantically grab their belongings. Unable to make out the words of heavily accented English, Des waited until the yelling had stopped before seeking out his father. Sonny was standing poised as though ready for an attack. The door to their room crashed loudly as it hit the adjacent wall. A Japanese officer and several troops filled the doorway.

"At eleven o'clock you will assemble in the field at the end of the road," the officer commanded in surprisingly accurate English. "Bring only what you can carry—nothing more."

A low moan tried to escape from Rosie's lips. She checked it almost immediately turning it into a weakly disguised cough. Sonny stood frozen in his earlier stance. Des looked for fear in his father's face and saw none. It was the moment he had overheard his father speak of with some of the other adults. In an atmosphere where no information was forthcoming, the captives were left to guess at their enemy's intentions. Rumours abounded. The local Chinese resistance offered tips and other occasional bits of conversation they picked up from their Japanese customers, none of it certain. Des had heard his father whisper of enslavement in Japan and even the possibility that the men would be disposed of.

Some of the men had contemplated making a run for it with the help of the Chinese resistance. The Chinese who lived in Indonesia were active here, and in their own country were locked in mortal combat with their ancient enemies from Japan. But there was nowhere to go. Even if they could manage the fairly simple task of escaping, it was almost impossible to avoid being caught. The colour of their skin, lack of money, language problems and the presence of Indonesian informers who hated the Dutch, were enough to doom their chances outside. For those who tried, the likelihood of survival after recapture was almost zero. People usually just disappeared, even when the Chinese resistance could confirm the fact of their recapture. Because of this, Des knew his father had decided to stay and face up to the threat.

Throughout the morning, the air stayed hot and humid. Its weight pressed down on the people as they gathered their few belongings. Des placed the toy brass cannon into a small white sack, and clutched it in his hand. As Rosie and Sonny had almost nothing to carry, they decided to bring as much water as they could, filling several glass bottles that Sonny had managed to collect.

They made their way to the field, passing through crowds of depressed faces and sobbing women. By now they all looked thin and hollow-eyed, men, women, and children, and many shuffled, unable to walk strongly any more. Des kept close to his parents, almost letting his mind wonder miserably which parent he would be forced to join. Instead, he numbed himself to these painful thoughts and listened to his parents as they discussed a plan of action.

"There's no escape," Rosie observed as she scanned the ring of armed Japanese soldiers circling the perimeter of the field.

Parked nearby were a couple of trucks. Des presumed the soldiers had arrived in them. That meant they had come a fair distance.

"It looks like we should be prepared for a long walk to wherever we're going," Sonny observed to his wife. "We must make the water last as long as possible."

Rosie nodded without looking at her husband. Her gaze was fixed on the circle of soldiers standing at attention, bayonets pointing up as they clutched their guns in both hands. Sonny gently pulled her farther away from the perimeter, guiding both her and Des as far away from the soldiers as he could.

A shrill whistle blew, then another. Suddenly the soldiers were shouting and blowing whistles from every direction, while dashing in toward the prisoners. They separated the families, pushing the men roughly away to one side. Because they were furthest away from the edge of the field, Sonny found the time to say good-bye to his family.

"Take care of yourselves," he said to both of them, wrapping his arms around Rosie. His lips pressed tightly together, he kept his expression stoic as he next bent down to hug Des.

"There's a good lad," he murmured into his son's ear. "You'll take care of each other, won't you?"

Des barely had time to return his father's embrace. Around him, the Japanese men seemed to take pleasure in the horrible scenes around them as they targeted more severely those who were most distraught, beating them with batons, screaming abuse. Wailing women clutched at their husbands and older sons only to have them ripped from their grasp. Determined not to give their tormentors the pleasure of seeing their sadness, Des and Rosie refused to cry as Sonny walked of his own accord toward the men. They stood proudly erect as Sonny took his place among his allies. As the crowd of fathers, brothers, grandfathers and husbands awaited their fate, their demeanour began to change. Heads were erect and some even smiled. When finally they were given the signal to move, they marched away rhythmically, united by the beat of their feet, then first one and then all the rest broke determinedly into song.

"*It's a long way to Tipperary...*" they sang, the jaunty words giving everyone courage.

The soldiers were hopping angry and ordered the men to stop. Des let his dread and despair give way to a small chuckle along with some of the other remaining children, as the soldiers rushed about in uncontrolled fury barking out orders to shut up. The men did not shut up. Instead, they sang louder as they marched, oblivious to the tantrums and batons of those in control. Finally their voices faded away as they disappeared from view. Des looked out at the now empty road, feeling as if they had just marched off the edge of the earth.

13. THE WOMEN'S CAMP

Des could tell that the ragged sound of the other women's sobs bothered his mother. Her lips were pursed with the edges pointing downward as if she were trying hard not to break down entirely. Still, she remained composed enough to offer him some consolation.

"We'll be alright," she said, with a fierce and angry look at the enemy soldiers. "We'll watch the guards, just as Dad told us to do, study their every movement, always watch. Then we'll be able to anticipate what they'll do next, and keep one step ahead of them. We'll survive."

He did watch them. The soldiers who remained behind seemed bored. Their bayonets were no longer poised to attack. As they stood at ease, calm and nonchalant, they displayed no hint of any trouble to come. Des guessed that the women and children were to be transported somewhere and not killed. They waited together, some of the women still crying, but most were too tired and hot in the heat of the rising sun.

Instead of taking them all away to some unknown new nightmare, though, the guards finally herded the women and young children back to the Palembang camp. Almost crushed by the wrenching separation, not knowing if the men were being taken off to execution, brutal labour camps, or some other horrible fate, some of the women could barely lift their feet, stumbling back to the camp in a daze of grief.

But Des drew strength from his mother's determination and courage. He walked as bravely as he could beside her, his heart turning to follow his father down that awful road. It took all his will power to keep it from breaking into pieces inside his chest.

Once back in the camp, as the sounds of despair and fear slowly faded into exhaustion, the women gradually tried to establish something that seemed like normal life, to carry on in hopes that the worst had not happened, and perhaps would not.

The house they had shared with so many other captives was now half as crowded, the men gone. Without Sonny as a shield, preserving some semblance of a normal family, Rosie knew she had to turn to the other women for mutual support, and she spoke with some of them in hushed tones in one of the larger rooms. Des cocked his ear, assuming his usual position for listening without drawing attention to himself.

Des counted the people in the room: including himself and Rosie, they were thirteen, all disoriented, tired, and strained. There was a pretty teenage girl there, a pale slim redhead named Betty he had noticed before, who sat quiet and withdrawn in a corner.

He overheard her name as his mother spoke quietly with the mother of another girl, a small six-year old. They were speaking about Betty's private grief. Betty had witnessed a terrible drama as her grandfather clung to her crowded lifeboat at the sinking of the Giang Bee. Seeing his grip weaken, she had cried and begged him to hang on, but finally he had given in to the inevitable. Seeing him descend slowly into the sea, Betty gave up a part of her soul, sending it into the briny deep with him, irretrievable, his final expression imprinted on her mind. She would carry the image of the last moments of his life within her, forever.

Des could see the drowning face in his imagination, and he felt a stab of pain for the girl. He felt all over again his own pain at losing Ah Wah and all the others he loved, but held to the comfort that he had his mother. Des and Rosie were to share a room with Betty and her grandmother, who was despondent at her terrible loss.

Normally, the difference in their ages would have kept him and fifteen- year old Betty apart, but Des was drawn to the shy girl with the kind manner. Though Betty was too private for him to get to know well, he liked her quiet intelligence, and her generosity. Like his mother, she was always helping inmates who were sick or elderly or just lonely and frightened. Somehow, in spite of all she had survived, Betty was always cheerful and positive, softly encouraging everyone around her.

The prisoners searched for routine wherever they could. Small chats with housemates as they prepared what food they had, petty gossip, concern for sick neighbours—all the symbols of pre-war daily life were duplicated in the compound. Des amused himself with the other children, using nature's toys as playthings. Clumps of sod, a branch from a bush, pebbles and pieces of worn-out shoe leather were kicked, thrown, collected and traded in the incessant search for an illusion of normality amid the brutality, sickness and death in their lives.

Their captors supplied only the barest of sustenance for their prisoners. Since nothing in the kitchens worked in the houses, the women had organized cooking fires and added whatever they could find to add to the pots of minimal rations. The paltry food was reduced to starvation level if there was even a minor infraction of the rules by one inmate. The Japanese soldiers seemed to love to increase their suffering. Des and the other children were thin and hungry, but surviving, some of them foraging when they could for any extra bits of edible grasses or fruits they could find. But for many the suffering was too much. Already weakened in body and soul by the series of horrors that had battered them since the escape from Singapore, more women and children fell ill every day.

Rosie, true to her original calling, nursed them as best she could, calling upon reserves of strength that amazed Des, as he watched her bathe hot fevered faces, and spoonfeed thin soup into quivering lips. She worked alongside a Dutch woman whom they had all chosen to be their camp leader, not least because she was a skilled doctor. Rosie and Dr. Holvek and a few others did what they could for their fellow inmates. But in spite of their efforts, there were always those who died, some contorted with pain, some in delerium, some who softly let their souls escape the bonds of physical existence, whispering into the ether.

Rosie bit her tongue often. With Sonny gone, her temper was like a frayed rope, pulled taut. She seemed poised to snap, and Des could see she was struggling to maintain her control. The house was too small for the disparate captives. Any furnishings belonging to the previous occupants had long since been plundered and the building stripped back to its bare walls. Some of the more fortunate prisoners were able to scrounge some grass mats to separate their bodies from the hard floor while sleeping. Rosie and Des had nothing. Their suitcase, carefully pared down to one from three so many weeks ago, was lost to the cold depths of the ocean that had almost swallowed them as well.

The cotton dress she had worn since they fled Singapore was now faded to an ashen hue from weeks of grime. Its yellow shades were indistinguishable from the rest of its printed pattern. The white handbag, whose broken handle caused Rosie to clasp it tightly to her breast for much of their time on the Giang Bee, was also long gone. Her flat walking shoes were falling apart and she had only the undergarments she had put on the day they fled to the docks.

Des had even less. Having sacrificed his shoes to keep the Giang Bee's leaky lifeboat afloat, he wore only his summer shorts and a light blue shirt, now both filthy and fraying. He pictured the men who had decided to leave the first island in the boat and try to find help, rowing through the island-dotted sea, his socks still plugging the holes made in the hull by Japanese bullets. He wondered if they had finally found safety, aided perhaps by helpful locals. Des liked to picture them boarding an English rescue vessel, their fatigue and hunger only slightly dampening their elation at knowing they faced a bright future in Australia, or even British India. He thought often of those survivors on the island who failed to board the Tappah. He wanted to believe they had met with a better fate than he and his parents now faced. He shuddered to think of them bearing the same expression he had seen on his father's face as he was taken away from his family.

Des's thoughts of everyone else's safety fell further into the back of his mind as his concern for his mother grew. Night after night he listened to her unsteady breathing. She seldom slept. During the day, he watched her struggle with tasks as she tried to help some of the older women inside the house. Co-operation among the inmates was impossible and they squabbled constantly, missing advantages they could have gleaned from teaming up for larger jobs such as cooking, and laundry. Sometimes Rosie snapped at them in frustration, her Welsh spirit impatient with such foolishness.

They might have cooperated on foraging efforts, but instead most of the women scrambled to grab what they could, often leaving the worst rations for those who were too slow to get the best for themselves. Damaged, dirty and often past its prime, the food was all but inedible. It was a far cry from the way he had been coddled on Rosie's strict diet of proper nourishing English food: creamy wheat breakfast cereals, apples, potatoes and red meat. Cookie was never allowed to serve Chinese or Malayan foods with their spices and rich flavours. Even rice was taboo. Now, Des could only dream about such mouthwatering meals, and Rosie fretted about her only child's lack of even basic sustenance. Des was starting to suffer truly terrible pains in his bowels.

The dirty rations trucked in to the camp offered paltry servings of the many tropical oddities that had been forbidden in the Woodford household. Outside the camp, the forest teemed with edibles but few had the knowledge or the ability to sort through the deadly blend of other toxic plants that grew up around them. In time, Des would learn to recognize the herbs and grasses that could be boiled along with the speckled rice of the camp. Wild roots and tropical fruits yielded themselves up over time to the hungry grasp of the prisoners who learned the signs of edibility. Wild yams and tapioca, shriveled to shadows of their groceteria counterparts, showed their upper stalks through the forest's secondary growth, tempting sharp eyes with the promise of a few bites.

"You must be careful," Rosie said to Des one day as she was laundering some clothing in a bucket.

Rosie had taken on the care of some of the older women in her quarters. In return, those who had spare garments gave her some to replace her worn out dress.

Des, who was chewing thoughtfully on some wild grasses he had picked from the other side of the roadway, looked quizzically at his mother. "Why, what do you mean?"

"I mean that you should be sure of what you put in your mouth from the forest. You won't want to get sick—not here. You must be careful of your stomach."

Des slowed down his chewing a little. "I am careful," he argued. I know what's good and what isn't. The Barding brothers showed me."

Rosie said nothing, merely sighing at the mention of the famous Dutch brothers who had distinguished themselves for their cunning and bravery during the Woodford's brief time on Bangka Island. She dipped the cloth in her hands into the soapless pail of wash-water. The corners of her mouth were rigidly fixed on either side of her lips, creating a thin parallel line which underscored her opinion of the Bardings. Their exploits were legendary on Bangka Island and had contributed greatly to the welfare of the inmates. Still, they were reckless and brave enough for her to know that their influence on a ten-yea-old boy could be dangerous. They had been taken away with Sonny and the other men.

"Still, bring back anything you aren't absolutely certain of," she said. "I want someone in the camp with more experience to look at it first."

Des swallowed what was left in his mouth and nodded obediently, before turning his back and heading off to find some other children from the other houses. He thought he could feel the steely Welsh eyes of his mother follow his departure, but he was wrong. Rosie had already turned back to her task, knowing that it was futile to counsel her child to be careful of what he ate in an environment where every meal was consumed as if it were one's last. She knew Des would eat what he could, or he would perish. She only hoped that in finding the nourishment that would sustain him, he didn't hasten his demise. She would not lose another child—not here—not this way.

The hardness of the floor against his bones bothered Des, subtly awakening him. He lay transfixed between a sleeping state and the live sounds of the women's voices.

At first, their words chopped dully into the background of his consciousness. Gradually they grew louder, rousing him more fully as they were joined by other intrusions to his senses. The pressure on his hip hardened and he rolled over. His head hurt too, its hollow pain echoing the emptiness in his abdomen.

The bickering of the women flowed harshly through the house, their disagreements over how much to cook, who was to do which task, what to share, when to trade, all fuelling Des's discomfort. He rose went out into the humid sun, which branded a sticky blend of moisture and dust to his skin. He was used to it now—just as he was used to sleeping without cover or bedding on the hard floor.

But he could not get used to the hunger. Mornings offered only his fill of tepid water, boiled and then left to sit in a steel bucket. He scratched viciously at old mosquito bites, avoiding, where possible, the fresh bites of sand flies and those of last night's mosquitoes. The sores festered, and when he scratched, the itch became a burning pain, as blood from each bite ran down his legs.

Des did enjoy the freedom he had to roam the camp. A few of the younger children from the other houses on his street joined him to search for fruit just outside the boundaries of the camp. Des noticed that the Dutch and English born children his own age usually kept clear of him and of each other as well. He knew they had little in common with him and he supposed that old distinctions were being kept alive within the camp's social hierarchy. The adults were funny like that. Not even the common bond of being prisoners together would allow them to forget the assumptions of their up-bringing.

Today, he returned with nothing from his morning food search. The other children moped about behind him, bored with his lack of success. Around midday, they parted company and Des headed back to his house to see if any rations were available.

His mother was outside rinsing some of the women's clothes out. She glanced up at him tiredly, motioning him inside with a flick of her head.

"Is there something to eat?" Des asked, hoping her gesture had indicated a waiting meal.

"There is," was all she answered. "Betty has something for you."

Des entered the house. His eyes needed a second or two to re-adjust themselves to the dimness within. Betty sat with a couple of the older women in a corner of the room, her eyes showing a rare spark of enthusiasm. As Des approached, Betty handed him a small tin plate. On it was a small piece of sweet potato and something else Des thought he would never see within the confines of the camp. It was laced with a tinge of gray but its familiar consistency allowed him to recognize it immediately.

"An egg," he exclaimed with wide-eyed surprise. "Wherever did you get that?" His mouth watered. He wanted to swallow the egg in one greedy bite, but somehow stopped himself from lunging toward it and inviting a nasty rebuke from the women.

"Don't ask questions," Betty cautioned, her voice hushed, "and don't mention it to anyone. If the Japs hear you talking about eggs, it could spoil everything."

"But who gave it to you?"

"Let's just say that we were able to arrange a trade."

"Who with?" Des asked again. "Where are the chickens? How could anyone keep the Japs from finding chickens in here?"

"They came from outside," whispered one of the older women. "Now be quiet and eat it. There'll be no more talking about it."

Des took the food from Betty and sat on the floor to eat. The sweet potato and egg melded together inside his mouth, stirring an exquisite comfort inside him. He gobbled it down, licking the dish over and over until the last traces of food had vanished and all he could taste was the warm acrid metal of the plate.

14. THE MEN AND THE DOG

Almost all the guards showed no sign of compassion for their victims, whom they very clearly held in utter contempt. There was one guard in particular they called The Dog. Des knew that when The Dog was on duty, it was best to stay busy and avoid catching his notice. The Dog had a fierce temper and an unpredictable mean streak. He seemed to enjoy beating up children. More than once, Des had seen him single out a child for no apparent reason, meting out his wrath in measured blows until the child was knocked senseless, or the other sentries gathered to stop him.

It was all even harder to bear without the reassuring presence of his father to shield and cushion Des from the awful reality around him. Worse, they had had no word of what had been done to the men, whether they had been taken to labour camps, or to some secret place of execution. Des's sleep was tortured by imaginings of

Sonny and the others, taken to a field, the guns being raised….he shut his mind to the image, and forced himself to picture his father alive in a prison bunkhouse somewhere.

One hot afternoon Des was playing listlessly at a game of marbles he'd improvised with stones, when he heard a shout.

"There they are! It's them! It's them!"

He looked up and ran over to where an excited woman was shouting, as the others crowded around her, craning their necks to see. Des heard the cause of the excitement before he saw them, tramping feet in a tired march. Then he saw, on the dirt road that ran alongside the camp, the ragged line of emaciated prisoners approaching, each hollowed faced searching the women's camp for a glimpse of a wife or mother, a sister or a child.

Des ran to the house to tell Rosie.

"Mum, Mum, it's them! It's the men! Maybe Dad's with them!"

He half-dragged her out to the balcony as she followed him out, her heart in her throat. They watched and watched, as the sorry parade went by, hopeful when someone else spied a loved one, choking down their own disappointment when there was no sign of Sonny.

Every morning after that they stood out on the balcony of their small crowded house, in desperate hope of seeing Sonny with the men on their way to whatever slave labour project the Japanese had devised for them. In the evening, they stood vigil again, to watch the men dragging themselves back to prison after a day of backbreaking work, in desperate hope of seeing Sonny. They imagined locking eyes and perhaps receiving some disguised acknowledgement from him. Some of the men had tried to communicate by waving wildly, breaking step or even calling the name of their loved one, only to be set upon by their guards and mercilessly beaten.

The morning was cool as the sun cowered behind a cloudy white sky. A night of rainfall had washed the dust from the ground, leaving a musty smell in the air. Dampness penetrated the houses and seeped into everything, inviting insects and mould. Des woke early, just as the sound of the men's footsteps broke the air. He ran to the balcony where he found his mother already poised and staring out in anticipation of seeing her husband, if only for a minute, while he passed by. Several others also stood on the balconies of the neighbouring houses shouting and waving, trying to attract the attention of their men. Some of the men chanced a glance up toward the balconies, others even sneaking a brief wave of their hand. Finally, Des spotted his father and pointed him out to Rosie.

"There he is!" Des squealed, nudging his mother with his elbow. "There's Dad!"

"Where?"

Des pointed toward the rear of the group. "There he is! There he is, beside the short man with the blond hair. Second row. He's very thin, but I can still tell it's Dad." He lifted his hand and waved wildly.

Rosie too, saw Sonny and waved her arms back and forth, hoping her beloved husband would be able to pick out his family from among the many figures on the balconies. She looked at Des and back at her husband. Sonny seemed to be peering intently at the group of houses where Rosie and Des were standing.

Most of the guards escorting the men were in front of Sonny. Only one walked behind the group, bayonet in hand, set for any skirmish or break in ranks that might occur. Sonny looked, squinting into the hazy morning. His face finally broke into a smile before he turned his gaze forward, never once breaking stride or faltering in his gait. He merely raised his left hand in front of him, out of view of the guard directly behind him, and moved it back and forth.

"He's waving," Des said, flapping his own arms harder. "He sees us!"

"Yes, he sees us," Rosie said pulling her arm down to her side and looking at the camp's sentries, who were taking no notice for the moment.

Des could see the sentries too, most of them bleary-eyed and bored. Des looked back at his father who still stared rigidly ahead. The women from the other houses were still calling and waving. The noise level increased and Des could hear the excited cries of three Dutch sisters, the Colinnes, who had climbed up onto the roof and were waving frantically producing the most noise. Yelling and shouting in Dutch, they unfurled a bright orange banner, the Dutch national colour, and raised it over their heads.

"What are they saying?" Des asked.

"I don't know, but they had better be careful," answered Rosie, looking down at the sentries. She pulled Des back into the house as the men's footsteps grew quieter with distance, finally disappearing into the quiet sounds of the women's activities.

Rosie picked up a bucket by the doorway. "Come Des," she said nodding her head toward a tract of secondary jungle across the road, "let's go to the stream and get some water."

Des was happy to go with his mother. They headed toward the edge of the road, Rosie swinging the empty bucket with Des at her side, barefoot and shirtless, a lift in her step now that she knew Sonny was still alive. As they were about to cross into the bush, a shout rang out from behind them. The voice was dreadful in its familiar snarl. They both reeled around together. Running toward them with bayonet fixed toward them was The Dog. His eyes were narrow slits and his lips were pursed so tightly together they seemed to vanish, leaving a jagged scar where his mouth should have been. It became instantly clear that The Dog wanted them to halt. Rosie stopped, frozen, in the middle of the road. With all the panic of a child, Des fled to the opposite side nearest the bushes, desperate for cover from the pointed end of the bayonet. He turned and looked back at The Dog, who now stood by Rosie. His face was crimson-bronze with fury. Des cowered by the bushes ready to flee.

Rosie's leaden feet were anchored to the ground. She stared at the surly, irate guard in utter disbelief at the lack of provocation for his actions. She stared at the point of the bayonet. All thought seemed to leave her. Time stood still for her as she waited for this malevolent person to say or do something that would prompt the laws of physics to work again.

"Bow," Des whispered under his breath, willing the message to his mother's statue-like frame. He looked heavenward and mouthed the word again. "Bow. Please, let her bow." He knew from experience that this was what the guard expected as his due. Even children were brutally dealt with if they failed to give obeisance.

Rosie still did not move. The Dog lowered his bayonet and began to scream and wave his arms around, pointing in the direction of the Colinne sisters' house. Rosie gained control of herself enough to figure out his meaning. She pointed first to herself, shaking her head, then to her house. She was standing arm outstretched, and finger pointed when The Dog gave her a thundering smack across the face, snapping her head sideways and nearly causing her to lose her footing.

Des's physical reaction to this assault mirrored his mother's. His face burned fiery red as he fought back an immediate impulse to attack this monster. He checked himself, obedient to a small voice within him that knew this move would be instantly fatal to him. He saw that his mother too had turned bright red. The colourful Welsh temper that had survived her capture and imprisonment, even now was ready to well up in spite of her best judgment. It was instinctive to her and threatened to imperil her now. If she hit this particular guard, she was as good as dead by bayonet. Her right hand curled up into a fist. Des knew immediately what was to follow. He was only twelve feet away but screamed out in his loudest voice.

"Mummy, no! Please no! Don't hit him!" Des's voice was high pitched and shaky with fright.

Rosie seemed to calm herself slightly. She looked back at Des, then at the guard.

"Please Mum, don't do it. For my sake," Des shouted again.

By now, some of the women from Rosie and Des's house as well as some of the adjoining houses were running up to provide moral assistance. The guard, surrounded by the growing crowd of angry women, appeared to change his attitude. The angry look he had worn was replaced by an expression of resigned contempt. He turned and walked away, leaving the women to tend to Rosie's rapidly swelling face. Des joined the women who took Rosie to see Dr. Holvek.

The following day, Des could hardly recognize his mother. The side of her face was swollen and her left eye was almost shut. Over the bone and around the orb glowed a massive black bruise. Des had never seen such a serious black eye in his life. Betty and some of the other women tended the wound as best they could.

Dr. Holvek, who was a formidable woman, would take up the matter with Captain Mahaji, the Japanese officer in charge of the camp, who ranked higher than their resident Commandant. Word had spread that Captain Mahaji was well-educated, and more decent and civilized than most of his men. Surely he wouldn't tolerate such undisciplined, sadistic behaviour from his guards. Even now, after all they had witnessed of the enemy, their belief in humane instincts had not been snuffed out.

Together, Des and his mother waited for news of Dr. Holvek's meeting with Captain Mahaji, the next time he came to inspect the camp and his staff. No information arrived but as the days passed, it became clear that The Dog was gone. Rosie wore her black eye without shame, waving proudly at Sonny, mornings and evenings, from the crowded balconies of the prison camp. The Colinne sisters' banner disappeared, but the women's determination to communicate with their men never waned.

Des was glad The Dog was gone. His mother's run-in with him had been a close call. Des had stopped questioning why they were always able to move successfully through so many close calls. He would live, or he would die. Providence would offer no explanations. It was merely the way things were now.

15. THE SWORD

After witnessing The Dog's assault, Des's resentment festered for weeks. He thought about revenge much of the time, but knew that any overt act on his part would bring the wrath of the guards down upon his mother as well as himself. Feeling powerless, he became ill tempered and cranky. Sometimes he assuaged his hatred of the guards by mocking them with a broad animated smile, so absurdly false that his friends worried for his safety. To their relief, the guards seemed not to catch on. From time to time, with some of the other boys keeping watch, Des would pour sand into the tanks of the Japanese vehicles. Still, his anger lingered. With each act of mischief, the urge to do even greater damage increased.

One morning, as he was helping his mother attend to her cooking fire he noticed a car drive into the camp. It was a large vehicle, dusty from its trip through the Indonesian bush roads, but still appearing grand enough for Des to guess that it must belong to an officer. It stopped a short distance away from the Commandant's building. Des heard the motor cut out and watched as the driver's door sprung open. Out stepped a well-built Japanese man, impeccably arrayed in an impressive officer's uniform. This was the first time Des had seen Captain Mahaji himself. A gentleman of the highest order, he had been educated at Oxford University in England, and his English was as polished as the beautiful sword that sometimes hung at his hip. He also seemed to have time to speak to the children who gathered a safe distance away to catch a glimpse of this most curious enemy who spoke and acted so well.

Later, Des asked his mother about this man. He looked civilized, but since the incident with The Dog, Des trusted none of the enemy.

"That's Captain Mahaji," she told him. "They say he's a reasonable man. He went to Oxford, you know."

"What's that?" he asked.

"It's a school in England."

"Why didn't he stay there and fight for us?"

Rosie didn't answer right away. Instead, she picked at a loose thread on the threadbare dress she wore night and day. "Maybe he couldn't." she answered.

"Why? What does that mean? Couldn't what—fight for England? Why would he want to fight for the Japs if he was in England?"

Rosie shushed him. "He's still one of them, but he understands us—and he's reasonable."

"If he's so reasonable, why would he ever have left England?"

Rosie put a pail of water onto the fire to boil. A mute frown held her face rigid. Des knew she was through discussing the matter. Somehow this made him seethe with resentment, increasing his hatred of the enemy.

From time to time Captain Mahaji returned, splendidly attired in full regalia. Des fumed as the younger children fawned over him, smiling as they stared hopefully at him, vying for his attention. They believed him to be kind. For Des, there was no amount of kindness or manners from these people that could erase the sound of the guard's palm as it collided with the soft skin of his mother's face, sending her reeling to the ground. Captain Mahaji could comport himself with as much elegance as he wished. But he was still one of them.

On one very hot day, the captain arrived in his shiny car. Des noticed he failed to put on the sword he usually wore, opting instead to leave it in the back seat of his car. Because the sun was so strong, Captain Mahaji instructed his driver to park the vehicle in the shade a short distance away from the Commandant's building. When the driver darted around the edge of another building toward the officers' latrine, Des could not believe his luck. With no one else in sight, he crept to the car, and stole Captain Mahaji's sword. By degrees, he made his way back to his house, hiding behind walls and long grasses until the coast was clear. He hid the weapon for an hour or so in the secondary jungle across the road from the house. When he was certain no one was inside, he retrieved his prize and ran into the house.

Alone with the sword, Des took the opportunity to examine its deadly beauty. He pulled the blade from its long sheath, revealing its mirrored length. Beams of light from the window glinted as he turned it over. The steel handle, etched beautifully to mimic ancient silk wrapping, fit magically into his youthful hand. He lifted it high above his head, feeling the sword's power. A blue and brown tassel attached to the handle caressed his wrist as it danced above him. Hearing footsteps on the veranda outside, he hastily sheathed it again, noting the smoothness with which it glided into the case up to its copper hilt.

Several soft raps at the front door were immediately followed by a familiar strong voice of calling his name. It was Kenny, one of the boys Des had become acquainted with in the camp. Kenny had been taken captive along with his parents and six brothers and sisters. His mother was a gentle person, who had a reputation as a wonderful cook, though here there was little material for her talents. But she was kind to the children, was a friend to Rosie, and Des liked her. After days of feeling lonely, knowing only the younger boys, Des had finally met up with Kenny, who quickly became his idolized big brother in the camp. Four years older, Kenny was already five and a half feet tall, bronzed by the sun, and still sturdier than most of the thinning boys, with wavy dark hair. Always ready to help the others, Kenny was a natural leader, calm and confident, and inspired Des with hope for their survival.

"Yes Kenny. I'm here. What do you want?" he called out, stalling for time as he quickly reached out a back window and secured the sword in a safe spot under the roof.

"Let me in," urged Kenny.

"I'll come out. Wait a sec." Des rushed down the stairs and out the front door. "What's so important?" he asked.

Kenny looked annoyed. "I guess you think you caught yourself a nice prize there, do you?"

"What do you mean?"

"Come on now. I saw you take it."

"Oh that," Des shrugged, feigning disinterest. Inside he chastised himself for allowing himself to be seen with the sword. Kenny was a trusted ally, but he could have easily been seen by the wrong person.

"Listen," Kenny whispered, drawing closer to Des, "word has it there's going to be a huge deal made of this. The Jap Commandant has said that he's willing to overlook it if the culprit returns it."

Des grew concerned. "Does anyone else know?" he asked.

"I don't think so, but just the same you'd better take it back. If you don't, they'll bring in the *Kempeitai* and turn the place upside down. They'll make us all pay, even if they don't find it. Besides, the Captain could be in a heap of trouble too."

Des's body quivered. His stomach tied itself into a burning knot, as he remembered the stories he had heard of the dreaded *Kempeitai*, the Japanese military police. If Captain Mahaji was transferred, he could be replaced by someone much worse. He chastised himself for not thinking of this. He dreaded the thought of a week's starvation for the prisoners, a common punishment for many infractions. Now he felt miserable.

Shrouded by the night's darkness, Des later crept out from his house, the beautiful sword clutched nervously in both hands, and made his way to the little room where the prisoners' leader Dr. Holvek, slept. Silently, and with great care he placed it beside her sleeping form, holding his breath as the scabbard made a small dull tap on the planked floor. She heaved a dreamy sigh but otherwise failed to stir.

Des made his way back to his place. Somehow, returning his prize made his tension increase. Over the next few days, he scoured the faces of the women to see if he was suspected. No one said a thing about it. He interpreted even the most perfunctory glance as an accusatory glare. When one of the adults did speak to him, his ribs tightened around his chest, squeezing his blood and flushing his cheeks.

Rosie noticed her son's odd behaviour and questioned whether he was well.

"It's the usual trouble," he answered, grateful for the suggested explanation. "My tummy hurts a little more than usual. That's all."

Rosie tilted her head and looked into her son's eyes. Her gaze softened as she tried to conceal the fear she bore for her son's health. In these brutal conditions, robust adults succumbed to sickness and death every day. What chance would a small boy have, already weakened by years of poor digestion? Des read her thoughts. Now he really did feel sick, knowing his small lie made her suffer. Still, he would not tell her about Captain Mahaji's sword.

16. UPROOTED AGAIN

A new pall hung over the camp, in spite of the blazing sun. For days, there had been no appearance of the men going bravely by on their way to their hard labour. No one knew what had happened to them. No one told the women if their husbands and sons were still alive, or not. All their grief of loss at the separation was relived with renewed fear.

Des and Rosie clung stubbornly to the belief that somehow, somewhere, Sonny was alive. Des knew his father would want him to be strong, and not to give up hope, but inside, he felt a flame in his heart grow dimmer, wavering in dread. He longed for Sonny's comforting presence and firm voice, for the strong arms that enveloped him and gave him courage. Tears began to well up in his eyes, but Des was too tired to cry, wasted now by hunger, as the weight fell off his once sturdy muscles, leaving thin ropes of sinew hanging from his bones. Even his hair became dull and lifeless, and his face grew pinched. The shoulders his Dad would have hugged were knobby and bony. He was vaguely astonished that he could be so thin and still live. Rosie too, and all the others, were growing thinner every day, their eyes more sunken. Many more fell ill, easy victims of dysentery, malaria, beri beri, and all the other parasites of the region. Des feared his mother would drop on her feet, as she tried to tend to them all.

Then the nightmare worsened. Screamed commands from their captors once again rousted them out of their quarters, and they were driven like livestock back to the field where the horrible separation from the men had taken place. Dazed, they all trembled with hope and fear—hope that by some miracle they were to be reunited with their men, fear that they were about to join them in death somewhere.

Just as they had with the men, the guards started to shout at the women and children, commanding them to follow one of the trucks down the road. A few soldiers remained on foot to goad the prisoners. The truck then sped away, leaving the crowd to make its way. Guards beside and behind the women and children prodded and shouted, commanding their captives to keep moving.

As they stumbled along, Des was struck by the sounds of misery all around him. Several women were still sobbing their torment, interrupted by the consoling voices of some of their comrades. Some carried sacks with a few belongings they still had from the Tappah. Some of the Dutch colonials actually still had luggage that they dragged along, guarding it possessively. Most, like Rosie and Des, had nothing at all except the clothes they wore.

Kenny and his mother and sisters walked as bravely as they could. Behind them, Betty helped her grandmother along, silent and stoic.

Des stayed silent too. He knew that Rosie was clinging to the last vestiges of self-control. The soles of his feet burned over the road's hot surface. He had eaten nothing since the day before, nor had he taken a drink from one of the water bottles he carried. They plodded on weakly, bedraggled and miserable. When his mind could no longer wrestle with the gritty dryness in his throat, Des removed one of the bottles from his sac and took a drink. It had warmed in the day's heat but still felt good as it soaked his mouth and filled his empty stomach.

"Not too much," cautioned Rosie. "Remember what Dad said. We must always make it last."

Some of the other women looked longingly at the water. One young Dutch mother with two small girls asked in English if she could have some for her children. Rosie took several more steps in silence. At first Des thought his mother was prepared to ignore the request. Instead, she sighed, closed her eyes against her own selfish temptations and handed over one of the glass bottles. From time to time, a soldier would shout out an order in Japanese. No one seemed to understand or care what he was saying. Sometimes the soldiers would exchange a few words with one another and laugh, appearing to take great delight in the prisoners' suffering. After an eternity of walking, some of the women fainted, annoying the guards no end. Those women who were stronger tried to help the elderly and weak.

A group of Indonesians, carrying large stocks of bananas, passed by them, reminding Des of his hunger.

The prisoners stared longingly at the food, but the Indonesians kept their heads down, refusing to meet their gaze.

"Maybe they'll drop a bunch or two," Des said to his mother, knowing the fruit would go far to ease their hunger pains.

"Those poor people may be suffering. They could be short of food too."

Des could only watch as the bananas—not quite ripe—passed by, so close that he could smell their waxy skins. As he continued to consume the bananas with his eyes, loud shouts ripped through the air.

"The Japs want the bananas," Kenny said. He and Des were talking together for awhile.

The Indonesians were ordered to stop, powerless to prevent their occupiers from robbing them. As a couple of guards ran towards the fruit, the Indonesians dropped their load and ran off into the bush. Des looked on resentfully as the soldiers filled their stomachs with their green booty, never once offering any of it to the starving captives.

"They'd never get away with that if the officers were around," Rosie mumbled to the woman next to her. "I hope those miserable Japs get a huge belly-ache," she added, causing laughter all around.

Their own hunger sated, the soldiers embarked on a round of songs. The foreign lyrics were indiscernible to Des but like the others, he understood the tempo of their warrior tunes. In front of him a true-blue, colonial high society type by the name of Mrs. Geer, gave the soldiers a thumbs-up sign, delighting them into a louder chorus. Then, in a voice loud enough for all to hear, she yelled.

"Could you slope-heads possibly sing Rule Britannia for us?"

Des saw his mother cringe, but the Japanese soldiers, failing to understand English, smiled even harder as they kept on singing. Rosie breathed a sigh of relief and joined in the women's laughter.

"Mum," Des asked innocently, "what does slope-heads mean?"

Rosie ignored her son, turning her head up in a gesture that told Des he would not receive an answer.

"It's a derogatory term for the Japs," a woman behind him said. "They don't like it."

Their mirth died down as the gruelling march continued. Two trucks passed by, carrying a load of Chinese men guarded by several Japanese soldiers. Unlike other trucks that periodically passed them, the men on board did not shout and make fun of the women as they passed. Des saw everyone around him grow sullen.

"Those poor fellows must be on their way to their doom," a Dutch woman loudly observed.

Rosie would not speak to Des. Several times, he asked her where they were going, how long they would stay. She grimaced and waved his questions away. Des could not help persisting in spite of the risk of provoking her irritation. His heart ached with the crushing pressure of not knowing. Without his father, he had no way to tell if they would be alright. He missed the steady reassurances of Sonny, even when they were wrong. But he hadn't been very wrong, had he? They were alive.

In silence now, the women walked for what seemed like an eternity. Too tired and hot to complain, they reserved their strength for the arduous task of putting one foot in front of the other. Finally they reached their destination.

It was an abandoned rubber plantation, the vats and refining equipment sitting cold and still, the sheds empty. There were several big wooden dormitories that had once housed the workers who stayed on site. The prisoners were lined up and counted. Boys and girls were separated into age groups. Since Des had his mother, he was placed in quarters with her, crowded with dozens of others in the humid dormitories.

The Japanese had merely seized the plantation and surrounded it with barbed wire, creating an instant warehouse to store their human inventory. The security measures were hardly necessary, as escape was impossible. Dense jungle and resentful villagers willing to betray their former Dutch masters served as effective barriers to any self-liberation.

While Rosie claimed a small area of the floor around a bunk for the two of them, Des went outside to look around. Several spots around the periphery had sentries posted. Here, many of the guards had been conscripted from the local Indonesian population. But the nearest one was Japanese. Later, Des would see straight black hair jutting out in badly barbered shards from his round head, but today, the soldier had topped himself with the same brimmed canvas hat worn by the other guards. Not very tall, and podgy in the middle, his general form was one of roundness. Even his chubby face was rotund, his eyes disappearing into bulging balls of flesh over his cheeks when he grinned. Dubbed 'Moonface', he quickly distinguished himself from some of the other guards by his approachable manner with the younger boys. The young girls, by contrast were forbidden by the mothers from ever being seen near the sentries.

For several days, Des investigated his surroundings, only entering the quarters he and Rosie shared with so many others when he needed to sleep. Sometimes he occupied himself by collecting firewood. A road separated the plantation buildings from the secondary jungle and dense bush surrounding the camp, and there was stream flowing through it that provided drinking and washing water. Des and his mother often crossed the road together, filling up a bucket from the house. The bucket was a possession brought in by one of the Dutch women. While Des and Rosie arrived at the internment camp with only the clothes on their backs and the air in their lungs, some of the Dutch Indonesians who had managed to bring luggage and some possessions guarded these possessively—as if their lives depended on it.

Tamarinds, mangoes and jackfruit grew on trees just outside the camp's periphery where barbed wire forbade them access, but sometimes Moonface allowed the children out to pick what they wanted. The rations that were trucked in were far from adequate, and Des and his playmates contributed the spoils of their hunt for edible fruits, roots and herbs to the supplies for the camp.

17. OZAKI

Des sat on the veranda steps, freshly awake and squinting against the strong morning light. An elderly diabetic woman had died during the night, distracting his mother.

"Get us some water," she said, before Des's mind had time to adjust itself to the new day. "I've got to see what I can do for Mrs. Donnelly's daughter."

"Not much, I'd wager," Des mumbled under his breath as he rose to fetch the steel bucket from beside the steps. He was beginning to resent her constant attention to others.

"Did you say something?" Rosie snapped.

"No," he answered.

Des filled the pail from the river that ran through the thick growth across the road from where they lived and brought it back, placing it beside their cooking fire area. He wondered why she would want him to bring water just to let it sit and attract mosquitoes while she comforted Mrs. Donnelly's spinster daughter. He left before she could return with more impractical errands for him to do.

He walked the periphery of the camp, careful to avoid drawing the attention of the guards. Rage still simmered deep and constant within him, often conjuring up images of his mother's body reeling to the ground under the sadistic hand of The Dog. Now he hated them all. Sometimes the other boys would playfully smile and tease the younger guards who would nod or smile in discrete movements designed not to betray any diversion from their wooden stance. Not Des. He trusted none of them.

Rambling across the compound, he came across Kenny and a group of the boys playing with a tennis ball. Des liked one of them in particular, Ron, a tall slim fellow with olive skin and straight dark hair. He was usually quiet and pensive, even a bit of a loner, without either of his parents. His father had stayed in Singapore, and he didn't speak of his mother. The boys assumed she had not survived.

As the boys tossed the ball around, Des noticed one of the guards watching. Des had never seen this one before. Japanese soldiers were often smaller than their European counterparts but this one was smaller than most. His youthful face did not display the usual impatient boredom of so many of the other sentries. In fact, amazingly, he looked amused.

"You play," he said quietly, but loud enough for Des to hear.

Des looked at the guard, who motioned with his eyes toward where the youths were tossing the ball. It was unusual for the guards to speak English, except when shouting orders. Was he being ordered to play, he wondered?

Ron threw the ball to Des, calling out "Think fast!"

Before he could react, the frayed gray ball split the air beside his ear and headed toward the guard. The ball bounced a few times, losing momentum, until in a bumpy roll, it came to rest in front of its unintended target. Des watched as the guard lifted his rifle. Puzzlement and panic clenched his chest, then dissipated at once as the guard turned his weapon upside down and connected its butt squarely with the ball, sending it neatly into the air and into the hands of the closest boy. A gleeful laugh escaped from the guard's smiling mouth, in shrill tones that made the children also laugh.

They played for hours in front of the guard, purposefully letting the ball fly his way from time to time, yet careful not to attract the attention of his superiors. His knowledge of English was only rudimentary, but the boys were able to glean some information from this unusually friendly enemy.

"How is it you speak English?" Des asked warily. In spite of the other boys' affection for him, Des was suspicious.

"I Christian," was the reply.

Des had never heard of any Japanese Christians. "How can you be Christian?"

"Yes, Christian."

"But how?"

"Yes. How," he answered, and then added. "Don't worry, next week war is finished."

Throughout the day they learned that the guard was from the port city of Kobe and that he had three siblings, the youngest of whom was Des's age. Later, he told his mother about the strange guard who seemed so kind.

"Oooh," she cautioned. "Be leery of him. He could be gathering information for his superiors."

"What information?"

"I'm not sure—illegal camp activities, perhaps."

Des thought of his afternoon playing ball with the guard, recalling how the man seemed so genuinely friendly. "He's a Christian too," Des added.

"Is he," she stated drily. It was not a question. "Just the same, you'd be best to stay away from him. You know better than to trust them."

The next day, Des sought out the other boys. Some of them had also been forbidden by their elders to associate with the guard. But the open space near his sentry box was the best place to play and they found themselves drawn to him yet again. This time, the guard himself beckoned to the boys. Scanning the area to see that he was not being watched, he pulled a small sack from inside the sentry box and handed it to Kenny. Inside, were some glass marbles and several handmade tops, each spun with about two feet of string. Des and Kenny and Ron were delighted and quickly taught the younger lads how to use them. For Des it was a special gift, a shadow of the one Sami had given him, that was lost in their flight from Singapore.

"What's your name?" Des asked the guard, letting down his defences.

"Ozaki."

"Thank you Ozaki."

For several weeks they watched for Ozaki to be on duty, careful not to attract the attention of the other guards and officers. Sometimes he would be there during the day and slip in the odd bite for them to eat. Once he astonished them by bringing in some bananas from a nearby Indonesian grove. Des was thoroughly impressed as he knew such a gesture could have dire consequences for Ozaki. When he was on night duty, Ozaki would stand in the dark, several feet away from his lit up sentry box to avoid mosquito attacks, and sing.

"What were you singing about?" Des asked one evening as he passed by the area.

"Japanese love song," he answered.

Des and his friends liked to listen to these songs and found much entertainment in Ozaki as he crooned in his high-pitched, lilting voice, the spell interrupted by an angry yell whenever a mosquito bit him.

In spite of his mother's admonishments, Des couldn't help dropping his guard around Ozaki. Nothing any of them did seemed to irritate him and so one day, they dared to ask Ozaki something they never would have asked of any other sentry. Des and Kenny approached him.

"May we go over there and pick some of the star fruit?" Des asked timidly, motioning to some trees about 60 feet outside the barbed wire barrier.

Ozaki swung his head around toward the heavily-laden trees.

"Yes please, may we?" Kenny added.

Ozaki's expression took on a worried tone. "Oooh, no, no, no," he said. Cannot do. Not all of you. Ozaki in too much trouble if guard commander see you."

Des and Kenny feigned exaggerated pouts, even though they had been certain from the beginning that their wish would not be granted. Ozaki appeared flustered and disappointed by their reaction and seemed to relent.

"Maybe one boy can go."

Des halted his antics and fired his gaze incredulously at Ozaki. "Only one of us?" he asked, trying to push his luck.

"Only one. But not now. You are too many. They look at you."

The small group of boys sat sullenly in the hot afternoon dust for about an hour, talking and playing. It seemed to Des that Ozaki had a great deal of sympathy for them and they were determined to make the most of it. But they had not forgotten the star fruit, or the fact that at some later time, Ozaki might allow one of them to pick some. Suddenly, they were startled by Ozaki's shrill yell.

"Go," he grinned, pointing to a tree. "Go to heaven."

Within seconds two boys were designated to stay behind and look out while Des and Kenny slipped past Ozaki's sentry box to the outside of the camp. They picked as much of the fruit as they could carry, stuffing it into their shorts and filling their hands, even pushing an extra one into their mouths before running back to the fence and slipping in undetected.

That evening Des shared the star fruit with Rosie, but thought it wise not to tell her of Ozaki's involvement. To his relief, she did not ask Des how he obtained the sour, under-ripe fruit, and he was glad not to have to lie to her.

The next week, Ozaki was on guard again in the same location, where the boys liked to play. He watched them for a while with his usual amused grin. Finally he spoke.

"Next week, I have night guard duty. You come then and I bring sugar cane."

"He's joking," Des said to the others. "His lit guard-box would be seen from the guards' office too easily. He'd never get away with it."

"Yes, yes. Can do," said Ozaki. "You come next week. Get sugar cane."

"When?" asked Ron.

"Wednesday. Come Wednesday—six o'clock."

Des and the boys waited expectantly for the next few days to pass. Some were doubtful that Ozaki could succeed at such a daring delivery. Sugar cane was bulky and easy to see. Ozaki was bound to be asked questions by his fellow sentries. Just the same, they planned their strategy for the big event.

"Only a few of us should go. If all nine of us show up, we might draw too much attention to ourselves." Kenny always had a sense of the practicalities.

"We can do it with four,' said Des. "That's enough for two to look out and two to get the cane from Osaki."

They all agreed and Des was designated to be one of the four on the sugar cane detail.

Together, they hung around in sight of the sentry box but still a safe distance away. At six o'clock, as the sun was setting, they watched as the changing of duty guards took place. To their disappointment, it was not Ozaki who took over the post, but another young Japanese soldier. Des was immediately suspicious.

"Do you suppose something has gone wrong?" he asked Kenny.

"I don't know. Let's hang around, just the same."

Des began to wonder if this had all been a trap, as his mother had suspected, and her warning words echoed in his mind. Nervously, the boys continued to watch the sentry box while going through the motions of childish play to throw off any suspicion. The sun had completely set now. Moonlight and incandescent lighting from the camp blended together casting murky shadows in which the boys played and plotted. At about eight o'clock, the unknown sentry called to them.

"Come over here," he said to them in English.

The boys held back, distrustful and suspicious that their plan was now foiled.

"Come here," he called to them again.

Des crept forward a few steps, still maintaining a careful distance. After several minutes, he saw some movement and heard a rustling. Ozaki stepped out from behind the box, out of uniform and appearing quite agitated.

"Silly boy. Come here," Ozaki said, in full view of the unknown guard.

The boys were now convinced this was a trap and stood frozen in their alarm. Des felt sick that he had not heeded his mother's advice. He poised himself to run away, along with his three comrades, when he saw Ozaki drag a large sack into view.

"Come, quick," Ozaki said, beckoning the boys to collect it.

The unknown sentry walked away from his post and into the darkness. Now was their chance. Des and Kenny quickly trotted up to Ozaki, who was bathed in nervous sweat and clearly agitated. As soon as the boys had collected the sack, Ozaki ran into the darkness without uttering another word. As soon as they had dragged their booty back into the safety of the shadows where the other two had stayed as lookouts, the other guard reappeared and took his place at his post.

Des stayed only long enough to retrieve his portion of booty from the sack, which held the promised sugar cane, and some sweet potatoes too.

When he brought it all to Rosie, he knew he had some explaining to do.

"He's really a very good person, Mum," Des told her.

"You may believe that, but it could all be a set up to see who is and isn't part of the Resistance."

"What resistance?" asked Des, not sure of her meaning.

"I don't know, but they don't need much of an excuse to suspect us of having one," Rosie cautioned. "More than ever now, you must be alert to these possibilities. Maybe this Ozaki is good, but you have no way to know this for certain. You're better off having nothing to do with them."

Des found it easy to follow his mother's advice. For three weeks, Ozaki was nowhere to be seen around the camp. Des wondered at Ozaki's disappearance and hoped he hadn't been caught. Then one day, Ozaki appeared on day duty, as usual wearing his customary grin and playful expression.

"Was it good?" Ozaki asked.

"Yes," Des answered, "it was very good. Thank you very much. The sweet potatoes were very nice too.

Ozaki's grin broadened to a large toothy smile.

"But," Des continued. "Who was that other guard that let you bring the sugar cane? Why didn't he report you? Weren't you nervous about that?"

"About other things, yes. But not him. He is from my village. He too regrets this war—regrets very much your suffering. Too much misery. Much regret."

"He doesn't hate the British?"

"No hate. I no hate too. My uncle likes British. He live in Singapore too before the war. Have camera shop. Very good business. British very good customers."

Then, Ozaki leaned in closer and lowered his voice. "If we get a good opportunity, my friend and I, we will run away."

18. LIFE AND DEATH IN PRISON CAMP

Des lazed in the dirt against a wall of a building near the barbed wire barriers encasing his world. His legs were drawn up to his chest, his cheek atop the knobby ridges of his knee bones, a brooding posture that let him feel the scorching impact of the morning. He had escaped from the dreary den of women that was his home, leaving his mother to fetch the morning water and prepare a fire on her own. He valued his nights on the floor of their cramped room, listening to Rosie's night breathing if he woke in the dark, knowing that for those few hours sleep allowed them some respite from the grim truth of their situation. But sometimes, like today, the house could be a second prison, a dank cage of clucking hens who overwhelmed his small space. He had heard Rosie's voice call after him as he crossed the road a short distance away, but ignored her, knowing she would assume he had not heard and give up.

A tiny ant crawled across his ankle, disappearing behind his leg to the underside of his calf. He brushed it aside and it fell to the earth where it resumed its trek without missing a beat. Des placed his hand in front of the ant, barricading it. The ant merely continued up onto Des's palm and down again over the other side, not stopping even for an instant to notice its change of terrain. Des thought of killing it, but let it go, watching it make its way to the wall where it disappeared into a crevice.

"We're not so different, you and I," he muttered.

"What?" a voice blurted from above him. "Who are you talking to?"

Des looked up to see Kenny standing over him with another of the boys, a big rawboned blond fellow named James. Des wasn't sure about James, who was always sad, and sometimes a bully. Today he seemed friendly enough though, and he was with Kenny, so Des shrugged.

"No one, "he answered. "I was just thinking out loud."

"That could be harmful to your health," Kenny retorted. "Sometimes the walls have ears."

Des stood up. "What are you two up to?"

"We came to get you," Kenny said.

"Where are the others?" Des asked. A band of younger boys were usually to be found in the shadow of the older ones.

"We gave them the slip. Something's up with the Resistance, "James said quietly. Like Kenny, James had some of the natural qualities of leadership, and whether they liked him or not, the boys generally respected him.

"Something's usually up with them," Des retorted. By now he had learned of the indigenous Amboinese and Eurasians who were sympathetic to the Dutch, and who were rumoured to help the male prisoners obtain supplies and pull off acts of resistance within the men's camps, like the one where Sonny had been before the daily march of the men past the women's camp in Palembang had suddenly stopped.

"Come," Kenny beckoned motioning his head toward the road that led to the camp's main entry gate. "Let's walk. I don't want anyone else to hear what I'm going to tell you."

They strolled along the road, careful not to attract the attention of the guards. Occasionally one of the boys would pick up a stone and hurl it playfully at a tree, careful always to appear as children, playing children's games.

A couple of guards stood erect, guarding the entrance to the camp at the end of the road. Another young officer, unknown to Des, stood beside them barking orders in Japanese.

"See that one?" Kenny whispered, nodding toward the unknown officer.

"Mmm-hmm," Des nodded discreetly.

"I heard he's for it."

"Why? Who from? What did he do?"

"I don't know for certain. I heard my Mum and sisters talking. When I came along, they stopped talking and I couldn't get anything out of them."

Des had seen Kenny's sisters and mother often around the camp. Kenny's mother was much older than most of the other mothers and was always seen in the company of one of her daughters, who were much older than most of the boys. He looked up to Kenny who was four years his senior and was amused to see his idol so babied and protected by a swarming family of doting women.

"But I know something's up," Kenny went on. "One of the women in our house had a nasty encounter with that Jap a couple of days ago. She's been laid up ever since and no one will talk about it. He must have done something pretty horrible. She won't speak to anyone and there's always someone at her side."

"Will she be all right?" Des asked.

"I don't know. Maybe. But I do know that they're trying to get a message out to the Resistance. There may be some sort of revenge."

Des felt his stomach flip. Revenge was fine for the men and the Resistance. But he had never seen the women plan such a thing. They had no experience in such matters. It could be a debacle. The Japs would punish everyone if they thought such a plan had originated in the camp. He hoped his own mother was not part of any plot for revenge. As kind as she was, when her Welsh dander was up, she could be formidable. He would never forget how close she came to lashing out at The Dog.

Now Des was worried. "Find out what you can," he said.

Try as they might, none of the boys could find out any more about the situation. Rosie showed no sign of any special tension, and after a couple of weeks they decided it must have all blown over. If there was any act of defiance carried out, they never knew of it.

Des went off to fetch a bucket of water from the stream and headed reluctantly back to the quarters he shared with Rosie and so many others. Most of them were easy enough to get along with, but there were some who were bitter and quarrelsome, and it made the horrible situation worse. Des's shoulder ached. In the short walk from the small stream across the road, his strength had somehow managed to leak away like splashes of water over the lip of his bucket. He thought of complaining to Rosie. As he entered the cramped dormitory, her back was to him. He wanted to approach her but hesitated. She was bent low over the reclining form of the same elderly woman she had been caring for since their arrival in Sumatra. Des thought she must have heard the soft padding of his feet behind her, for she turned and gazed at him, her face frozen into a stern caution not to come any closer. She shook her head rapidly from side to side.

"Leave the water outside the door," she commanded, "and don't come any closer. Mrs. Palmer has passed on."

"I told you so," retorted an acid Dutch voice from the end of the room. "You shouldn't have wasted the medicine on her. She was diabetic. Nothing could help her."

Rosie glowered at the sharp-featured woman. "Should we waste any on you when your time comes?" she retorted.

"Why even ask when you know there won't be anything left by then." The woman huffed out of the house.

"I don't know why that harpy has to be so trying," Rosie said to no one in particular. "She sits here on her high horse with two suitcases, brimming with items she hoards away while many of us have nothing but rags. She doesn't lift a finger to help with the sick ones—oh, but can she whinge!"

Rosie looked down at the rigid corpse before her. She had nursed the kindly Mrs. Palmer for five weeks, brought her food saved from her own rations and discarded scraps that some of the inmates still, unbelievably, felt were inedible. When Mrs. Palmer's legs began to swell and ooze with bloody pustules, Rosie dressed them with salve brought by a Dutch prisoner. In the last couple of weeks, Mrs. Palmer's comas grew more frequent, often requiring Rosie to send Des desperately scurrying to scrounge any source of sugar he could lay his hands on. More than once he had combed the secondary forest for edible berries only to find them picked bare by other hungry inmates. Sometimes he could beg a piece of jackfruit or lime from the ladies in the food preparation area. Often he would resort to scavenging bits of rotten bites from the rubbish heap near the camp's perimeter.

Des knew his mother was wrong to nurse the woman so long. He heard the other inmates scold her for wasting resources on those whose death was inevitable. Finally, no more food scraps could be found to keep Mrs. Palmer from the merciful grasp of her own demise. Now, Rosie bent over her, fixing her eyelids and placing Mrs. Palmer's hands across her chest before delivering her into the hands of her cremators. Des saw his mother's hand caress the dry skin of the dead woman's arm, running it along the bone to the elbow, finally catching hold of her sleeve. Rosie paused, holding the fabric between her fingers, feeling its texture. Des's heart leapt as he saw her grasp the lower part of the dress with both hands, stretching it out on either side as she examined its fullness. He knew what she was thinking and ran back outside almost spilling the bucket of water at the door's edge.

When he returned later, Rosie was clad in a different dress but not the one previously worn by Mrs. Palmer. Instead, the mean-spirited complainer Rosie now always referred to as *'that woman'* wore it. Rosie's new frock was less fine—more utilitarian. It fit her loosely, its roomy drape emphasizing her diminishing size. All of them, women and children, were shrinking into skeletal figures, and as Des looked in dismay at his once beautiful mother, she caught his eye and beckoned him with a wave of her hand. Des neared but did not ask about her dress.

"We are moving,' she said flatly.

"All of us?" Des asked, realizing the silliness of his question.

"Of course."

"Where,"

"I don't know. They never tell us anything."

"Are we going to another island? Are we going to Dad?" Des asked

"I don't think so. But you must prepare for a long walk. Eat as much as you can today. Look further into the bush. Find anything edible you can, and eat it."

Des's pulse quickened. "What about you?" he asked.

"Don't worry about me. I don't need as much. If you find extra in the forest, you can bring it back. I'll be fine. I don't use as much energy as a ten year old."

"I'm eleven now," he corrected her. "My birthday was on March the tenth. It must be way past that now."

"Eleven. Oh darling," she murmured. "Don't you worry, one day we'll be free again, and you'll have lots of happy birthdays. You'll see."

She held him close, then released him with a sigh. A faraway look swept across her features. Her eyes moistened barely, not as tears, but enough to add a glistening shine which weakened her tough resilience. Des was uneasy at this sudden change in mood. He knew enough not to ask what was really in her mind. He walked away, staring over at the bungalows and dormitories of the prison camp that had served as his neighbourhood since their arrival so many weeks ago.

He did not want to move. Moving brought more uncertainty to his world. Each time it happened, he left part of his childish soul behind, replacing it with the emboldened desperation of a reluctant warrior conscripted into a fight for his life. He worried more and more for his mother as well. Each day he saw her stand up to an injustice in the camp, he feared for her life. He did not trust many of the other women and he could not trust the Japs. He had lost count of the number of times his heart jumped into his throat at the thought of being orphaned by a display of Rosie's indignation in the face of brutality. She was all he had in this world.

19. TAKEN FROM ROSIE

Rain bounced on the ground, sending muddy droplets into the air. Des and Rosie huddled under the overhanging shelter of their veranda. A dark cloud blackened the sky, masking every bit of sunlight and blue. Des had never seen such a complete darkening of his world. He picked up the edge of his mother's dress and casually rubbed the fabric between his fingers. Their captivity bonded them. In Singapore he had shared his life with the boys of his neighbourood and also Sami and Ah Wah, leaving his mother to coo with his frail baby sister, creating a private feminine world with her. When his sister died, he watched Rosie transfer her affections to little Ah Wah, buying the dresses and ribbons she could no longer buy for her own little girl.

In the camp now, he was all she had and she clung to him as if her very existence depended on him. Des too, felt closer to his mother. As the months passed he had grown out of his childish concern for his own comfort and transferred his worries to thoughts of Rosie's safety. He lived in fear of being an orphan and knew that his chances of outliving the war would be slim. His mother was his lifeline. The strength of her heartbeat bolstered his, giving him the power to face what was only a half-life of day to day subsistence in the camps.

Rosie reached down and placed her hand over Des's fingers on her dress. "I can't stop thinking about your father today," she said.

"I think about him every day," Des responded, feeling the comfort of her thin moist hand over his.

"I'm glad you do," she smiled.

"Sometimes I dream about him too," Des said. "He's in his light gray suit and has liquorice in his pocket."

"Does he give you some of it?"

"No. He gives it to you."

"Do I like it?" Rosie asked.

"You love it and fill your mouth full."

"And how do you feel about that? Aren't you disappointed not to share in the treat?"

"No," Des responded. "When you eat it, it's as if I had some myself."

"Des?"

"Yes Mum?"

"You will have liquorice again one day soon. You believe that don't you?"

Des paused, allowing a brief interlude of silence to stand out against the sound of raindrops splashing against the wooden roofs, tin pots and muddy ground, each creating a different note of a hollow melody.

"I don't know," he mumbled.

The rain fell all day and into the evening, making it impossible to light the fires for cooking outdoors. Des was given some weak tea made from leaves found in the secondary forest area across from the camp. It soothed the fire in his stomach, quieting his appetite for awhile. This was the time he must fall asleep. If he could not, then he would face another night of aching hunger. Des slept.

The next day streaming sunbeams and the jarring sound of parrots in the jungle jolted him awake. He stumbled outside, rubbing the last vestiges of sleep from his eyes. The sun had already dried the muddy ground, leaving the sweet scent of earth and forest to permeate his bleak surroundings. He watched the ration truck arrive, spilling what looked like a bounteous supply of fruit and vegetables onto the ground. Like ants, the women emerged from their holes, covering the supplies in hungry numbers, making it apparent that the delivery was nowhere near enough to feed all of the inmates. Later, when the area was clear again, Des approached. It amazed him that despite the hunger and deprivation, the women still chose to discard food that was deemed by them to be undesirable. Bits of rotten fruit and dried onion skin littered the ground. Des picked up as much as he could and brought it to Rosie to put in the rusty can that was her pot.

She made a small meal, which instilled some energy into her son. Shortly afterward, the familiar call came for them to assemble before the camp Commandant. Obediently, they moved to the open area a hundred yards or so away from their house. First they were counted, then Des stood bored while some administrative information was conveyed. He was abruptly called back from his thoughts by the Commandant's referral to the children. Some of the older ones were to be removed to a men's camp whose location would not be revealed.

Their captors had done this once before – taking away the oldest of the boys, without telling their mothers where they were going, whether they would be taken to their fathers and brothers, whether they would live. It was a torment that broke the women's hearts. Now, once again, the women were to return to their barracks and wait for one of their representatives to come around with a list.

Des could hardly breathe. His mother ran to him and escorted him back to their space, her arm covering his shoulder and pulling him into her perspiring side so tightly he could feel the tremor that coursed through her. When they were back at the house, she sat on the floor with him, hugging him close. He felt her draw in her breath, trying to steady herself.

"Des," she said, trying, as always, to be strong for him, "the Japanese have ordered that more boys be transferred to the men's camps. If you have to go, it would be better for you to be with them. Our British camp commander thinks so and I agree. And you would be with your father. We've heard the men's camps are much better, that they know a lot more about organizing to survive together."

She held back her own doubts and fears, trying to reassure her young son.

He was not pacified. "No!" he cried. "I'm better here with you! You can't believe the Japs. Or our commander! Dad may not even be alive! We don't even know for sure there's a men's camp. Why would you believe them? I can stay here and hide!"

Rosie's heart was ripping apart. She knew that what he said was true, but she had no choice but to let them take her son. Defiance would be fatal for them both. And she was still hoping that Des, being young, would not, in the end, be on the list.

She said none of this, only tried to convince him, and perhaps herself, that Des would indeed be with Sonny, and would be much better off. But Des felt betrayed. Even if Sonny was alive somewhere, Des had no faith that the Japanese even knew which family member was where, or cared about reuniting anyone. That night, trembling and hugging his knees to his chest, he plotted his escape, envisioning how he could run away through the forest, and live on what he could forage. After a few sleepless nights of feverish planning, he realized he could not survive, unless Chinese sympathizers would hide him for the duration of the war, and that was extremely unlikely. Miserably, he accepted his fate, but could not forgive his mother for allowing it to happen instead of fighting to keep him by her side.

"Don't worry," she said. "You're only eleven. There are others older than you. You're so small." Rosie let Des go abruptly as if convinced by her own words. "You are small. You are small. You are small," she moaned to herself.

Des sat, stunned, beside his mother. His heart raced, thumping its rhythm into his head and drowning out all thought. He knew that if he spoke, his words would release the panic that lay just beneath his silent exterior. He was still silent when a woman arrived.

"She has no list," Des thought. Relief washed over him, slowing his heart and soothing his worry.

The woman spoke to Rosie in a low voice. Des could not hear her, but he read the expression on his mother's face as surely as if the woman had shouted out into clear rain-washed air. Rosie's head turned to Des in an unguarded gesture. Her eyes held him, steely blue and pierced with pain. Des ran outside leaving his mother to her anguish.

Des woke to the reverberating pound of the Japanese gong. At first, he thought his eyes were playing tricks on him, encountering only deep blackness where there should have been the tinge of dawn. He twisted his palms across his eyelids and opened them again, realizing that the darkness was no trick. Immediately his heart went into his throat. A familiar hand reached out to him, groping in the blackness before finding his cheek. He heard a small gasp escape his mother's lips.

Japanese shouts ordered them out into the damp pre-dawn darkness. They all knew this was not the usual morning summons. Shivering with dread, Des saw Kenny and Ron and James stumble out to join the group. The tropical winds washed warmly over his thin body, as if trying to calm his shuddering, but still he quaked. The boys and their mothers were hurried roughly to the camp gate, where a truck waited with its engine idling.

A looming silence shrouded the group, broken only by a few soft sobs from some of the women. In the east, a sliver of dazzling red suddenly pierced the blackness. It cast a glow that reached upward into the sky, fading to hues of orange and purple that reached up to vanquish the darkness of the dying night. Shapes soon emerged into the strengthening light. Second by second, Des made out the forms of the frightened prisoners, realizing with shock that less than half of the boys within his age range had been selected for removal. Fright now turned to panic enhanced by an overwhelming sense of betrayal. Their own camp leader, not the Japanese, had made the selection, with his own mother's agreement. He looked at his mother in the dimness, focusing his growing despair onto her.

At this terrible moment, he blamed her and wondered in despair how she could let this happen. Rosie still clung to a belief in their commander's promises, but Des had been stripped of all innocence, and he feared he and the other boys were not going to their fathers or the other men at all, if they even lived.

The guards looked on in amusement as the band of boys hugged their tearful guardians. Kenny's mother held him close, whispering into his hair. Ron and some of the children who were orphaned earlier accepted hugs from the mothers of their comrades. Rosie wrapped her son in her arms, clutching him tightly to her withered bosom. Des let her cling for a moment, standing stone-like and inanimate before being rushed by the guards onto a waiting vehicle. Sitting on benches in the open air of the truck's cargo section, the boys did not speak. Several clung to whatever possessions they had brought. Des nestled a white cotton bag between his feet. It contained all his worldly goods consisting of a pair of shorts, nine glass marbles, a punctured tennis ball, the toy top from Ozaki, and the treasured ornamental brass cannon taken earlier from the house on Bangka Island.

Many turned to catch a last glimpse of their loved ones, believing that this could be their final farewell. Des sat rigidly beside Kenny, Ron and James, frozen in fear and terrible resentment, unable to turn and look at his mother. She was wrong to let him be taken away! He faced forward, showing Rosie only the back of his head. She was all he had, and she was sending him away.

He did not see her wave good-bye, nor did he hear the choking sob that rose from the depths of her anguish. His senses were shut off by the terror that now took hold of him. Tears welled up in his eyes, blinding him as the truck pulled away. Rosie stood at the gate watching and waiting for her only son to turn and see her once more, until the truck finally disappeared from view. Des never looked back.

20. THE BOYS' VOYAGE

For an hour and a half, the boys bounced over rough roads through forest and thick grasses. A Japanese guard sitting with them in the rear compartment tried to make conversation with them. He spoke first in Japanese, then, failing to elicit any reaction from them, he tried out a few words of Dutch. Finally, he spoke in English.

"You see new place," he said. "Ride is nice."

The young prisoners sat silently morose, unyielding to their captor's attempts at conversation. Eventually, the guard stopped trying to draw them out and resorted to torturing them by aping the sounds of a crying child. Anger rocked Des's mood, jarring him momentarily from his fear, and the ever-present pains in his abdomen. The expressions on the other boys' faces mirrored his growing rage. He clenched his fists against the urge to trade his own life for one brief opportunity to thrash this monster, whose face was twisted into a repulsive caricature of a sobbing child. The fat around the folds of his narrow eyes squeezed up, erasing them into thin lines that blended with the pursed wrinkling of his down-turned mouth. His nostrils flared. All of the guard's facial features seemed to cluster into the centre of his fleshy face, as he puffed and heaved exaggerated sobs. Des imagined himself jamming his fist into the middle of this contorted target, occupying his thoughts for a few moments with his fantasy before his anxious terror took over once more.

The truck halted, lurching them forward. During the ride, gray clouds had swept over the sky. In the muted light of the lingering dawn, Des could see that they were beside a small river jetty with a barge tied up alongside. About twenty Indonesians and a few Japanese guards in uniform were busy loading a cargo of produce. The children's mouths' watered to see all the crates of fruits and vegetables, and sacks of dried tapioca, chickens, and ducks, which Des thought must be for the Japanese garrison stationed at their destination. The same guard from the truck brusquely ordered the boys on board. They clambered onto the deck and were told by another guard, in English, to stay at a spot on the side of the barge in full view of the cockpit.

Still clutching his white cotton bag, Des, found a spot with Kenny and Ron where they made themselves as comfortable as they could on a few sacks of tapioca. James settled morosely nearby. They were left exposed to the sun. If not for the cover of the cloudy day, they would have been badly burned.

The sound of clanking metal, followed by a shudder from beneath, signaled that they were under way. Clusters of floating vegetation and other flotsam passed them in the murky water. Bits of driftwood bumped hollowly against the sides of the barge. The muddy banks of the river glistened wetly, bordered by rich green grasses and other plants that made their home by the riverside. The odour of livestock, mixed with the pungent smells of vegetation rotting in the season's dampness, penetrated Des's nostrils and accentuated the strangeness of his environment. These things bobbed past his vision. At this moment, Des realized it was possible to look directly at something and not see it. With eyes wide open, he stared out into his changing world and saw nothing, save for his own rippling fear reflected in the muddy river.

The passage of the morning hours did nothing to assuage the boys' anxieties. Around noon, a Japanese guard appeared. He led the group to a large drum of water.

"Drink," he said in English.

Des leaned over the drum and saw a slick of oil resting on the water's surface. Prismatic colours wound through it, stopping at the edges. With the aid of a broken coconut shell, Des and the others scooped the liquid and drank the only water they had been allowed that day. The acrid aftertaste distracted Des from other miseries as he consumed enough water to quench his thirst, hoping it would not make him sick, and add to the stabbing cramps in his belly. They were still gathered around the drum when an elderly Indonesian crewman appeared with some boiled sweet potato and fresh raw coconut. Des had not eaten for over twenty hours and even this meagre bit of food was welcome.

The crewman's face was wrinkled and weathered from a life outdoors. He patiently waited for the boys to finish eating before speaking to them in Dutch.

"Are you Dutch?" he asked.

"British," some voices chorused.

"England?"

"Singapore," Des answered, uncertain whether to trust this man with too much information.

The Indonesian puffed out his chest and smiled. "I been to Singapore many times. And Penang. Before war."

His smile faded slightly at his reference to the conflict. He continued in his broken Dutch. "I work many year on Dutch coastal ships."

Des finally felt secure enough to ask what they all wanted to know.

"Do you know where they are taking us?"

"We crossing straits to Bangka Island. You going Muntok Prison."

The boys' expressions reflected their dread. They all remembered the grim place they passed on their walk to the tin workers' barracks in Muntok months before.

"Men's prison," the crewman said.

"When will we be there?" they wanted to know.

"By evening, tomorrow—if boat doesn't break down."

The old man left, returning a few moments later with a tarp. He guided the boys back to their resting spot and set the tarp up for cover from the afternoon sun.

"Latrine is here," he said, pointing out a wooden box hanging over the edge of the barge. A hole had been cut from the centre of its underside to allow its contents to drop into the water.

When the man left them, Des felt less depressed and his anger somewhat diminished. Maybe they really were being taken to join the men. Maybe, just maybe, he would find his father.

A short time later, another guard approached and stood before them. The bayonet on his rifle glinted in the sun. He gestured threateningly with his fist.

"Place everything over there!" he commanded, indicating an area in the opposite corner of the foredeck. "Do not look over the side. Hurry, hurry! Go back to your place," he barked as the boys dropped their belongings where they were told.

Des placed his bag among the others. The brass canon clunked heavily on the wooden deck. There was an echoing hollow thud in his heart. He was bereft now of even this small treasure. Mental exhaustion finally overwhelmed him, and he slept. But instead of offering escape from reality, his dreams took him to more perilous places. Dreadful images tortured his mind. Food turned to dirt in his hands. He ran to safe oases that disappeared as he reached them. He relived the shooting of civilian Chinese traders he had seen murdered just outside the women's camp. One in particular, who carried a suitcase similar to the one his parents had when they first boarded the Giang Bee, was shot through the back. In his dream, he saw it from a vantage point inside the women's camp. This time, when the trader fell, Des ran through the fence to the man's side. He turned the body over and saw the smiling face of his father.

"Dad," he said, disbelieving his eyes. "I thought you were at work."

"I am," he said. You're just dreaming. It's not real. Go back to sleep".

Shouting pierced his sleep, waking him rudely. The barge was still and calm, and Des knew the engines had been shut off. It was late morning and it shocked him that he had been able to sleep for so long. He felt weaker than ever. On the shore, a Japanese truck, similar to the one the boys had been on earlier, waited with its motor running. He made his way to the pile of belongings to retrieve his bag. Some of the other boys were already there and Des stood back until they cleared the way. When it was his turn, he stepped forward only to discover his bag was not where he had placed it. After looking around at the few things left in the small pile, he decided to ask around in case one of the other boys had picked it up for him. Every child had his own property except for two, who like Des, found themselves without any goods.

"My bag," he croaked dryly. "Where is it?"

An Indonesian guard looked past Des and into the horizon, ignoring him as he would the bleats of an animal from among a hoard of livestock. The rest of the boys staggered onto the shore, disoriented and dazed by the sun. Screaming Japanese soldiers herded them into the back of a truck. Des held back, hoping desperately to catch sight of his only worldly possessions.

"Go!" he heard a voice bark rudely at him.

Des faltered. At that moment, he considered letting himself be shot by running back onto the barge. He had nothing more to lose, nothing more they could take from him. If they wanted his skin, they could have it.

But running back onto the boat held no reward. He knew he would never find his brass cannon, the marbles, the tennis ball, the gift from Ozaki, or even his shorts. All that he had now was inside of him, and he could no longer muster the will to save even this. Nor could he give it up either. Sacrificing himself required strength he did not have. For the first time in his short life, he knew what it was like to give up.

With leaden legs, he boarded the back of the truck and sat on the wooden surface of its flatbed. A familiar air penetrated his nostrils, jarring him. It was the sweet and pungent at the same time, and he remembered it from his early days in the garage on Bangka Island. He knew he was back on Bangka again, but this time they had not landed at Muntok jetty. They were at a smaller wharf at a more remote outpost.

The truck jerked forward, picking up speed on the dusty road until it was almost flying. Des and his comrades were tossed about like rag dolls as the trucks wheels seemed to find every pothole and rut along the way. For hours, they tore along through the countryside, allowing him to forget, for a while, his nagging hunger and thirst. Now he worried for his bones that slammed against the truck's flatbed, with scarcely any fat or muscle to cushion the battering. Raw panic gave him the strength to cling to the side of the truck. Others in the middle with nothing to hold onto clung to each other in a futile attempt to brace themselves against the relentless thrashing. Des wondered if the driver was a Kamikaze soldier, intent on killing himself and everyone else. His prior mood of resignation to his own fate gave way to an intense desire to survive the ride, or at least to avoid being tossed out into an unforgiving jungle of predatory animals and vengeful Indonesians.

Hours later, the tortuous journey ended with an abrupt jerk as the truck reached its destination. Muntok. For Des, there was no relief at the sudden cessation of the painful ride. Now his small frame quaked as he took in the frightening sight of his new home.

21. MUNTOK JAIL

Des's legs were like rubber as he stumbled off the truck. Cruel young guards shouted, and pushed the boys through the iron gates and into the dusty yard of Muntok jail. It looked even more menacing and overhwelming than before. On that first sojourn on Bangka, they had been able to breathe with relief when they passed by the gates and the massive stone prison. Now, it loomed larger and more appalling than ever, as they knew their fate lay within its walls.

More sadistic guards laughed and pushed laggards as the weaker boys tried in vain to move faster. Des knew he and his starving mates must have appeared grotesque. Barely clad, and weak from hunger, their bodies could scarcely perform the simple task of walking upright. Hunched over and exhausted, their gaunt faces wore no expression, as their vacant eyes blinked against a dusty breeze.

A sneering guard offered the boys some vermin-infested stagnant liquid. Though his swollen throat felt like sandpaper, Des refused, as did the others. Most knew that drinking such poison could lead to a slow and ugly death.

The sun had not yet closed the day. The boys stood bewildered and still, as groups of bony, exhausted, and desperate-looking men approached them in the waning light, asking for names, and word of the women left behind in Sumatra. The dazed boys gradually realized that some of these must be the fathers and brothers who had been taken from them. Several asked Des who he was.

"Des Woodford," he answered, still rooted to the spot.

"Woodford?" a voice said. "I believe your father may be here."

The words leapt into his brain, stimulating a dizzying hope. Des could only gaze at the man and try to steady himself as his heart pounded against his ribs. He barely heard when other men's voices asked him for word of wives, daughters and sisters. For some, he had good news. For others, he had no news, and those men went from boy to boy, questioning. Many were given the worst news possible. Des watched each of these men turn away in anguish, with despair and dejection in every retreating step.

Kenny stood with Des, looking desperately at every lean and hollowed face. Suddenly Kenny gave a shout and staggered into his father's arms. There was no familiar face for James. He went to a corner, alone.

Des scanned the yard, searching for Sonny's familiar, lean frame and wondered if he would recognize him from among the throngs of emaciated prisoners. He steeled himself to peer through the dusky light. Parched and starving, he quickly scanned the area for a source of water but saw nothing. Although hoards of prisoners were now approaching to see the newcomers, he felt alone. His beating heart seemed to sap the last remaining strength he had. His rubbery legs felt as though they would buckle any instant. He tried not to faint.

Then from behind him, a pair of arms wrapped themselves around his misery and spun him about. He felt his father's sinewy muscles embrace him, drawing him close. Des became more light-headed as he settled silently against Sonny's thin, quivering body. No words came forth from either of them as they stood, enfolded into one another. Des felt the shaking manifestation of his father's emotion, the staggered gasps as Sonny tried to speak, only to give in to the soundless aura that meshed the two of them into one.

At last Sonny drew back enough for Des to look into his father's tear-glazed eyes. Now the questions began.

"Are you healthy?" he wanted to know. "You're so thin. Have you been very ill? Did you have much to eat in your camp?"

"I'm thirsty," was all Des could manage. "Do you have clean water?"

"Yes, yes. We'll get some in a minute," Sonny said, still clinging to his beloved son.

"I…I…is your mother…," Sonny struggled for the words to ask what he dreaded to know. "Is Mum alive? Were you with her?"

"Yes. Mum is alive. We were together until they brought us boys here."

Sonny swallowed before asking his next question. "But is she well?"

"Yes. She's well. She's fine. Very busy like always… just like herself…like Mum always is."

"Not sick?"

"No, not sick. She helps the others. Please can I have some water now?"

Sonny led Des to the side of the jail's main building where a pipe was fitted against the wall. At least there was clean water in the prison compound. He turned on a tap at the end of the pipe and Des fell onto his knees, drinking greedily. All at once, he was seized by intense cramps, like a thousand knives carving at his stomach. Dark patches danced in front of his eyes, then circled around him as they spread their blackness over his vision. He felt nothing as his face hit the ground. In his next conscious moment he was cradled again in his father's arms.

The two of them were now on the wet ground, as rain began to spatter the prison yard. Together, they were one binary soul. Sonny's voice was no longer choked as it had been when Des first arrived. His words were soothing and confident as he rocked his only living child. "Don't worry," he comforted. We're here and we're alive. We *will* make it through this war. We will make it through—as a family—all of us."

For days, Des opened his eyes each morning expecting to see his mother's form lying nearby. The old Dutch residence in the Palembang had each at least been part of a real home at one time. In their first quarters, the veranda, the bedrooms, even the faint lines etched on a doorjamb, marking a child's growth, had all held for Des the imprint of a family's haven. Even the rubber plantation abode, although overcrowded, and filled with the aura of worry and death, had still registered something familiar in Des's heart and for almost a year, these had been his home, with an odd sense of normality. It was hard to believe a year had gone by, that he had grown so used to the situation, even had a strange sense of normal routine.

Everything was different now. The transfer to Muntok prison had stolen his illusion of home and security. Stone walls and cement floors encased the acrid odours of male perspiration, urine, disease, and death. About eight prisoners a day were dying of starvation, malaria, dysentery, beri beri and sheer despair. Here, the guards were brutal, and the prison was real. The rations were meager and scarcely edible, and basic bodily needs were served by basic Asian squat plumbing, all of it filthy. At least there was clean water, part of the original facilities provided by the Dutch.

His father's presence was a godsend, but Des knew that Sonny could do nothing to change their awful situation. The cells had originally been built for one or two inmates each, but now many more were crammed in, and spilled through the unlocked cell doors into the corridors and the yard. Locks were unnecessary. Even if they could escape past the guards and surrounding fence, they had nowhere to go. They were on an island; the colour of their skin would give them away to local Indonesians who bitterly resented their former Dutch masters, and anyone who resembled them.

At least the two of them were able to find space to sleep in a kind of covered veranda, where it was cooler than the crowded inner cells, but safe from the rain. Beside them was a good-natured, resourceful young man named Trevor, who Des had known back in their first days on Bangka. Sonny had taken to Trevor, who was only a few years younger than himself, and it was clear to Des now that the two had formed a strong friendship that was also an alliance for survival. Trevor was gaining a reputation for his selfless efforts to help others.

"Welcome to beautiful Muntok," he said to Des. "Your Dad has worried about you so much. Now we'll be able to take care of you."

Des immediately felt the warmth of his concern.

"Do we all have to go someplace and work for the Japs every day?" Des asked, afraid of the answer. "When you all went by our camp in Palembang some of you looked like you would never make it."

"No," Sonny reassured him." We're not sure why, but they don't have us doing slave labour now."

"They just keep us locked up here," Trevor added, "but we have ways of sneaking out and back in on foraging runs. We'll teach you."

Eventually Sonny and Trevor and some of the other men managed to find enough scraps of wood to build rudimentary bunks for themselves and their sons on the verandah. There were some thin straw mattresses that gave a small amount of comfort. Des slept easily that first night, exhausted, relieved, and safe in his father's love.

Summer heat turned to October rains that cooled the dry dust. The boys grew more despondent in the men's prison. Without their mothers to comfort them, they had to grow tougher among the men, and survive as best they could. Now Des was tormented by the way he had treated his mother when they were torn apart.

"But she should have kept me with her!" he said tearfully to his father, trying to explain what had happened.

"No, Des, she was right. You'll be much better here. We have a lot of men who know how to get past the fence to forage, how to make trades with some locals, and a lot of other things that we've organized for survival. Trevor is especially good at it. You'll see. We all look after each other."

Des remembered his pampered life in Singapore, with his parents and Ah Wah and Cookie to look after his welfare. There were rules about coming straight home from school, about staying within his neighbourhood, about what he could eat. This secure childhood world had now given way to a new imperative born of desperation. In Muntok, everything he understood was flipped in reverse. Here the children, whose size made them ideal for the task, were encouraged to transgress the rules, to dig holes under the boundary fences by night, and squeeze under the barbed wire to search for food. Des and his comrades learned that the one and only rule that mattered was to never get caught. The boys followed this creed with every action they undertook. Des's new inner code was accompanied by another self-imposed regulation: he vowed never to do anything to shame his father during their internment.

22. THE BANKER

Some of the prisoners were more self-absorbed than others, and as in their former lives, some of them could be outright horrors. Des and his friends soon learned who these people were and tried to avoid them. They especially despised a Dutchman named Van Leeuwin, a six and a half foot former bank manager with a shaved bald head. From the outset, this Dutch giant, accustomed to a life of authority and high esteem, made it his mission to act as though he were in charge. He condescendingly barked orders to everyone, and was almost universally despised. Somehow he had managed to manipulate, or threaten, a few minions to do his bidding.

"He believes he's superior to God Himself", James said one day to Des.

James had managed to find himself a space on the veranda with some of the other fatherless boys, and if anything was becoming more moody than ever, sometimes tough, other times despondent.

"I despise him," Des pronounced, stealing a glance at Van Leeuwin as he lounged nearly naked in the sunlight on his adjustable canvas deck chair, barely covered by a skimpy loincloth. "He acts as if he's on holiday and we're just a bunch of coolies."

"The other men hate him too," James added, "not just the English. I heard his own people can't stand him either."

"Well he must have some friends somewhere. He's got some books and a lot of nice clothes. I wish he'd wear them."

The boys moved on to other topics, talking tiredly as they scratched lines in the dirt with sticks. The morning sun ascended slowly over the eastern horizon casting long shadows over the dusty common area. Des and James meandered slowly through other groups of prisoners, trying to distract themselves from thoughts of food. They were startled to hear the booming voice of Van Leeuwin scream at them from just a few feet away.

"Stop casting a shadow on me you English loafing pigs," he screamed in Dutch, "or I'll thrash you to a pulp."

James and Des wheeled around to see Van Leeuwin staring up at them from his deck chair. His angry face glowed crimson as he glowered at the boys. In his hands he held a large thick novel which it was his custom to read while lolling around with certain other idle prisoners waiting for their next meal. Stunned, James and Des quickly moved away, shielding their own red faces from the shocked stares of the other prisoners.

Nearby, Des heard a distinctive Australian voice accompanied by the righteous support of some others with the same accent.

"If you touch one hair on their heads, you won't wake up alive tomorrow, mate," it said to Van Leeuwin with quiet authority. It was a promise, not an empty threat.

At this, Des and James moved away faster than ever, while stealing a glance at the group of defenders – a group of tiny Australian jockeys who had befriended Sonny. These feisty, wiry little men, especially one in particular, were later to become heroes to the prisoners, and were already famous for their foraging exploits, and quiet defiance of bullying of any kind. Their diminutive stature next to the brutish bald giant hardly seemed threatening, but no one raised a voice to challenge them. Instead, Van Leeuwin stormed into the jail block mumbling something to himself in Dutch.

That evening, as Des lay down with his father to sleep, he thought about the incident with Van Leeuwin. He considered telling Sonny about it, but his embarrassment at having been so harshly insulted kept him silent. As his thoughts sprinkled through his last moments of wakefulness, he entertained images of retaliation. His daydreams gave way to sleepy images that became dreams. By morning he could hardly wait to seek out James and plot their revenge.

With no breakfast to delay his mission, Des set out to find James whom he hoped would also have some ideas about how to get even with Van Leeuwin. He came upon his comrade on his way back from the latrine.

"Des," said James, "What's eating you? You look mad enough to kill."

"I am. I didn't get much sleep last night thinking about that pig Van Leeuwin."

"Yeah," James nodded, "I don't like thinking about it. We'd better stay away from him."

"Oh I'll stay away from him alright," Des echoed. "But first I want us to get even."

James' eyes widened. "Oh no," he said. "I couldn't possibly. You've got your dad to back you up. I've got no one. If we were caught, I'd be finished. You've seen how well connected he is. I don't want to get on his bad side."

Des sympathized with James. Like so many of the boys, James had no parent or other protector in the prison, and was frequently despondent and lonely. But Des also felt certain that they could pull off a successful operation against the Dutch giant if they remembered the number one rule and made sure they weren't caught.

"Don't worry about that. The jockeys won't let anything happen to us."

"No," James dug in his heels, "count me out. I don't want any part of it."

"I guess I'll have to take matters into my own hands," Des retorted, undeterred.

From a distance, the two boys watched Van Leeuwin emerge from the jail, accompanied by a couple of his toadies. In one hand he carried one of his precious books. The wooden frame deck chair swung loosely from his other hand. James and Des kept their distance, careful not to be seen looking in Van Leeuwin's direction. The hulking Dutchman set up his chair, paying meticulous attention to the angle of its recline, as if he intended to relax, while at the same time having the most advantageous view of the goings on around the camp.

Des watched with loathing as Van Leeuwin finished setting up his chair. Before sitting down, the hateful bully paused to survey his surroundings like a feudal lord inspecting his estate. He then placed one bare leg on either side of his throne and lowered his shiny naked bottom onto its canvas seat. His minions sat nearby on the hard cement while Van Leeuwin propped his book on his belly, just above his loincloth.

"You see," James said, "he's never alone. It's impossible to get to him. There's nothing you can do. Just forget about it and stay away from him."

Des shook his head. "There's always something. That lazy pig is going to get his."

Over the next couple of days, the boys watched Van Leeuwin's habits. At certain intervals, he would leave his chair and head over towards the latrine, returning shortly afterward to his reading. Des now knew what to do. That night he mapped out his plan in the silent darkness beside his father. He told no one, not even James, who lately seemed to be always in a constant state of worry and depression.

In the morning, he waited as usual in the distance, stealing only the most casual of glances at Van Leeuwin. A group of men sat on the ground nearby. They appeared to take no notice of their pompous comrade as he idled in his chair. Des walked around the area, looking about as if searching for other boys his age. Peripherally, he studied his subject, measuring vanity in every gesture the large man made. Resentment furrowed Des's forehead for a moment, before he remembered to look casual. There was no room for error. Any slip in his guard might be noticed. After about an hour, the big Dutchman slipped a small leaf between the pages of his book and rose. No one near him took notice of him, nor of Des. When Van Leeuwin rounded the corner of the jail's outer wall, Des circled widely around the chair and approached it casually from the back. Bending down, he made a small adjustment and was gone again before anyone noticed.

When he was a safe distance away, Des blended into a group of boys playing a listless game of catch with a stone, keeping one eye on the empty deck chair. Minutes passed. Des was on tenterhooks as he waited for Van Leeuwin to return. Anticipation turned to nervousness as he began to worry that Van Leeuwin might not return. Two of the other men got up and approached the chair. One of them lingered around it a moment as if deciding whether or not to steal a few seconds rest before his comrade returned. Des's heart nearly leapt from his chest as he considered all his careful planning going to waste on someone who had done him no harm. To his relief, Van Leeuwin appeared from behind the building, strutting arrogantly as he surveyed the camp. The two men noticed him and ambled away from the area.

Van Leeuwin returned to his deck chair, scanned his surroundings as was his custom, and promptly sat down. The chair's wooden frame collapsed noisily, dumping the majestic giant onto the floor. His large head cracked audibly against the cement. From across the common, Des and his friends could hear a roar of laughter resound from Van Leeuwin's own group, and when Des's mates looked over, unaware of his role in the joke, they slapped their thighs and laughed with the rest. Elated, Des laughed with the first real giddy joy he had known in months. Van Leeuwin's face was purple as he clumsily picked himself up. Not a soul lifted a finger to help him. His anger boiled up in a bellow of rage.

"You are all nothing but trash! One way or another, I'll see you all punished!"

At this the crowd roared louder. Now Van Leeuwin was sputtering and fuming, but in his loincloth he only managed to look ridiculous. He picked up his chair and book and stormed back into the jail, leaving all around to feel sorry for the prisoners inside who would bear the brunt of his fury.

The rest of the day, Des was on cloud nine. He hardly noticed his hunger or the nagging pain in his intestines. He had pulled off his revenge and its sweet taste was enough to soothe his appetite.

That evening as Des lay next to his father, he had almost put the incident out of his mind until Sonny's voice broke the silence.

"Did you have an interesting day, Des?" he queried.

At these words, Des knew instantly that his father must have been told of Van Leeuwin's comeuppance. Sonny was always fully knowledgeable about events around the camp. Nothing ever escaped his attention.

"I guess you heard what happened to that horrible Dutchman," he said by way of an answer.

"I heard."

"You should have seen it, Dad. It was really quite something to see him flat on his back with that stupid deck chair under him. I thought he would..."

"Des," his father interrupted. "That was a nasty thing you did to Van Leeuwin,"

"But Dad, what he did to me and James was worse."
"James and me."
"Fine. But don't you agree that he deserved it?"

Sonny's face wore an expression of sternness that reflected the evening moonlight, making him appear almost angry. He ignored Des's question. "I would make you apologize to him…"

Des gasped.

"…if it were not for the fact that Van Leeuwin is such a nasty, arrogant piece of nothing. What you did was wrong and I want you to swear you will never do such a thing again."

Des fumed, disapproving of his father's reasoning.

"If apologies are being passed around, Van Leeuwin should be the one to apologize to us. He was the one who wronged us in the first place."

Des waited in the dark for his father's rebuttal. Instead, an imposing silence draped itself over father and son, broken only by the incessant hum of hungry mosquitoes.

23. WORK AT THE TINWINNING

Perhaps it was the threat that the jockeys were protecting the boys, but in any case, the boorish banker left Des and his friends alone after that, except for the usual bad-tempered tantrums he displayed to everyone in camp. Des was still quietly pleased with his ambush, figuring he'd taught the bully a lesson.

It was small comfort though. Des suffered more every day from the effects of the of the paltry, debased rations, his tender insides, once used to being pampered with his mother's strict diet, now assaulted by the rough food of prison, and by his own digestive acids. The pain was constant, sometimes severe, like knives slicing into his abdomen, sometimes a low ache, but almost always there. All the boys suffered, but Des seemingly more so than many, with his delicate insides. Pain became a constant companion he pushed to one side, to get on with the business of surviving. Sonny grew more and more worried about his son, as Des grew even thinner, with lines of suffering etched around his eyes. Every day he looked older, eerily more like his father.

At the morning assembly, Des noticed familiar faces were sometimes missing, and never reappeared. Had they died? Had they been moved to another prison camp?

"We have to just carry on," Sonny told him.

But one day, horribly, Kenny's father was gone. The malnutrition, the seemingly endless fight for survival, and finally a severe case of beri beri had been too much for him. Much older than Sonny, he had been a true gentleman of the old school. Kenny was broken-hearted, and Des wept with him. The weight of their tragedy, the pure evil of what was being done to them, hit them full force. As they toiled to live every day, this dreadful place had become their normal daily routine, but Kenny's loss tore apart that frail illusion and showed the horror anew for what it was. The boys struggled to carry on, Des helping Kenny any way he could.

One day Nikko Barding, one of Sonny's Dutch friends, approached, his brow knotted in seriousness, and said "Des you're wanted over at the tinwinning."

Des and the other boys almost worshipped Nikko and his younger brother Jan, and would obey them without question. When they had all come to Bangka the first time, it was the Bardings who had taught the boys their first lessons in foraging and survival. Both Dutchmen were in their early thirties, almost six feet tall, bronzed and strongly built, though now wiry and bony from deprivation. The boys knew the Barding brothers were always looking after the welfare of others. Their exploits in foraging and hunting, in evading the guards and in creating makeshift tools and other miracles, were fast attaining legendary status.

"Off you go," Nikko said.

The tinwinning was a large, well-built concrete structure at the back of the compound, that had been the old quarters for the tin dredging workers, used now as a makeshift kitchen for preparation of the rations, such as they were. All the boys went there when the rations came, in the hopes of doing a few chores, and being given some extra scraps of food. Sometimes Des and Kenny were chosen. But since the tinwinning was out of sight, it was also possible to breach the wire behind it, to go foraging. Des wondered if he or another boy had been seen, or if they thought he'd been filching.

"Why?" he said, "has some food gone missing? We didn't do anything."

Nikko shrugged, but his eyes softened. "Go and find out for yourself," he said, with a thinly disguised twinkle.

At the tinwinning, Kenny and some other boys had gathered round, also summoned without explanation.

When the boys were called inside, they found Jan presiding over the scene. All of the camp's daily rations were piled in organized heaps, a riot of colour of green sprouts, tapioca root, bronze sweet potatoes, and peanuts. Unripened jackfruit and yams shone green and gold.

Jan Barding stood nonchalantly fiddling with the handle of his knife.

"You've been chosen to help on a regular basis,' he announced, "as long as you work hard. And no pilfering from the kitchen. You'll find that this place has benefits without doing that." Jan smiled broadly at them. Jan had a perpetual grin, his open, ingenuous face shining with some inner secret of life. Nikko told them he'd been like that even when he was a boy.

"Today," Jan said, "you'll learn to handle a knife, and then you'll be assigned a task, along with an adult."

Over the next few days, Des learned to peel and chop sackfuls of root vegetables. Then there was the jackfruit, the worst because the skin was tough and messy to peel. His hands stiffened and blistered and his arm muscles ached. White sap oozed onto his hands and knife, and dripped onto his pants, gluing them to his thighs. The boys also had the task of stirring the large boiling cauldrons over the open fires where the food stewed.

"Don't fall in," one of the adults warned Des, who was smaller than the others.

The huge vats were four feet wide and open at the top, and two feet deep. Des leaned back to make sure he would never fall in as he turned the big paddle through the mixture. It would seem to be enough food and nutrition to keep everyone healthy, but once it was diluted into a watery stew, and doled out in tiny portions, it was barely enough to sustain life. There was never any meat or fish to provide vital protein.

Since they were allowed to check and taste the food, and could eat some scraps, Des was able to eat about the equivalent of an extra meal. Now he found the evening rations were almost enough to tide him over without the familiar pangs of hunger to disturb his exhausted sleep. He knew that Sonny must have gone to the Bardings for help, as Des's intestinal pains had grown worse, and his muscles seemed to melt away.

"I've had enough," he said one day, passing a bit of leftover tapioca to his father. Sonny was showing signs of weakness sometimes, and now Des worried about him.

"No. You eat it," Sonny said, waving the dish away. "You're growing, in spite of all this. You need it. Why do you suppose you boys were invited to help in the kitchen in the first place?"

Des had known, in his heart that Sonny and Nikko and Jan had engineered the whole arrangement, when they saw how badly the boys were deteriorating. But to hear his father say it was a relief. He was meant to live, to grow up and some day leave this place. They would not give up on him. Now all he had to do was not give up on himself either.

24. FIGHTING BACK

Rations were cut. For two days, Des's belly moaned and churned. Something was always triggering the Japanese Commandant to punish the inmates it seemed. Des never knew what latest transgression would prompt another period of reduced rations. Illness frequently prevented Des from engaging in his usual habit of sneaking through the barbed wire. The inhabitants of the local *kampongs*, now alerted by experience, were on the watch for garden thieves. Sentries in the camp sharpened their guard, watchful for unrest in the camp brought about by hungry desperation.

They lined up for assembly. Des stood weakly in his usual place among the younger men. His arms hung at his sides, leaden and still. He could scarcely listen to the clipped babbling of his Japanese captors as they informed the inmates that rations were to be restored. In the back of his mind, he felt a nugget of numb relief swell, until the realization gripped him fully. He could eat today.

In front of him, a few feet over, stood another boy. He was taller and stockier than most of the others. In spite of the deprivation, David had managed to maintain some bulk, dwarfing Des considerably. His hair hung over his forehead, exposing only his sinister eyes and snarling facial features which aroused themselves into a frenzy of jubilation whenever his considerable cruelty was expressed. Des was his favourite target. David turned his head, sneaking a glance at Des, briefly penetrating him with a look that required no translation. The trucks of rations were arriving at the tinwinning. As always many of the boys would go over to it in hopes of extra scraps if they could do some of the extra chores in the kitchen. Des knew that Nikko and Jan had worked a miracle, with all their influence, to get regular work in the kitchen for him and Kenny and a few others.

When the prisoners were dismissed for the day, Des set off for the tinwinning with the rest. The tinwinning complex was joined to the main compound by a canopied walkway. A guard was posted outside each end of the passage, but not within it, giving the prisoners a small oasis of privacy. As Des went through the walkway towards the tinwinning, he saw David, already waiting there.

"Slow poke", he scoffed, stepping in front of Des.

Des peeked back at the guard who seemed oblivious in the oppressive morning heat, and to the clear threat from David.

"Go away," Des said, knowing he was wasting his breath. Reasoning with David was impossible and any attempt at conversation only seemed to provoke him. Des tried to step around the bigger boy but was grabbed around the neck in the powerful crook of David's arm. Head-locked, Des was drawn downward, doubled over and bent until he was forced to his knees, his forehead in the dirt. David released his prey from the headlock position. He then stepped over Des's hunched back, straddling him. Scooping his arms up from underneath, he pinned them behind Des's back, stretching his tendons until they felt they would tear. Des cried out in pain, attracting the attention of the guard.

David let go. He was satisfied now, having established his superiority over the much smaller and lighter boy. Many times more over the dismal weeks, this performance was repeated.

"Why don't you fight back," asked Kenny one day. Being older, Kenny was not on David's radar.

"I can't. My father won't allow me to hurt anyone," answered Des. "He says we all have it tough enough in here already without fighting amongst ourselves."

Kenny's eyes widened. "That's unbelievable. Does he know what David's like? If anyone deserved a thrashing, he does."

"Are you going to do it?" Des asked.

"No, I have no quarrel with him. He mostly goes for the smaller boys. Do you know why that is?"

"So he can get more of us without tiring himself out so much?"

"Well maybe a bit of that," Kenny said, grinning. "I was thinking it was because he's not all that good a fighter. I've seen him go at it and he always uses the same wrestling moves. He just uses his bulk."

Des looked thoughtful. "I'd sure like to get back at him."

"You can," Kenny assured him. "You're quicker and more agile."

"Yes, but I'm not stronger. And he sneaks up, so he takes me by surprise."

"I could show you what to do. Don't play at his game. Make him play yours. He doesn't throw a lot of punches because he doesn't know how, or he doesn't want to get hurt. If you could draw him into a boxing match, I'm sure you could win—especially after I show you some moves. He needs to be taught a lesson and if you don't stand up to him now, he'll just keep beating you."

"I don't know. What if I lost? He'd kill me."

"He's not going to kill you. You could yell blue murder and attract the guards' attention. He wouldn't want that. Besides, you mustn't lose. When you go after him, you have to do it knowing that you'll get him. Once you make the decision to fight him, you can't stop until he's beaten. I'll show you how, if you want to do it. What's it going to be? Are you willing, or not?"

"I am," Des answered. He trusted Kenny absolutely.

Des studied hard, learning Kenny's boxing moves. He was taught to jab and punch all the while ducking and weaving to avoid being hit. He learned to go for the face first and to use any opening possible to land a punch. During the secret training sessions, Des felt confident. With Kenny's encouragement, he felt powerful enough to conquer his tormenter. In the meantime, David kept up his sudden attacks in the camp. Each time he leapt onto Des, crushing him into painful immobility, Des's confidence drained away and he wondered if he would ever be able to use the skills Kenny was teaching him.

"You're ready," Kenny said one afternoon in the tinwinning. They were preparing the rations for the day's meal. Des's job that day was to peel the grimy skins away from a load of tapioca roots. The other boys were assigned to various other tasks, and Kenny was to stir the paddles around in the giant cauldrons once the food and fire had been prepared.

Des hacked away at a root with the kitchen knife. "I'm not sure I'll ever be ready. I'd just as soon avoid him."

Kenny said nothing. He merely shrugged and returned to sorting the rations.

The delivery to the tinwinning had been smaller than usual and Des finished up his work quickly, earning him a bellyful of extra rations and an early dismissal from his duties. He padded across the kitchen complex toward the jail area, feeling full and content. With him were Nikko Barding and a few others, also returning from their kitchen duties. A Japanese sentry stood guard at the edge of the canopied corridor, lazily distracted by his own thoughts. He stared sternly at the group of kitchen workers. Fortified by his recent meal, Des ambled along the walkway, his steps lighter than some of the older unfed men.

His foe appeared like an apparition, unexpected and out of place. David stood glaring at Des, anticipating the thrill of thrashing the smaller boy, his lips stretched into a smile that contradicted the intention in his eyes. Des saw him and swallowed. In his happiness at being well fed, he had forgotten to think about David. Both boys stared at each other as Des continued walking past his tormenter, looking back over his shoulder. David began to follow him, shoulders set, menace in his every movement. Des turned around, this time facing David squarely. Nikko turned to watch Des confront his nemesis.

Des knew that there was no retreating now. He stared into David's mean eyes and saw a glimmer of surprise. His first strategy was successful. He had caught his opponent off guard by meeting his stare straight on. Now David no longer controlled Des's behaviour. Des would retaliate and there was no better time than now.

David rushed at him with arms upraised to drag Des down onto the ground and use his favourite wrestling hold. Now his contorted face was in close proximity and open to attack. Des clenched both fists and put as much power into them as he could manage. He let go with two swift punches into David's face. It was easier than he thought and he felt soft flesh give way easily under his thrust. His knuckles landed on the bones of David's eye orbits. David covered his face with his hands in shock; then Des saw a smear of blood as his opponent dropped his hands. Stung to tears that ran down his cheeks, David lunged again in blind fury, again meeting a similar onslaught, until more blood mixed with the tears.

Des's weapons were his brains and fists. Although David was bigger, his arms were shorter, leaving Des with a longer reach. Practices with Kenny had shown him that he could count on an energy limit of about ten minutes. He had just eaten and unlike David, who had not been given extras from the tinwinning, he would not be as weakened by hunger. Adrenalin pumped through his body. He tried to remember all of Kenny's instructions.

David would have to be beaten before Des collapsed from exhaustion, so he was to conserve strength and make every punch count without any fancy prancing about. In addition, to maximize the effect, Des would have to take the fight to a knock-out. The thought of this frightened Des momentarily, shaving the edge off his nerve.

The fight continued with David's attempts to grab being met with forceful jabs to his face. Des wanted to pummel him all over but stuck to Kenny's instructions to only go for the face.

The guard's attention was aroused now and he looked on with delighted amusement as the bully received his due. Nikko cheered Des on, adding to his confidence. In the first couple of minutes, the flesh around David's eye grew, swelling it shut. Alarmed at his own power, Des wanted the fight to end. He hoped David would stop lunging at him. Over and over, the young bully kept coming at him. The blood was smearing over David's face and along with the swollen eye, made him look grotesque.

"We can call it quits now if you like," Des offered, landing another blow to his opponent's other eye.

David said nothing but kept up doggedly, in spite of his ebbing strength. Des too was tiring but held the upper hand. Time after time, David would lunge in and be rebuked with crushing jabs to the mouth, nose and eyes. In no time, Des had closed David's other eye and had his mouth bleeding from inside and out. Kenny had been wrong. It was well under ten minutes and Des was feeling totally spent.

He kept the advantage by waiting for each attack and greeting it with more well-landed punches. Finally, with the other boy blinded and bleeding he came in close to meet his opponent face to face

"Your day is over, David," Des said calmly, trying not to show his exhaustion. He no longer felt angry at David who stood in the middle of the corridor, laughed at and jeered by the audience who took a great deal of satisfaction at seeing the larger boy get what he deserved.

Des walked back to the jail. Word of the fight soon reached Sonny who was more than forgiving of Des's breach of his rule never to hurt others. That evening, he was discussing the fight with Kenny, who was bitterly disappointed at having missed the battle, when they were approached by David's older brother. Eight years senior to his younger sibling, Phillip was the lamb to David's lion. At first, Des thought he was in for more trouble but Phillip merely congratulated him on his victory.

"He had it coming for a long time," Phillip consoled him. "I don't blame you one bit."

Later, when Kenny and Des were alone again, they spotted David, who ran off to stand next to Phillip. He stood humbled into silence as the boys approached.

"I'm sorry," Des offered, genuinely regretting the damage he had done, which David now wore crusted and puffed upon his distorted face. "You won't have to worry about this happening again. If you want, I'm willing to be friends."

David shrugged but did not raise his eyes to meet Des's look. He hunched in closer to his brother as Des and Kenny left. Des sensed his former foe peering at him through his blackened eyes as he headed back to his quarters. He walked taller, as if a burden had been lifted. His oppressor vanquished, he felt triumphant.

25. SCHOOL

Feelings of demoralization and depression continued throughout the early weeks, especially for those boys like Ron with no relatives present. Confinement in a prison yard, after such freedom to come and go within the women's community, was difficult for their boyish souls to tolerate. One morning, as they walked through the grounds, Des and his comrades were called into a group by some of the adults and abruptly informed that school classes would commence the following week.

For Des, this seemed like the final straw. Were his own people now turning against him? Hadn't he been through enough? He ran to find Sonny.

"Dad," he panted, "They're making us go to school here! Can't you do something?"

"About what?" Sonny asked.

"About the school. Haven't you heard about it? It's a terrible plan. We have enough to do just to stay alive."

"Yes son, I know about it."

"What? How long have you known?"

"For awhile. And I very much condone it."

Des almost sputtered. "But why?"

Sonny's expression was sympathetic. He sighed and turned to look directly at his son. "It's for your own good. Children should go to school."

"But we have no blackboards, no chalk or books. How can we learn?" Des was trying logic he thought might work on his father. For him, the whole idea was ridiculous.

"Learning doesn't come from those things. It comes from here," Sonny said, pointing at his temple.

"Then why do it at all? We don't need the lessons either. We can learn other things—things that will help."

"It's only for three hours in the mornings. You can cope with that, can't you?"

"Who's going to be our teacher?"

"Father Coufutt."

"Oh," Des muttered, thinking Father Coufutt might not be so bad. He'd seen the priest from time to time in conversation with Sonny and thought him quite friendly. They certainly could have made a worse choice.

"But we're not Catholic," Des blurted, invigorated by a fresh argument. "What can a priest teach us?"

"Father Coufutt is a highly educated and qualified theologian."

"What's a theologian?"

"It means I have no doubt he'll contribute much to your general knowledge, if nothing else."

Des gave up. He had five more days until the start of classes next week. He hoped he could put his disgust behind him enough to make good use of the free time.

Des wandered the jail yard seeking out his friends. He found Kenny and Ron and James moping listlessly by a stone wall and knew immediately that they had also been told the same sad news.

"I can't imagine why they'd want to do this to us," Ron complained. "We have it bad enough already."

"That's exactly what I told my Dad," said Des, shaking his head.

"And what's worse, the lessons will be in Dutch," interjected James. "We'll be the only English, non-Catholics there. What a treat."

"Maybe we shouldn't go. There's nothing much they can do about it if we don't," said Ron.

"I don't know about that," countered Des, "I for one wouldn't want someone else to be given my job at the tinwinning."

"They wouldn't do that to you," Ron said.

"Maybe not, but there are plenty of good Dutch schoolboys who might like a turn at it."

Word spread of the new school. Dutch and English boys alike dreaded its commencement. At last the morning arrived when Father Coufutt stood before them in the open air of a canopied deck. Des sat cross-legged between Ron and Kenny, not bothering to conceal his resentment.

For his part, Father Coufutt seemed in high spirits. He had donned a pair of tan trousers that seemed less worn than most others Des had seen in the jail. A faded green cotton shirt draped his withered frame exposing a tanned jaw through its open neck. Not handsome, Father Coufutt wore a friendly countenance making him look not at all unpleasant. Des thought he seemed eager to begin his mission.

With no books, paper or blackboards to stimulate his view or break the monotony, Father Coufutt's lessons seemed endless. Des often daydreamed but Father Coufutt's chopped Dutch words continued to penetrate his thoughts. To entertain himself, Des began to listen to the teacher's pronouncements on God's influence on nature, looking for inconsistencies or gaps in logic. There were many. Des questioned everything and was angered by Fathers Coufutt's tendency to quash all debate by declaring most situations as merely one of God's mysteries. After several weeks, attendance dwindled down until the entire idea was declared a bad one and to no one's surprise, the school was cancelled.

26. WAITING FOR THE DURIAN

Each morning dawned, sending only one thought to Des's mind. The search for food was automatic and relentless. Anything edible was yanked from the ground without a thought for taste or appearance. Des and the other young boys were small enough to sneak beneath the barbed wire enclosing the camp, but only under cover of darkness. During the day, Des contented himself by scouring the grounds around the perimeter. Sometimes he could spot something in the distant fields that could be sought out during the nightly forays. The other boys competed with each other for the privilege of returning with a parcel left by a Chinese sympathizer. More often than not, however, nothing could be found and they would be reduced to eating paltry rice rations, gritty with dirt and sand, enhanced only by the presence of weevils and their larvae.

Des was almost getting used to the general announcements that rations were to be either diminished, or cut off completely for almost any misdemeanour imaginable. He paced the confines of the entire prison compound, scouting obscure places behind buildings and through areas of weedy grasses. Fruit trees grew outside the prison boundaries, their harvests reserved for the Japanese officers who lived in handsome Dutch-built houses nearby. They were all out of his reach including one very tall tree that grew behind the tinwinning. But this tree was different. It grew out of sight from the jail yard and was not connected to any other residence or property of his Japanese masters. Although he could not touch it, he could see its small buds sprout from sparse green branches that grew from the familiar looking bark with the gray patches. It was a durian tree. One giant limb extended over the fence sporting its pride about thirty five feet above his head: a durian fruit, larger than any others he could see on the entire tree.

Since he had found the durian tree, Des had closely watched the one fruit, which dangled high above his head, ready to fall one day into the prison yard. Mature durians were knobby, prickly-looking ovals, plump as footballs, famous for the almost rotten, pungent smell and taste that some said was like heaven, and others swore was like hell. Right now, it looked like heaven come to earth to the starving boy. Des knew the durian fruit could not be picked, attached unbreakably to the tree until ready to fall of its own accord.

Des went to the durian tree daily. With each visit, the tree seemed to extend its arms out more and more over Des's head, promising to sacrifice its fruit in return for his patient company. Afraid of being spotted, Des snuck past the front of the tinwinning to the back, where the durian tree grew, unnoticed, a short distance over the fence. He was connected to this tree now, bonded by a mutual promise. He needed only to wait with it.

Des knew the durian tree would drop its fruit as surely as he knew the days would pass. Nocturnal breezes rocked the ripening fruit by night. By day, a gentle afternoon wind swayed its mother's leafy arms, tempting Des, as she held fast to her offspring. Each morning, Des checked the tree, only to find the durian fruit still clinging stubbornly to its branch. The stillness of the tropical mornings ensured no possibility of the tree's movement. Afternoon was the time to wait. Every day, he lay on his back on the grass a few yards away from where the durian hung. His mind often wandered but his eyes never wavered. He stared at the fruit for hours on end, watching the leaves fan their protégé.

Alone with the tree, Des could lay back and watch the dappled heaven above its branches. All around it, the blue vastness was no different from the Singapore sky of Des's memory. In the grass, he could shield his gaze from the colourless buildings of the prison camp. Here, if only for awhile, he was not a prisoner, but just a boy in the grass on a warm November day, peering upward, his face licking up warm, passing breezes. The prickly touch of the grasses beneath him was like any other he had felt. He was reminded of the wonderful days when he and Ah Wah and Sami gathered the rambutans and papayas and other fruits from their garden. The sun's heat baked his skin to glowing copper as it had for ten years before the day he had fled with his parents into the streets toward the docks of Singapore as the Japanese bombed the city.

Then to his dismay, James came into view. He too, Des soon understood, had seen the durian, and was equally determined to be present when the tree dropped its prize. Though they were friends, in the camp there was competition as well as cooperation in the search for food. Des said nothing but lay in his place while James took up a position a short distance away from him. He felt his stomach clench and bile rise in his throat. If it had been Kenny, he might have felt differently, but he was not as close to James, who was often a bit distant, and sometimes a bully.

This was *his* durian. Des was tied to it by a contract of nature. The tree would use the sunlight and soil. It would grow its fruit over this isolated section of the prison, out of sight of the guards, and Des would wait for it to fall in its own time. He had kept his side of the bargain, returning day after day, earning the right, with time, to reap the benefit of his consideration. Now James was here to frustrate the deal and Des had no authority to which he could appeal. This contract was forged by nature's hand; only nature could govern its execution.

James was a difficult boy for Des to fathom. Although he was one of their group in camp, Des was a bit wary of him. Starving like all of them, James was still bigger, being two years older. He had grown still moodier and often meaner with imprisonment. Des did not want him as an adversary. He wished he could reason with him—explain that the durian was his, that he had earned it as surely as if he had planted its seed and harvested it himself. But he knew that asking James to stop waiting and voluntarily give up the durian was like asking him to give up breathing—to give up life. Nature's law would not abide this. Des waited out the hot afternoon with James, silent and fuming, never once allowing his eyes to fall away from the fruit on the branch. His muscles were tensed and ready to leap simultaneously with the rustling that would herald the durian's fall. He could sense that James too, was ready and watching the branch, poised to jump and thrust his heavier frame first upon the oval orb. The afternoon waned and the warm gusts ceased to blow. The durian did not fall.

Des was the first to leave, walking around to the front of the building where some of the older men were gathered. After a few minutes, James emerged from his watch, smiling slyly as he spotted Des. In a minute he had disappeared around another building leaving Des to seethe in the company of his own hunger.

27. THE DURIAN FALLS

The day opened with the simplicity of a child's yawn, stretching and releasing its light into the humid air. Birds danced across the open sky, teasing the prisoners below with their freedom. Forbidden fruit trees shook their leaves temptingly on the other side of the barbed wire.

Des emerged into the open air, wiping sleep from his eyes. Already, his mind was turning to the durian. He had eaten well yesterday, compared to the usual prison fare, but for some reason, that only stoked the fires of his hunger. His stomach burned as he worried about the durian and the possibility that he had missed its descent, leaving one of the men at the tinwinning to stumble across it. He looked around for James and spotted him walking back from the latrine. Their eyes locked as each boy resolved to be the first one to intercept the durian. Des started to walk in the direction of the tinwinning but was interrupted by the blast of the prison horn, summoning the inmates for assembly. He fell into place, joined by his father and those other prisoners who were mobile. Clouds gathered above to mercifully shield them from the already oppressive sun.

The counting at assembly was tedious again this day. Finally it was done and Des fell out with the others, threading his way through the mingling groups of men. He had lost sight of James, but made his way over to the tinwinning and down the side of the building. Des quickly found the durian still hanging on its branch. It seemed heavier today as it hung lower on its branch. The surrounding foliage was silent and still. With no breeze to rock the durian, Des knew it would spend the morning sheltered in its lofty haven. Satisfied that the durian was safe for the time being, he walked around to the front of the building again where he was given some tapioca and a piece of star fruit by one of the kitchen helpers.

Later that day, Des found himself back at the durian tree. James was there, sprawled languidly on the tufts of grass a short distance from the overhanging branch. Des said nothing to James, only folding his own legs under himself, settling behind James and a little further away from the durian. A tropical breeze fluttered the tree's foliage. The durian swayed, but resisted the wind's efforts to jar it loose. The boys scarcely looked at it anymore. Their senses were attuned to the rustling leaves. When the durian fell, they would know.

It happened without drama. No sound of fruit separating from its stalk cracked the air. No extra strong gust of wind shook it audibly. Instead, it was suddenly there on the ground, announced only by the soft thud of its arrival. James was up first, as Des knew he would be. Both boys ran to it, with James firmly in the lead. Des had always known James would be there first. He had thought about it often, knowing James was faster and stronger. Des never had even the slightest chance of being the first one to the durian. He held back now, and watched James reach their prize, standing over it and then bending to seize it. He grasped its knobby hull with both hands. Des made his move the way his mind had mapped out many times. With the urgency of desperation, he ran into James as hard as he could. James's bent position left him no opportunity to keep his balance. He was sent flying forward toward the barbed wire, his hands easily slipping free from the durian. Now it was Des's turn to snatch the prize. Before James could right himself, Des was off with the durian, running as if for his life, past the tinwinning and into the main compound where he was safe with his father and his friends. He had done it. He had won the durian and defeated his adversary. His elation made his head spin. He had the durian; he had everything.

Its terrible smell somehow made it even more precious, the awful odour hiding the wonderful delicious fruit inside. As he shared his bounty with his father, Des relished it with deep satisfaction. It was like his life in captivity: something so dreadful that revealed, from time to time, unsuspected wonders like friendship and generosity that were all the more precious for being wrapped in suffering.

28. KOEFER AND BLUEY

Des sat quietly next to Sonny and his friend Trevor watching them sip gritty coffee. Trevor was almost like family now. Six feet tall with rusty-coloured hair, Trevor was always amiable and smiling. Des liked him and was a bit in awe of his exploits. A mining engineer by profession, he spoke Indonesian and knew the culture and the terrain, including the jungle, which meant he was a tremendous asset when they went foraging outside the camp. Over and over, he risked his life to get medicines from friendly collaborators outside, for the sick and dying inside the hell of the prison compound. Des knew his father felt like Trevor was a kind of older son, and that they planned to work together after the war.

The sound of the men's matter-of-fact talk about events within the prison soothed him. If he closed his eyes, their voices could make him feel as if he were somewhere else. But his eyes were open this evening. Of all the places they could be, he loved that his father and Trevor chose to pass time in the shadow of a large water storage tank. Away from the evening's starlight, Des felt sheltered and invulnerable to the glaring eyes of the night sentries. He slapped at the mosquitoes that found him.

Nikko Barding approached them from across the yard. In his hand was a jute bag, rounded somewhat on the bottom by the weight of its contents. Trevor and Sonny stopped their chat and stared at the bag. Des's curiosity was piqued. Possessions in the jail were treasured and few. It was unusual to see someone carrying them so openly at night, even one of the respected and capable Barding brothers. Nikko sat down next to Trevor, setting the sack next to him. The men chatted casually without any mention of the bag or what was in it. Soon, Des too lost interest in it. After some time had passed, Nikko turned to Des.

"I have a present for you," he said, gently lifting the bag onto his lap.

Des looked first at Nikko and then at the bag. He watched as Nikko reached his hand inside the stiff cloth, and gingerly pulled out two tiny chicks, each the size of Des's fist. For a while, no one spoke, least of all Des who was stunned into awed silence by the impossible gift. Then, Nikko reached into the bag once more and removed a smaller pouch.

"This is corn to feed them with," he said.

"They're mine?" Des asked breathlessly.

"Yes, they're both for you. You're to give them a bit of the corn twice a day," Nikko told him.

Des stared in amazement at the two fuzzy babies as they pecked unsuccessfully at the too-large corn kernels

Nikko had strewn on top of the jute bag. He was grateful for the darkness that concealed the welling tears in his eyes. He rubbed them dry with the back of his hands, not wanting to miss a single movement of his new charges. They were beautiful; and they were his alone. He felt his heart lift until it seemed it would soar out of his body. He couldn't remember the last time he had felt truly glad. Only a short time ago his misery had been complete. Now, he had his father; and something else of his own as well—something else to love—and he did love them. He loved them instantly and so completely, he thought he would burst with joy.

"They're your responsibility now," Nikko said, and the gravity of his statement crashed upon Des's elation. He thought of his captors.

"But how can I hide them from the Japs? When they see all of this, they'll know you've been outside."

"Don't you worry about that," Nikko assured him. "Tomorrow I'll bring you something to hide them in."

"What?" asked Des.

"I've made a bench. It's almost finished. It's got a ventilated space under the seat, and you can actually sit in it yourself. The Japs won't twig to what's going on."

Des's joy was back, this time pulling at his emotions until tears ran freely down his cheeks.

"Thank you, Nikko," he whispered hoarsely. "Thank you for this."

Nikko leaned over and gave Des a firm hug. Then, without a word, he rose and disappeared into the darkness. Sonny and Trevor sipped their coffee, their eyes visible over the rims of their cups as they silently stared at Des. In that moment, it struck Des just how lucky his father was to have such loyal friends whose talents and kindness seemed unlimited.

At dawn, Des awoke with bones hurting and muscles aching from night on the thin straw mattress of his bunk. His discomfort dissipated as he remembered his chicks. He reached for the bag and opened it. The chicks were wide awake and upon seeing the light, began to chirp hungrily. Des drew out a small handful of the corn, and realized they would never be able to get their tiny beaks around such large kernels. He slipped the chicks back into the bag and while his father still slept, and took the corn outside to a place where he knew some rocks were piled alongside one of the buildings. Laying the corn on one of the larger rocks, he took another in his right hand and pounded several times until the kernels had crumbled enough.

When he returned, out of breath, he opened the bag enough to expose the chicks and placed the crushed corn into the sack. Their loud peeping gradually quieted as they set upon the corn, ravenously gobbling up every bit.

Next, he scoured the jail yard and found an old lid from a milk can, which he filled with a small amount of water. When he set it down in the bag, the birds immediately drank their fill. Des watched, rapt with devotion. He picked up one of the tiny birds. It was black with an unusually long neck and large blue eyes. He thought wistfully of his days in Singapore when Sami and he had raised baby chickens and ducks. One of them, he remembered, had looked similar to this one. The small bird sat calmly in Des's hand. Raising it to his lips, he kissed it gently on the head.

"I'll name you Bluey," he said, placing it softly back onto the bag. He then picked up the other chick noting its light brown patches amid a pale beige background. Des thought it unusually pretty as he examined a raised tuft of feathers growing cutely on the crown of its head. "And you will be Koefer," he said, giving it a kiss in the same manner as he had done for Bluey before placing it beside its sibling. "Koefer and Bluey," he whispered. "I love you."

The softness of the chicks' downy feathers on Des's cheek soothed him to his core. He drank in the softness, allowing the feeling to fill his heart. They remained docile and contented while he petted and caressed them, and he thought of nothing else but how glad he was to have them. Eventually he put them into their bag, removing the smaller pouch of corn, to give them more room to squirm. He knew the pouch of corn would never be enough to keep his chicks well-fed and healthy. Now he started to worry about how he could replenish his supply. It would be impossible to hoard any of the rations, with inmates all around him dying from starvation and sickness on a daily basis.

Des was still brooding when Sonny awoke and gave him a morning hug.

"Good morning," he said.

Des murmured a distracted "morning Dad" failing to reciprocate the affection.

"What's wrong?" his father asked, "Is something bothering you?"

"I'm worried about Bluey and Koefer."

"Who?"

"Bluey and Koefer. That's what I've named them. Bluey has blue eyes and Koefer has the little tuft of feathers."

"I see. You mean your babies," Sonny kidded him. "Are they all right? Are they eating well?"

"Yes, quite well. That's the problem. I don't know what I'll do when the corn is gone. I don't suppose they'd eat grass. Our own birds back home never would," he said.

Sonny put his arm around his son's shoulder. "Don't give that a second thought. I can assure you there will be plenty of food coming. You're not to worry about it."

Des looked into his father's eyes and saw he was telling the truth. His concern dissipated, relaxing his frown into a smile. This happiness was enough to see him through the morning with only a few sips of tea. Bluey and Koefer's wellbeing took precedence over anything else, distracting him from his own hunger. The chicks were his tonic—a life-saving elixir—and he would be theirs. He was eager to face his responsibility for them. It would be his joy.

Around noon, Des sat in the yard with his bag of chicks. No one bothered him. It was as if the birds helped to form a protective shield around him. He assumed all of this had something to do with Nikko's reputation around the jail. Both he and his brother Jan were formidable hunters and gatherers. They were heavily involved in the resistance efforts and respected by both the Dutch and English alike. As much as they shone like brilliant stars among the captives, the Bardings were at the same time almost invisible to the Japanese, seeming to elude suspicion or capture on their many forays outside the jail. To Des, they were heroes.

A lull in the normal jail-yard buzz caught Des's attention. He looked out into the yard and saw Nikko crossing through the centre of the crowded compound, openly carrying a wooden object. Stopping at Des's spot, he handed him the promised bench as well as a fist-sized granite rock.

"Oh thank-you Nikko," Des gushed. His words felt hollow and insufficient.

"Lift it up," Nikko said indicating the seat of the bench.

Des put his fingers under the rim of the seat. It pulled up neatly, like the lid from a box, revealing a hidden compartment with a built-in food tray and a place for water. The space inside the bench was roomy enough to house Bluey and Koefer while they grew.

"You can hide them inside until they're bigger," Nikko told him.

"And this?" Des asked, lifting the rock. "What's it for?"

"To crush the corn. You must take them to a corner of the yard, away from the others to let them peck from the bare ground and get some exercise. This is natural. It is better for them."

"I gave them some corn I crushed up this morning."

"Good, good," he nodded, obviously pleased.

"Nikko," Des said, "why did you carry the bench across the yard in full view of the others? Now so many of them will know."

"Exactly," he answered, smiling. "It will be a warning to them not to bother either you or anything that may be inside the bench. They will know I am interested in its safety. Now give me the bag. I'll introduce your new friends to their accommodation."

Des watched like a proud mother as Nikko gently lifted the two chicks one at a time from the bag and placed them in the bench. He then showed Des exactly how much corn and water to place in the small feeding compartments.

"See?" he beamed. "They're happy here and will lay many eggs for you.

"Is that so?"

"Yes. You see, this one will be a hen, and this one a rooster."

"Their names are Bluey and Koefer," Des interjected, pointing out each bird in turn.

Nikko chuckled as he nodded approvingly. "Bluey is the rooster. He will defend Koefer as they grow up. This is how it is with them."

Together, Nikko and Des walked back to the place where Des bunked with his father and Trevor. Sonny brought Nikko a steaming hot mug of sugarless coffee. For Des, he had a treat of tapioca cake. Des gnawed hungrily on the heavily salted biscuit, which had been compressed to rock hardness. It was enough to fill his shrunken stomach, satisfying him.

"Where did the cake come from?" Des asked, full of curiosity about such a rare treat.

Sonny just shrugged and looked at Trevor who merely looked upward, appearing not to notice.

At dusk Nikko returned to check on the chicks. This time, he brought with him some cooked rice he had saved for them from his sparse evening meal. Des thanked him again, giving the rice immediately to Bluey and Koefer.

He watched happily as they gobbled the rice. Now he could save the corn kernels to crush and strew in the yard so they could practice their foraging.

"I'll come by in the morning," Nikko offered as if reading Des's mind. "We'll find a good spot for their first hunting and pecking lesson. They'll need to learn this to survive."

Many times in the night, Des awoke with fretful thoughts of his young charges. He listened for noise from the bench, unsure whether to worry at the silence from inside, or be reassured that Bluey and Koefer were fast asleep and content. Although Sonny and Nikko had both promised there would be enough food for the birds, he knew that promises made within the prison walls were often hopeful deceptions that crumbled under the pressures of survival.

"Des," he heard his father whisper gently, "Wake up. You don't want to sleep through your chicks' first lesson."

Des opened his eyes. "Koefer, Bluey," he muttered.

"They're fine," Sonny said. "But I think they may be hungry."

Des could hear the busy chirps inside the bench and reached for the pouch of corn. In less than a minute, he had crushed a few of the kernels for them and filled the water tray and settled back to watch. Together, Koefer and Bluey pecked at the grains. It amazed Des how they seemed to co-operate, never fighting over the food. He smiled as the toffee-coloured tuft on Koefer's head wiggled and bounced with each peck. She then began to peck at the water, splashing tiny drops into the air, some of which landed on Bluey's back, spreading shiny smooth dots over his fluffy black body. Within seconds, they were finished the corn and peeped for more.

"You'll have to wait a while," Des said to them.

Soon, Nikko arrived. Des gathered up his chicks in the jute bag and followed Nikko to a secluded spot near the outer walls of the jail's perimeter, then carefully placed each chick on the ground while Nikko stood back and observed. For nearly half an hour, the birds seemed confused, sticking close to Des.

"See," Nikko observed, "they see you as their protector already." He sprinkled some cooked rice over the ground a few feet away from Des.

Des chuckled as he watched Koefer and Bluey immediately scurry to the rice. Bluey ate only a couple of bites before trotting back to Des and hopping up onto his lap where he nestled contentedly, seeming to take no interest in the second breakfast. Koefer continued to eat until all the food was gone.

"Talk to them," Nikko said. "They must learn to recognize your voice and learn your commands."

"They won't understand me," Des scoffed.

"No, of course not. But they will learn to respond to your voice. Keep talking to them constantly. They'll learn to do what you want them to."

After another half hour with the birds, they walked back to Des's sleeping spot. Des was quiet, his thoughts filled with doubt about the chicks and his own ability to train them.

"Des," Nikko said, "Koefer and Bluey will be fine. I'm sure they'll thrive under your care. They're adapting well. Don't worry."

After a couple of weeks, Des had fewer doubts. Bluey and Koefer began to respond to his commands to come in and out of their bench and bag. Each time they did, Des rewarded them with a few tidbits supplied by either Nikko or Sonny. Soon, like loyal puppies, they followed Des around everywhere and were completely at ease with Sonny as well. As the birds grew, the inmates knew not to interfere.

Sometimes at dusk, Nikko would arrive with a half coconut shell containing a few bites scrounged from his evening meal.

"They're growing well," he observed one day as he sat around with Sonny, Des and Trevor. "I wonder how long it'll be before Koefer lays an egg."

"Hope it's before the end of the war," Sonny chimed in. "The sick around here need eggs and more to survive."

"You're doing so well with your chicks. We'll have to start a farm together after the war," Nikko told Des.

"That's a great idea," laughed Trevor, "and just for a change, we could use the Japs for slave labour."

They all burst into hysterical laughter.

29. TRAINING THE CHICKS

One afternoon, three of the Australian jockeys, the small men with the big hearts whom Sonny had befriended earlier, arrived together with some rice, sporting huge grins on their faces. Wally Bagby, Porky Donnelly and his brother Mickey, and Jimmy Martin put on their best exaggerated manners and politely asked to be introduced to the pets. Des proudly presented Bluey and Koefer who were now beginning to lose their downy coats in favour of soft smooth feathers. The birds allowed the jockeys to hold them.

"You'll have to let us know when they get big enough to ride," Porky joked.

"And don't worry about food," Jimmy Martin added. "We'll stop by every day with more than enough."

Sonny gave them each a small supply of smuggled tobacco and the jockeys pranced off, laughing and joking as was their custom, occasionally stopping to bow to one another in mockery of their captors.

The next evening, Nikko stopped by. It pleased Des that he took such an interest in Bluey and Koefer, acting like a friendly uncle.

"My, they're getting big," Nikko said, admiringly.

"Yes, they are," Des responded proudly, "and they still follow me everywhere."

"Yes, I've noticed," Nikko agreed. "I think the time may have come to teach them to function more independently, don't you think?"

Des studied Nikko's expression, trying to read his meaning. "Why? I can take care of them."

"Yes, you've been doing well with them. But you know how unpredictable the Japs are," he said. "We could be shifted out without any notice, forcing you to abandon the birds. You know this is their way. If this happened, you'd want them to be able to survive without you, wouldn't you?"

Des looked at his father, hoping for a sign that Nikko was wrong—that Bluey and Koefer would never have to survive without him. Sonny looked back at his son, nodding slowly, in agreement with Nikko.

"Listen to Nikko," Sonny told Des. "He has a plan."

Nikko turned to face Des directly. "You know the drain over by the wall near the edge of the grounds?"

"I think so. Do you mean the one with the iron grid covering it?"

"Yes that one. You can teach the birds to go through it to the other side…to leave the jail grounds."

Des was horrified. "But they'll get lost. What if they don't come back?" His voice was on the verge of cracking.

"I don't think so. From my experience, it's in their nature to forage around during the day. But they like to return to what's familiar at night. They know you. I think they'll come back."

"But you're not certain."

Nikko smiled. "Yes," he said. "I think I am certain."

Nikko and Des agreed to meet early the next morning at six o'clock by the drain Nikko had chosen for its position away from the view of the sentries. Des arrived with Koefer and Bluey following in his wake and sat down with Nikko, who was already crouching by the drain.

"Talk to them. Tell them to go," Nikko said.

"I don't think this is a good idea." Tears welled up in Des's eyes blurring his vision. He wiped them with the back of his hand and picked up Bluey. "What if they don't come back?"

Nikko put his hand on Des's forearm. "Please," he said. "I know what I'm saying. This is a very important matter for the chickens' survival in the long run. You must trust me on this."

Blinded again by fresh tears, Des released first Bluey and then Koefer between the bars of the drain. They stood frozen at first, uncertain of their new surroundings.

"Talk to them. Tell them to go," Nikko urged.

"Koefer, Bluey, go," Des said, struggling to make his words clear through his sobs.

Finally the birds seemed to understand and disappeared into the drain.

"Keep talking to them. It will help them get their bearings. They'll know where to return, hopefully."

Des fired a stinging glance at Nikko.

"Certainly, I meant. They'll know where to return. I'm sure of it. Keep talking to them."

For five minutes, Des talked, cooing to them and encouraging them to go. When Nikko stood up, Des knew they were gone. A feeling of terror swept over him, compressing his heart. He wanted to shout into the drain—to call them back. Now Nikko put his arm around Des's shoulders, guiding him back to the jail.

"We'll come back at five and you'll call them. Don't worry, they'll come. You'll see."

Time crept by slowly. Not even the distractions of a busy day at the tinwinning could speed up the hours until five o'clock. Koefer and Bluey occupied Des's every thought as he helped stir the food in the large vats. Simmering rice grains brought images of his young ones pecking at their food inside the bench. He hated himself for letting them go so easily that morning and wished he had called to them more and let them hear his voice. He wanted to run to the drain and call them back—to tell Nikko it was too soon for them—too soon for *him*.

At five o'clock, he was released from his duties and sped to the spot where he had abandoned the chicks. Nikko was already waiting by the fence. They sat down on either side of the drain and listened for sounds of the birds.

"Call them," Nikko said. Beads of perspiration shone through the curly wisps of hair on his forehead. He wiped them away with his forearm. "They're probably not far away."

Before Nikko was finished talking, Des had already pursed his lips in the shape of Bluey's name.

"Bluey, Bluey, Bluey," he called, and then listened. Nothing—not a sound echoed back except for the silence that trailed in the wake of his desperate calls. "Koefer, Koefer, Koefer," he tried.

Panic rose up in him and he glowered at Nikko who displayed no reaction except for the worried wrinkle on his brow.

Des called again. "Bluey, Bluey, Bluey." Over and over, he repeated their names. "Come Koefer, come."

The sun dropped behind the trees outside the perimeter of the jail. After forty-five minutes of calling, Des was frantic. Periodically, Nikko interjected with words of encouragement, angering Des and increasing his desperation. The silence in the drain offered no hope. Outside the jail, not even the trees cared enough to buoy his hopes with small rustles. Nearly an hour had passed but Des was prepared to call all night if necessary. With every breath, his distress increased, along with his anger at Nikko.

"Bluey, Bluey, Bluey," he called with growing hoarseness.

Several more minutes passed. Then, out of the silence a flurry of noise heralded a riot of activity in the drain. Koefer and Bluey emerged together and flew into Des's arms, nestling their quivering bodies into his torso. Des hugged them happily, noting their crops were stuffed tight with food. He wept freely from a mixture of relief and joy while he petted them and spoke to calm them down. A pair of arms—Nikko's—distracted him with an energetic hug. Des looked up and saw Nikko grinning from ear to ear.

"You see," he said, "you must trust me."

With his birds safely returned and settled down, Des walked back to his sleeping area. Koefer and Bluey toddled behind like loyal puppies while older inmates gawked in amazement. Des thought his father appeared somewhat astonished to see him return with the chicks. He noted that Sonny had obviously also been outside foraging himself, probably with Trevor, when Sonny offered both him and Nikko each a couple of bananas.

"I must admit, Nikko," Sonny said, "I didn't expect to see them return ever again."

"Woody," Nikko answered, using the name by which Sonny was known among the inmates, "You are learning how we can survive with nature in the world of the jungle. Trust me."

This was the second time within an hour Des had heard Nikko utter these last two words. They jolted him, imprinting an echo on his memory. He *could* trust Nikko—would trust him with his own life, as well as those of his pets.

The next day, and every day afterward, Des let Koefer and Bluey out through the drain. It pleased him to set them free, knowing they would return each evening to the sound of his voice alone. The adult inmates teased him, referring to his birds as dogs with feathers—and many brought food for them.

"I know you want to make them happy, but don't feed them so much. You want them to remember how to hunt on their own, don't you?" Nikko cautioned.

Des curled up his hand, covering a few grains of rice he had held out to Koefer. He knew Nikko was right, of course and that Koefer and Bluey would not want to forage if they were fed well inside the prison.

"I'm sorry Nikko," he said.

"You don't have to stop feeding them completely," Nikko added. "Sometimes, they need to be reminded they have a good reason to come home too. Just do it occasionally. Today is fine. Wait a few days before you do it again."

Des nodded, relieved to have Nikko's approval. He had learned so much from Nikko and looked forward to their time together training Bluey and Koefer. The chicks were growing so fast and looking so healthy, Des couldn't help feeling both proud and grateful. Koefer and Bluey were devoted to each other as well. Des knew he'd wake up to find an egg or two one day soon. Perhaps he'd even let Koefer raise a chick of her own.

30. SAVING SONNY

Des loved being busy. His work at the tinwinning, friendships with Ron and Kenny, Nikko's tutelage with the birds, and the comfort and company of his father all made the daily burden of survival bearable. Although he was unable to quell the incessant pain in his belly, he often felt the keenness of other more pleasant sensations as a soothing tonic, helping him push the pain into a place where he could ignore it.

He was so distracted that he failed to notice how lethargic Sonny was becoming. One morning, when Des returned from releasing the chicks, he found his father lying on the floor. Sonny lay motionless, his eyes closed as if asleep. His face and arms were beaded with sweat. Des could hear his father's panting breath.

"Dad," he said softly, touching his father's forearm. It felt hot beneath his fingers and the muscles twitched in minute quivers Des had not noticed at first.

"Dad," he repeated a little louder. "What's wrong? Wake up."

Sonny opened his eyes slightly but said nothing. Now Des's throat tightened as his heart pounded. He ran out into the jail-yard and met Trevor approaching in quick strides. Trevor's slim, rugged face was creased into a frozen mask.

"Trevor!" Des cried. "Something's wrong with Dad!"

"I know," Trevor said, hurrying along with Des into the jail. "I've got some tea and rice. It's all I could get."

"What's happened to him?"

"I'm not sure. We were working in the jail yard yesterday. I saw him pull back after picking up some firewood. I think something bit him."

Des felt a hot wave of panic. He had seen other prisoners show similar signs of illness after being bitten by poisonous insects. "Are you sure?" he asked Trevor.

"Either that, or it could be malaria. In any event, we've got to tend to him. Be a good lad and get the fire going, will you?"

"Malaria?" Des echoed. "No, it can't be. He wouldn't. He's too strong. He's…" Des felt tears well up and stop his words.

"It might be nothing much at all," Trevor offered consolingly. "Let's see how he is tomorrow."

The next morning, Des awoke to find his father much worse. He shivered and shook more than ever now, reinforcing Des's fears of malaria. In the afternoon, some of Sonny's friends stopped by with some precious quinine, smuggled in at much risk to those involved. Des watched as Trevor coaxed the medicine into Sonny, whose fever seemed to grow worse by the hour. The following day, Sonny's friends gathered around with Trevor and Des.

"The quinine was useless," Trevor said to the men, "and he won't swallow anything.. I doubt the rubbish we're trying to feed him would help anyway—it isn't enough. He's getting weaker. There's not much else to do."

Des fell into a cold panic at Trevor's words. He wanted to throw himself at Trevor and wail like a baby, demanding Trevor not to say such horrible things. Instead he began to shake, feeling the cold sweat of his own brow slide over his tearless face.

In the evening, Nikko came over, as always, to share the evening meal with Trevor and Des. They ate in grim silence, wordlessly understanding each other's deep anxiety. When they were finished, Nikko reached over and enfolded Des with tenderness reminding him slightly of his father's many warm embraces. He surrendered numbly to Nikko's gesture. After a moment, Nikko spoke.

"It's time to sacrifice the chickens," he whispered softly. "It could save your father."

Des nodded mechanically and without hesitation. He knew his father desperately needed real nourishment, protein, for his body to fight back.

"It must be done first thing in the morning," Nikko continued."

"How?" Des asked, releasing himself from Nikko's grip. He looked first at Nikko and then at Trevor who sat holding his forehead in his hands. "I can't slit their throats," he said, remembering how he had once been told it was done in Singapore.

"I'll break their necks," Nikko said. "It will be painless for them."

The three sat for a long while in the evening's quiet while Trevor and Nikko sipped warm water from metal mugs. Des's mind pondered the possibility of saving his father and how it was to be done. As evening's dullness faded into black night, his mind focused clearly. They were his birds and he would sacrifice them for his father. He would allow only one person to do it.

"Nikko, Trevor," Des said, "I have to do it myself."

Des's words released the tension of the silent night. Now, both Trevor and Nikko had much to say. Nikko talked about how he would prepare a soup for Sonny to drink. He estimated that each bird weighed about two pounds. Trevor slipped his arms around Des, holding him tightly.

"I'm proud of you. Very proud. I'll be here with you tomorrow too. Nikko and I both will help. You can kill Bluey first, at dawn."

Des nodded. He had no words.

"Koefer must be kept inside her pen all day," Nikko continued. "Don't let her out to forage. You will kill her the next morning, if your father is still alive."

Throughout the night, Des listened to the sleeping sounds of Nikko and Trevor. Their even snoring contrasted against Sonny's shallow inhalations nearby. He dared not sleep as he tried to lengthen the night, wanting it to last long enough for a miracle that would save them all.

31. SACRIFICE BY A YOUNG MAN

"Des."

The voice stirred him. Trevor handed him a cup of warm water.

"He's alive," Trevor said, answering the question Des could not ask. "In a minute, when the coffee is cool enough, we'll see if he can hold down some liquid."

"Give it to him now," Des said, not wanting to wait another minute before trying to revive his father. He saw Trevor nod at Nikko who then got up and poured some of the weak coffee into Sonny's metal mug. Des added some of the warm water from his own cup to cool down the still steaming brew. From his pocket, Nikko removed a tin container that held a small but precious cache of sugar.

"This will give him strength," Nikko said, pouring most of the crystals into the mug.

Sonny was motionless. The beads of sweat that indicated a body working hard to survive were gone. Now he was dry and sallow.

"Woody," Trevor whispered gently. "Des is here. He wants you to drink a little."

Sonny's eyes opened slightly. Des saw the edges of his father's mouth twitch upward and thought he was trying to smile. Slowly Des fed him the sweet coffee, pausing after each sip to be sure that it would not come back up.

"He's holding it down. That is good," said Nikko. "Perhaps he'll hold down some soup too."

Without a word, Des went over to the bench and removed Bluey. The feathers on Bluey's back and chest had lost their fluff, and Des stroked their sleekness. Bluey was always calm in his arms.

"Give him to me," Nikko said. "I'll show you how to hold him and where to pull and twist."

Des handed Bluey to Nikko and watched as Nikko held the base of Bluey's neck where it joined his body. Nikko then wrapped his other hand around the thinnest part of Bluey's neck just under his head.

"Now you twist and pull. You'll hear a crack. Make sure it's forceful enough so that a second try isn't necessary."

Des cringed at the thought. "I'll do it right," he assured Nikko, hoping the conviction of his statement would make it true. Nikko handed Bluey back to him. Des cleared his mind of all thoughts, except for those of his father. He told himself that for only an instant, he must rid his mind of everything. All his concentration must be directed toward making his own muscles do this one task—twist and pull. That is what Nikko said. He would remove himself from everything else. He would save his father's life. For this moment alone, nothing else would matter. He forced his hands to move into position on the bird's neck. Taking an extra second or two to make certain he was properly braced, he twisted and pulled with all his might.

It surprised him how little force he needed. The strength Des put into it nearly caused the bird's head to come off. Bluey's limbs fluttered for a moment before falling still. Des felt dizzy and nauseous. He retched a couple of times before gaining control of himself.

Trevor ran to him and swept him into an embrace. "It's all over, my young man," he said. "It's all over."

Des felt surprisingly calm. The agony of losing Bluey was surpassed by something else. Three words from Trevor lingered inside his brain, drowning out the anguish he thought would be too difficult to bear. *'My young man'*, he kept hearing. Today, Des did feel like a man.

Within a couple of hours, Nikko had cleaned the carcass and prepared a soup to which he also added some bits of sweet potato and wild herbs collected from outside the jail. Nikko held Sonny up while Des fed spoonfuls of the nourishing soup into Sonny's mouth. Trevor approached with the Dutch doctor who studied Sonny's condition.

"Give him some of the liquid first. If he holds it down, follow it with some of the solids. Just a small amount, though," the doctor instructed before scurrying away again.

Des was relieved to see Sonny hold down first the broth, and then bits of the sweet potato and meat. The aroma from the chicken wafted into his nostrils, rousing his own hunger for an instant, before he realized that this was the odour of Bluey he was smelling. His appetite vanished.

"Just a few spoonfuls to start with, Des," Nikko advised. "He should have some every three hours."

Throughout the day, friends of Sonny came to see him, pausing to visit only briefly before heading off again with worried expressions. Des wondered what they knew that he didn't. By evening, Des and Trevor had managed to feed the entire small batch of soup to Sonny, most of which he kept down. When the sun had almost set, Nikko arrived with his brother Jan. They approached Sonny's side and seemed relieved to see Sonny awake and more lucid than he had been the day before. He was sweating now, but the trembling hadn't returned. Nikko bent in close to Sonny.

"Woody," he said, "Des is taking good care of you, isn't he?"

Sonny managed a weak grin.

"You'll soon be well," Nikko added, "if you can hold down the food and drink he gives you."

Sonny seemed to understand, and nodded before closing his eyes.

"We'll let him rest," Nikko said to Des and Trevor. "His fever still hasn't broken. That's the telling point, according to the doctor. If it persists much longer, I don't know if…"

"Shhh," interrupted Trevor, "there's no need for that."

In the morning, Des woke before the sun was up, and listened for his father's laboured breathing. Hearing it, he closed his eyes to concentrate, not knowing whether to be relieved by the sounds of life coming from Sonny, or alarmed by their gravity. It was easier to be encouraged. Sonny was alive and as long as he still breathed, there was hope. He watched the sun rise over the distant jungle outside the jail, remaining quiet so as not to wake Trevor and Nikko. He knew today he would have to kill Koefer. He dreaded it. For now, he was content to wait until the men woke up.

A short time later, Trevor approached Des and before he could speak, Des stood up and walked to Koefer's bench. Nikko joined them and watched as Des cuddled Koefer one last time before causing her to suffer the same fate as Bluey.

"This may be the most important thing you ever do," consoled Trevor.

"I was thinking that very thing," Des answered, wiping his moist eyes with the palm of his hand.

As he had done the day before, Nikko cleaned and boiled the bird's carcass into a broth. This time, there was no sweet potato. Instead, Nikko threw in a few grains of leftover rice from his own meal the night before, along with some edible grasses. Sonny's fever continued throughout the day, with Des and Trevor taking turns feeding him the soup. Occasionally, he was lucid enough to manage a smile at Des, but did not utter a word as Trevor tried to bolster him with encouraging words. Des noticed Trevor's thin drawn face brighten artificially as he spoke.

"We need you here with us, Woody. I know you want to see us beat those Japs. You can't do it lying down, now can you?"

Des sat on the hard floor, and listened to Trevor with his father. Again and again, he was amazed at how many caring friends Sonny had. Des could now see him as the men saw him, not just as the father of his childish ideal, but as a remarkable man with amazing qualities of courage, resourcefulness, and loyalty. He had seen his father take absolute constructs of good and bad and turn them upside down, as hard it was to change his own code, making such traditional wrongs as lying, deceit and theft into tools for good. He had also seen men and women who failed to relinquish these steadfast truths, perish.

In the evening, Des fed the last of the soup to his father.

"Get some sleep, Des," advised Nikko. "You've done all you can. The rest is out of our hands."

Exhaustion made him sleep, uninterrupted by dreams or bouts of wakefulness. It was only the rattling snores of Trevor and Nikko piercing the morning light that finally woke him. Before he opened his eyes, he listened to the din of male inhalations sawing through the air. He recognized the sharpness of Trevor's breathing and the deeper rasps of Nikko. There were also the slumbering noises of the other prisoners further off down the verandah and in the cells and hallways of the jail. But another sound caught his attention, one he recognized in his deepest memories, like the sounds of his own father's noisy sleep. He opened his eyes and bolted over to where his father lay. Sonny's expression was serene and peaceful. There was moisture on his forehead but it was the normal shine worn by all who experienced the heat of Bangka Island's sun.

Tears of relief clouded Des's vision. "Dad?" he choked.

Sonny opened his eyes. "Des," he answered weakly. "How long have I been asleep?"

Trevor and Nikko bantered lightly with one another all morning. Nikko found the doctor and informed him of Sonny's change.

"I must say," he said, "I'm very surprised at this, considering how long the fever has lasted. He should not be alive after such high temperatures." He looked at Des. "You're a good boy. He's a very lucky man to have such a good son."

Over the next few days, Des and Trevor watched Sonny's recovery with amazement. Des was sad to see Nikko return to his own sleeping quarters with his brother, Jan, but understood that Nikko had a much greater role around the jail other than nursing Sonny. When Sonny was able to walk, Des accompanied him outside into the fresh air for an early morning stroll in the yard, his father leaning on his shoulder. He felt truly like a young man.

"You're a good lad to wait around on me as you did," Sonny said. "I've lost so much time."

"Don't you remember anything?" asked Des.

"Certainly. I know that I woke up sometimes and you were there."

"And Trevor and Nikko too—and your other friends as well. Do you remember seeing the doctor?"

"Was it as bad as that?"

"You were very sick and we were worried. I was worried."

They continued along in silence for a short distance, occasionally nodding to some of the prisoners who happily waved their best wishes. As they neared their own sleeping area, Sonny suddenly stopped and put his arm around Des's shoulders.

"Des," he said, "where are your chicks?"

"Gone to Heaven."

Des heard his father's audible gasp. He was pulled into an immediate embrace and locked there tightly with all the force that Sonny's weakened condition could muster.

"Thank you," Sonny sobbed. Des felt his father's wet tears against his own dry face. "Thank you, thank you, thank you," he repeated, over and over, holding his grip on Des.

They embraced, father and son, ignoring any lack of privacy or sense of propriety. Des dared not break the embrace as his father held him for what seemed an eternity. When they finally separated, he felt their new bond. He knew this bond would remain forever, unbroken, for the rest of their lives.

31. MOVING FROM MUNTOK

It was late in the nighttime when Des and Sonny and their fellow inmates were rudely awakened and forced outside into the moonless chill. Sonny was still weak, but able to walk. Nikko and Jan and Trevor were nearby to help if he faltered. Des stayed by his father, proud to be the one whom Sonny depended on the most. His friends Kenny and Ron were close to their group, Kenny with his brothers, and Ron bravely on his own. James too, walked wearily along with them. He had accepted Des' victory in the contest for the durian. It was part of their code of survival. The guards herded them all out of the compound into the jungle.

They plodded along disoriented and spent, wondering if they were being taken to another camp. Or was this their last walk toward another fate that had always loomed over them?

Des had been sustained by a child's naïve hope that the Motherland would return to save them. This was the promise of his schooling. The British Empire would always be there. With her formidable allies, England would rescue them. He had learned her history, sang songs of her glory in the classroom. Now he wasn't so sure. They had been at least seven months in Muntok. But seven days or seven years, it was all endless time, waiting for rations, waiting for the war to end, waiting for rescue and for life to begin again.

In the dim light of dawn they realized they were once more at the main port of Muntok, and were being forced to make the awful trek along the huge jetty to a waiting barge. Des shuddered with dread, and then felt a small flame of hope inside, that perhaps they were being taken back to the women's camp in Sumatra to be reunited.

Crowded again onto a filthy boat, finding what comfort they could on old tarpaulins or in sheltered corners, they once more endured the long hot passage back across the Strait, up a steamy jungle-edged river, and finally they moored at a rickety dock. None of it looked familiar. They were not going to the women's camp. Des's heart sank lower than ever. Were they going to be slaughtered in the jungle somewhere, after all this? The guards barked orders and roughly shoved them towards a dirt road through the heavy growth, forcing them all to keep going.

Des and Kenny and the other boys struggled along with Sonny, Nikko, Jan, Trevor and the ragged group of men. At last, collapsing with fatigue, they arrived at the end of the jungle road. In the dimness, Des could make out wooden sheds with thatched roofs. He and his father found a place to sleep alongside the others on the raised sleeping platforms that ran the length of both sides of the building. In the morning, he would find the strength to explore his new surroundings, and learn new ways of survival. But right now, inside, his heart wept with utter exhaustion and misery, as he curled up beside his father's warmth.

The new camp presented a host of new problems. Sonny cautioned Des before he even stepped outdoors.

"Where are you going," he asked.

"To look for water. I'm thirsty," he answered.

"Wait, I'll come too."

They went outside. Dawn's glow spread itself weakly across the new surroundings creating pockets of shadow among the rows of houses. Des spotted his friends, Kenny and Ron, and joined them ahead of his father as they made their way around the camp. To their delight, they came across a swiftly flowing stream about twenty feet wide. Des's tongue felt large and dry within his mouth, reminding him more than ever of his need for a drink.

As if reading his mind, Sonny warned him. "Don't drink that."

"Why not?" Kenny and Ron were now looking at Sonny as well, anxious for an explanation. The water was clear and beautiful.

"We don't know what is upstream. For all we know there could be an entire *kampong* nearby using it as a latrine. We have no way of knowing if this water is safe to drink." He looked directly at Des now. "You are to never drink directly from this stream. Do you understand? You must wait for me to boil it first."

Des nodded. His two companions remained respectfully silent in the presence of his father's sternness.

A short while later Sonny had collected and boiled some water. Des drank it slowly, savouring the relief after the long journey. The prisoners' committee called a meeting of all dormitory leaders to get the new camp organized as quickly as possible. It seemed the Japanese were not supplying any rations here, so it was doubly important to scout the perimeter for potentially safe places to exit and enter the camp without detection. Des, Ron, Kenny and a few others scouted the area, pinpointing the guard posts to find spots where they might slip away undetected.

They found five places where the fence could potentially be breached, and watched these points daily, making sure the guards behaved consistently in their duties. Des noticed that most of the guards were Indonesian.

"Who are these new guards, Dad?" he asked.

"They're Indonesians. This is their territory."

"I can get by them," Des offered bravely, emboldened by his success at such exploits in the last camp.

"Not just yet," his father said. "Their presence is a disadvantage to us. They know the terrain better than the Japs. They're also more alert and in tune with the environment and jungle noises. Take your time. Try to make friends with them and see what they are about."

Des went off to do as he was told. The other boys had also been given the task of chatting with the guards to gauge their friendliness and their ability to be bribed. It was thought to be less risky for the younger boys to approach the local guards, acting like curious children everywhere. But the guards remained aloof. To a man, they all stood motionless as the boys played and smiled about them, trying to get them to talk, but careful not to anger them. Des thought they looked nervous, even fearful of their Japanese superiors. If this were so, it would be another negative element to contend with.

In time, the various exit points were made use of and the boys found two sources where non-poisonous roots could be obtained outside the barbed wire fence. One location proved useful by providing fruits and tubers growing wild in the jungle along the perimeters of the camp. Another area presented a more dangerous challenge, but had the potential for a much better yield. The cultivated gardens of the nearby native *kampongs* presented the boys with a source of food along their edges. During the night, Des and his friends would stealthily slip into the gardens and take what they could. There were even some abandoned *kampongs*, which they preferred, as the occupied ones brought the threat of being chased by angry inhabitants with machetes. The settlers in these occupied hamlets had a justifiable anger at the prisoners, many of whom had been their Dutch masters prior the Japanese occupation. The Indonesians had no love for them.

32. ON THE MOVE AGAIN

A deafening noise of gongs and shouts in staccato Japanese commanded the prisoners to line up.

"It's moving day again," Des heard one of the prisoners nearby mutter.

They were barely established in the new camp, and now were being forced yet again to march through the jungle paths to an unknown fate. Des knew they would have to muster every last bit of strength to walk. The sick would leave their grass mats and rise if they could, or stay behind to die. For many who set off, it would be the last walk of their lives. Some would get no further than the perimeter of their prison before collapsing, some mercifully picked up and carried by a loyal friend. Others would die where they fell, listening to the footsteps of the living tramp past them as they drew their final breaths.

Des plodded with Kenny and Ron and James at the front of the ghastly parade, then fell behind to join Sonny and Trevor. He tried to talk.

"Save your breath," his father told him. "You'll need it to walk."

Sometimes Des could retreat into the rhythm of his own steps, traveling to a place where only his thoughts resided. Occasionally, he could even go where all thinking ceased to exist, and time passed quickly. More often, the minutes were eternities, and every footstep marked an eon of pain and desperation.

Finally they arrived at their new prison camp, part of a rubber plantation called Belalau, a kind of workers village surrounded by barbed wire. With the usual harsh shouting from their captors in their ears, Des and his friends sagged into the compound with the men. Like the rest, Des and Sonny found places for themselves in the old workers quarters and falling to their knees, lay down to sleep where they fell.

The younger prisoners had survived better than the men. So many were missing. None of them were sad to notice that one of the missing was Van Leeuwin, the camp bully. No one had seen him on the march, and no one knew, what had become of him. Des never saw him again.

Like his friends, Des was emaciated, and weary of the constant brutality while they struggled to live. In addition, the constant pain of hunger they all experienced was worse for him, as his fragile insides suffered even more, with increasing bouts of agony that made him want to cry out.

Despite all this, nature continued to run its unrelenting plan for his adolescence. He was now thirteen years old. His bony shoulders broadened, and his muscles hardened into knotted lumps on his slender frame, refusing to be consumed by his system's need for energy. He had been a robust boy of ten when it all began, and he had grown only a little, development stunted by the constant deprivation. But inside, he felt he was a young man.

In Belalau, they found that latrines had been dug for them, probably by local Indonesians working for the Japanese. Des heard some of the men remarking that their captors only provided these because they feared an outbreak of cholera would spread to their own men if there weren't at least basic hygiene. And basic it was: long trenches covered by wooden planks, with holes cut in about five feet apart. For Des they had an even more awful aspect. Every visit to them was painful, as more of his lifeblood seeped away. He hoped now that maybe they would be able to find some decent food in the surrounding forest, and he might get better. The rations supplied in this camp were barely sufficient to keep even half of the inmates alive. Their survival was staked entirely on the abilities of Des and others like him who could still forage.

Nikko Barding was in charge of the team of boys. He gave his approval to their excursions but told them not to antagonize the guards or start any excursions until he signaled.

"Wait until I give you the nod," he told Des one afternoon when he and Ron were planning a foray. The boys skirted the riverbank, ambling along its edge until they reached the entry point into the camp. Five single strands of barbed wire around the perimeter stretched across a river, anchored on either side to wooden posts planted in the ground. Incredibly, the area seemed to be unguarded. This was an unusual oversight on the part of the Japanese and the young foragers made the most of it.

Receiving Nikko's signal, the boys slid into the water and swam easily underwater below the fence, emerging on its other side just outside the camp.

They had been counted as usual by their captors that morning and the day offered many free hours to plunder whatever supplies were available in their wanderings. Like snakes, they slithered through the tall Sumatran grasses, avoiding detection and plundering all the booty they could gather from the gardens on the fringes of the *kampongs*. Des was following behind Ron carrying three sweet potatoes and a paw-paw toted in the knotted legs of a pair of pants.

"Shhh," said Ron, stopping abruptly in his path.

Des heard nothing but stopped moving and cocked his ear. The sun's angle indicated that it was early afternoon, and tropical winds already marked the passage of midday.

"What is it?" Des whispered to Ron.

"Shhh," Ron hissed more sharply now. "Listen, don't you hear it?"

Des twisted his gaze around, searching the grasses for a sign of a five foot iguana that had menaced them just a few days earlier. He saw nothing. Only the hissing winds rustling the waxen leaves of the mango trees in a distant garden made any audible noise.

"I don't hear any…," he began, beginning to suspect that Ron was toying with his nerves.

The flow of his sentence was cut off suddenly by a change in the wind's breezy hiss. Another sound, similar but of a different rhythm floated just under the distant swishing of mango leaves. It was moving closer to the spot where the two boys crouched. They held their position, scarcely daring to breathe. In a moment, the noise was loud enough for them to make out a nasal rumble under the breathing. Des identified it instantly and stayed frozen, not even daring to announce to Ron what it was. Together they saw it emerge from the grass and into a village garden, not thirty feet away from them.

The boar sniffed the air and stood frozen, as if uncertain whether its promised meal justified ignoring the presence it knew was nearby. The boys dared not get up and run; risking a charge by an angry boar would be too dangerous. As well, they might be seen and chased by machete-wielding villagers. They held their positions, hearts beating wildly as they waited for the boar to make its move. The beast's hunger seemed to win out over its caution and it finally turned to root through the fallen mangoes spread before it. Des wished he had a machete himself. Wild boar was an item he would gladly add to the camp's menu.

They waited for what seemed like hours, although they knew this could not be so as the sun seemed to merely inch along the afternoon sky. At last the boar had apparently eaten its fill and trotted back into the grass toward the denseness of the jungle.

Next, it was Des and Ron's turn to pillage. They gathered what they could, grateful for the mess left by the boar. The residents of the *kampong* would blame the animal; the camp inmates would not be suspected. They carried all they could back to the river just outside the prison fence, holing up by the water's edge until dusk. Inside and further downstream, a small group of boys splashed and played in the water in front of the watchful guards. They could have been anyone's children playing as children do in the refreshing waters of a tropical stream. Within the camps however, outward appearances of normal living masked a deadly serious purpose. Just under the water, barely breaking the surface, floated melons, paw paws and other buoyant fruits the foragers had found and sent down the stream. They were intercepted discreetly by the boys and carried into the huts for distribution. The heavier vegetables and roots were floated downstream on logs and picked up inside the camp close to the fence and away from the guards' notice.

Once the last of the supplies had been safely floated downstream and spirited away to add to their provisions, Des and Ron removed their shorts and passed them through the barbed wire. Slipping into the stream, they ducked underwater, emerging again within the camp, where they dressed and walked back to their huts, past the Indonesian guards. Nikko discreetly nodded his approval.

"I want you to reconnoiter another section of the fence line," Nikko told Des and Kenny one day. "Stay put on the edge outside and whatever you do, don't annoy the Indonesians on guard duty. Their presence may turn out to be a good thing."

"A good thing?" Des repeated, wondering how any guard in the camps could be a good thing.

"Yes. It may be possible to bribe them in some way or other. This is their island. They must hate the Japs as much as we do."

Ron looked pleased. "Then they might want to help us?"

"Maybe not," Nikko answered. They don't like the Japanese but they hate the Europeans worse, especially the Dutch."

"All of them?" asked Des, hoping to learn of at least a few potential allies.

"No, the Chinese-Indonesians are sympathetic, but you'll never see them working in the camps. The best we can hope for is to continue trading our Dutch guilders. Some of us also still have some goods left to trade. The Amboinese are okay as well."

Nikko glanced around him, checking to see if his conversation with the boys was being noticed. Reassured, he turned back to them.

"I want you to sit here by the river's edge and monitor the guards. Just sit here and don't let them see you staring."

Des and Kenny sat, motionless into the evening. As the sun descended, shadows glanced off of the rippling water, contrasting with the boys' stillness. They gazed into the water, bored with the guards' inactivity.

"What's that?" Kenny blurted, suddenly excited by a passing presence under the water.

Des saw it too. A long black rope-like object glided along near the bank, followed by several others. Most were about two feet long, but Des thought some of the others would have measured at as much as three feet.

"Snakes. They must be snakes—and we were just swimming there today," Des gulped, horrified at the thought of tangling with them.

The boys' alarm turned to fascination as the snakes glided languidly ahead of the current, charming them with their fluid movement. For a moment Des was mesmerized. His memory carried him back to Singapore and the dozens of times he had let the moving waters of his youth thoroughly captivate his attention. He stirred himself back to the present. It was no use dwelling on his days in Singapore. That was another time—another era. His childhood was gone, eaten up by the events of the past three years, replaced now by an incessant search for sustenance and the wait for liberation.

Later that evening, they reported what they had seen to Jan Barding

"Snakes?" he repeated to the boys. "I don't think so. It's highly unlikely that any snakes of that size would travel around in groups."

"But we saw them. They slithered along under the water. They had no fins or legs. They weren't fish at all."

"What colour were they?" Jan asked.

"It's hard to tell. They looked pretty black, but it was getting dark."

Jan tilted his head, scratching his narrow chin, "You'd better show me tomorrow. We'll go over there at the same time and have a look. They're probably eels. If they are, you boys had better keep them secret," he said with a wink. "If the others find out, they'll be fished out in no time."

Des kept the eels a secret all the next day and pointed them out to Jan just as the sun was lowering. The younger Barding brother confirmed it. They were definitely eels. Now his normally cheery expression grew serious.

"Secrecy is imperative," he said leaning in close to Des and Kenny. "Do you understand me?"

They understood implicitly. Everyone was always a mere step away from starvation. The rules were simple. They ate what they found, or they perished on the insufficient rations. A few spoonfuls of tapioca might temporarily ease the screeching pain of stomach acids as they eroded their insides, but only protein would keep them moving.

A few days later, Jan gave them each a device for fishing. Des examined his, running his fingers along its edges. It resembled the T-shaped corkscrews he had seen his parents use when entertaining guests. Fastened to its end was a piece of wire about a foot long. A different kind of wire, stiffer and thicker had been curled at one end, creating a hook. This was tied to the end of the thinner wire.

Des looked around. They were alone, safely hidden from curious eyes. He and Kenny both held their crude fishing rods up, swinging and dipping them into the air as if casting for marlin.

"Careful," Jan warned. "You must keep these hidden. No one must know what you are doing."

The boys put down their tools.

"We need bait," said Kenny. "What shall we use?"

Jan Barding drew closer. "Once you have found a secluded place to hide these, you can go and find some snails."

Des thought of the hundreds of snails that clung to the underside all the plant leaves around the river. Finding snails would pose no problem at all.

"Next," continued Jan, "you will de-shell the snails and use the flesh to bait the hooks. When this is done, slip into the river—and this is very important—making certain you are not observed. Swim along the riverbank and look for nesting holes about three inches in diameter, either just below or just above the water's surface. Next, slip the baited hook into these holes as quietly as possible."

"How long do we wait," asked Kenny?

"You don't wait," answered Jan. "Leave the hooks and wire in the holes and return after dark. Then, slip into the water and carefully pull out the hook. If you are lucky, you will have hooked an adult eel. If not, there will be nothing. The hooks are too large to catch the small ones." Jan stood back, glancing around to make certain they were still unseen. Satisfied, he leaned in once more. "Listen to me now," he cautioned. The severity of his tone was enhanced by his clipped Dutch accent.

"Do not take too many—two or three a week at the most."

"But why?" Des asked, disappointed at not being able to eat his fill with plenty to share around his shack.

"There are not enough of them. They will be gone in no time if you are found out, or if you get too ambitious with the fishing. You are to share them among yourselves," he said, referring to the other younger boys in the camp.

Des and Kenny went out many afternoons and evenings, drawing in several eels. They were delighted to see their rudimentary fishing rods perform their task brilliantly. They brought in eel after eel, careful, most of the time, to stick to the limit. They shared what they caught with some of the other boys and even tried to offer some to Jan and Nikko who usually refused.

"Keep it. You need it more than the adults. We have our snakes," said Jan.

Des cringed. So far, and in spite of his searing hunger, he had been unable to face the thought of eating snake meat. The adults were somehow more daring in that regard and availed themselves often of the plentiful snakes around the grasses and secondary jungle surrounding the camp. Most were harmless, but some were deadly, and foragers were careful.

The protein energized the boys. Des found that he struggled less through his daily outings in search of food. He came alive on the meat, learning through experience the direct connection between his own strength and the creatures he ate. His body usurped the eels' sinewy strength, making it his own. The cooked eel sat well inside his belly, hardly disturbing the needles that seemed to reside deep inside his bowels. It helped him eat less of the splintered sandy rations, dumped by the truckload into the camp. For awhile, the bounty almost eradicated the blood in his waste.

Now the river was his friend. It protected him as he monitored the sentries' movements while pretending to play with childlike abandon in its waters; it gave him cover to slide noiselessly under its waters below the five strands of barbed wire; it nourished and watered him, saving him from starvation and allowing him to grow, and it carried the pilfered morsels from outside the fence along its surface to waiting mouths. This small artery meandering its way through the camp was his life's blood.

33. LEECHES AND LOVEBIRDS

Des and his friends were scouting a section of jungle outside the camp looking for tapioca roots and other edible plants and fruits. Kenny, Ron and Des led the way followed by a couple of younger boys eager to assist. As they plodded along, pushing aside ferns and branches, they heard the sound of voices.

"Shhh," hissed Des, instantly stopping the party. They crept silently closer to the voices.

"I see them," whispered Ron.

"Are they from our camp?" asked one of the younger boys.

"I think so," answered Des. "Yes. I recognize one of their men. He's a friend of my father."

The man Des knew stood with another man, apparently on the lookout while the rest of the group were huddled around something, their backs to Des's view. The boys crept closer, without attracting the attention of the two prisoners acting as sentries. The boys decided on a prank. Circling around unseen to where they could approach from behind the guards, they snuck in close. The huddled men were busy with something on the ground, which kept their attention focused and away from the boys' movements. On signal, they all leapt out of their hiding spots shouting, startling the men who turned around in horror of their discovery. The stunt did not have its desired effect. The adult men were not amused and made it known in no uncertain terms that they did not appreciate such dangerous games.

"What have you got there?" Des asked, trying to deflect the men's anger. They had killed some prey and were working feverishly over its carcass.

"A monkey," one answered. "Would you care to try some for lunch?"

"Where did you get him?"

"We felled her with a slingshot."

Des and the boys cringed as they gawked at the animal, its skin mostly removed, exposing the all too human-like shape of its flesh beneath. Nausea mixed with repulsion as Des took a step backward. The other boys also recoiled, their expressions souring as the blood drained from their faces.

"You're welcome to join us," offered another man.

Des and his posse declined the offer, choosing instead to spend the afternoon hunting for wild yams beneath the soil.

Later that afternoon, they approached the perimeter of the camp and waited to see if the coast was clear for an undetected re-entry. The Indonesian guard had shifted over from his usual post and was now outside the perimeter talking to a young woman.

"She must be from one of the *kampongs*," Des suggested quietly.

"What are they saying," whispered Ron?

"Hard to say. It's in Indonesian," answered Des. "We'd better wait here until they go away."

But they did not go away. Crouched silently within their vantage point, the boys watched as the sentry helped the woman undress herself and proceeded with his unwitting demonstration of adult romantic love.

"What's he doing," whispered the youngest boy?

"It's pretty evident, isn't it," answered Kenny, who was the oldest and fully understood this visual opportunity.

"I thought breasts were only for feeding babies—not adults," said the youngster.

Kenny almost split his sides at this comment and had a hard time keeping his laughter under control. He was jolted out of his mirth only by the sight of his friends crouching alongside him. Leeches clung to their skin everywhere. He looked at his own arms and torso and found them also covered with large bloodsuckers. Unable to do anything for fear of alerting the lovers, they had to watch the leeches grow larger as the minutes passed. Mercifully, the sentry was speedy at his diversion and shortly returned to his post. Des brushed frantically at the leeches, unable to dislodge them.

"Follow the woman," Kenny ordered, selecting a few of the boys. "See where she lives. If it's not too far, maybe we can use it as another food source."

They would all just have to live with the leeches for now. Finding more food was imperative.

"Watch out for black bears," warned Des, who had been told by Nikko Barding to always keep an eye out for such animals.

Half of the boys trailed the woman, keeping a safe distance behind to avoid detection. The rest of the boys kept an eye on the guard until the entire group could reunite and return into the camp together. They still pulled ineffectively at the feasting leeches.

More than an hour passed. The group did not return from their excursion. Des became alarmed. Darkness came and with it mosquitoes who nipped and stung in swarms. He sat with his comrades scratching and slapping at the bites. The leeches were getting larger. Soon the boys would have to return to the camp without their friends. At last, the others were seen cautiously but triumphantly approaching. They transported a heavy load of bananas that they had found after pinpointing the exact location of the Indonesian woman's hamlet.

"The pickings are pretty good, and it's very small. Only four huts," Ron offered. "The bad news is that there are also two dogs there."

"Did they discover you," asked Kenny?

"No. They saw the woman and met her but luckily, we were too far away for them to notice us."

The group returned to the camp via the cooling waters of the river. Des's father rolled a leaf into a cigarette and daubed Des's leeches with the lit end. One by one, they fell away from his pricked and bitten skin, leaving a blood trail in the wake of the more stubborn suckers. Some of the other boys with fathers in the camp also had the comfort of a parent. Kenny, who had lost his own father so painfully, at least had his brothers. The rest, whose fathers had been left behind to face an uncertain fate in Singapore, or had died in the camps, merely picked at their own sores and pulled away their own leeches. They never complained, these young men who could look to no one but themselves for survival. Des saw them in the stark glare of his pity, bringing into sharp focus his own unmitigated luck at having Sonny. He was not alone. He had never been so. He had watched James, Ron and so many others floating without an anchor. Adrift, they bounced like flotsam, free and unfettered, but ultimately solitary.

34. COFFINS FOR THE RESISTANCE

Des had ample time to observe the changes in his father. Before the fall of Singapore, Sonny was a bastion of propriety, and law-abiding to the extreme. For Sonny Woodford, there was no gray zone in any situation—only black or white. He taught his son to follow the rules. Thinking back, Des had first started to see the changes to his father aboard the Giang Bee. Sonny was one jump ahead of the others when it came to serving the interests of his family. The meal of sandwiches and Ovaltine had been secured early, before the actual mealtime, as a precaution against the hoards of evacuees who would want to find provisions.

Des knew that along with the Barding brothers, his father and his friend Trevor were particularly respected and held in high esteem by the other prisoners, even back in the days in Muntok jail. As he matured, Des realized it couldn't just be because they admired his father the way he did. The reasons became evident one evening as Des overheard his father and Trevor talking.

"We're agreed then. It's on again for tomorrow," uttered Sonny in a low voice.

"I see no reason not to go forward. The guard seemed oblivious," responded Trevor.

"I saw him too, but I just want to be certain he wasn't just pretending not to notice. Even if he was willing to overlook it, he could tell one of the others who could report it in turn," cautioned Sonny.

"I don't think so," Trevor said, "He didn't have that look about him."

Sonny sighed softy, pursing his lips. "Tomorrow, half of them will be full. We'll put different men on the off-loading detail. Today's men were pretty unfit. They almost gave it away."

In the dark, from his nearby vantage point, Des suddenly knew the meaning of a scene he had witnessed that morning. Curious, he had watched as some prisoners off-loaded a delivery of rough-plank coffins that their captives had purchased from the Chinese traders, ready for the corpses produced by their policies of starvation and cruelty. They were constructed of flimsy wood and Des was astonished to see the prisoners staggering under the weight. The coffins must have contained smuggled goods.

Over time, Des learned that his father and Trevor were two of the operators of a highly organized smuggling cell. Various items of value that the wealthier Dutch prisoners had brought into the camp were traded for sugar, dried peas, canned goods and essential medicines. The

Chinese, who held no love for the Japanese, were willing to compromise their own lives in order to carry on this illicit trade, in addition to supplying the camps with their normal rations. If caught, Des knew these traders would be tortured and executed, unless they could adequately bribe the Japanese. He wondered if the guard today had been bribed, as he seemed oblivious to the struggling efforts of the prisoners to carry what were supposed to be empty coffins.

The next morning, Des was determined to speak to his father alone, but Trevor seemed to always be around. Finally, when Trevor slipped off to the latrine for a few minutes, Des confronted Sonny.

"What is it, son?" Sonny asked, seeing the worried look on Des's face.

"I don't want to become an orphan," Des blurted, suppressing the tears he felt were ready to well up.

"Don't you worry about such things," Sonny said.

"I *am* worried," Des insisted.

"You aren't about to become an orphan," Sonny said, his voice softening. "Look at me. I'm still alive and well after more than a year here. The British army will come for us one day. You'll see."

"No. It may be too late for you then."

"Why ever would you think that?" asked Sonny.

"I heard you and Trevor talking last night," admitted Des.

Sonny's attitude changed. His placating smile faded and his eyes closed briefly before opening to reveal a conspiratorial look. He placed his hand around Des's upper arm and pulled him closer in a gesture of trust.

"Des," he said, "you must be brave. We *both* must be brave. In this place, it's necessary to act in the best interest of the sick and needy. If we are to come out of this intact we must preserve our humanity."

Des was not persuaded. "Please," he implored, "if not for my sake, then for Mum's. Think of her. Think of how she'll feel if she comes out of this and you're not there for her."

For a moment, he saw his father's expression flatten before displaying a firmer resolve.

"It's not that simple." Sonny's voice lowered a tone. "The safety of many others would be compromised if not for the resistance efforts. We all have a role to play—you as well."

"Me?" Des asked, incredulous that his own father would ask him to become involved in something so dangerous.

"Yes. As someone so young, you could be our eyes and ears in situations where we older men would be suspected. All you need do is observe any unusual behaviour you see around the camp."

"Among the guards?"

"Yes but not only them. The prisoners as well."

"You mean some of them would…"

"I'm afraid so," Sonny answered."

"But why?"

"Because they are afraid to face the consequences of getting caught. They think by turning us in, they will be spared."

"Wouldn't they be?" asked Des.

"No. The Japanese never respect cowardice."

35. FORAGING FOR LIFE

Des, Kenny, Ron and James were gathered by a bend where the river widened slightly before changing direction to penetrate the camp. The guards could see them, but were used to the sight of the young boys playing noisy games beside the cool water. The group was careful to look innocent, tossing stones into a circle traced in the dirt.

"We've got word from the scouts," Kenny whispered.

"Good news, I hope," countered Des, hoping for news of the Allies' progress against the Japanese.

"They've spotted what they believe is an abandoned *ladang* a farm about a mile upstream. It has a large crop of tapioca and other fruits ready for harvesting; looks as if the inhabitants left in a hurry."

"Brilliant!" blurted Ron. "What unbelievable luck! Let's get to it then."

"Not just yet," Kenny cautioned. "We'll watch it for a few days. The villagers near it may be setting a trap for us. I'm sure word of food thieving has spread. And if it's not the locals, it could also be the Japs in charge of that area. Better to play it cool for a few days and keep an eye on the situation. I've sent out a couple of the fellows to see if any other nearby hamlets had been vacated as well.

"But why would they leave without taking anything?" ask one of the younger boys?

"They wouldn't.... unless they were forced. At the other camp, I heard of hamlets that were forced to move if the Japs thought they were too close to a prison camp, or if they believed that the locals and the prisoners were trading with one another."

Des shuddered as he remembered the sight of the Chinese man running across the field after leaving a package for the inmates in the women's camp. He could hear the explosive crack of the sentry's rifle as it found its mark. He had known death in the camps, seen it swallow first the infirm, then the healthy as months and years of deprivation took their toll on the prisoners. But this was the only time he had seen the hands of his captors so directly spill the blood of someone outside the camp. It told him no life was safe.

The boys planned their raid.

"James," Kenny said. "You'll carry the harvest from outside the camp. Find something to cover that head of yours. It shines like a beacon."

James ran his fingers through his gleaming blond crop, pushing it back from his forehead as if trying to hide it behind him. Des stood next to James. He stretched himself, craning his neck a little, hoping for an assignment outside the barbed wire. At fourteen years of age, he was somewhat taller, but years of malnourishment had delayed his growth. He tried not to show his disappointment as Kenny assigned him to sentry duty inside the camp with Ron.

In a few days, the scouts' verdict was back and the *ladang* project was approved. Des found himself crouched by the river's edge next to the barbed wire boundary. The Japanese had still not caught on to this gap in security, and no guard was within view. Dashes of orange near the hazy sky's horizon, heralded the sun's impending retreat. Three of the smallest boys stood off a few yards down river, splashing and laughing as they provoked each other with their play. Des and Ron stared out from the camp, watching for a glimpse of the returning party.

At last, James was seen, struggling awkwardly under a large banana stalk. The green fruit spread copiously from its central pole. James' knees seemed almost to buckle under its weight. Des signaled to the boys downstream, who on cue, clambered onto the river bank and assembled a few yards offshore. Des and Ron kept their eyes fixed on James, waiting for his signal so that he could gently drop his bounty into the river at the same time as the younger boys ran to the river and jumped, causing a splash loud enough to divert the nearest guards' attention away from any noise outside the camp.

Before he could launch his cargo, James lost his balance. Des saw him teeter for a moment, trying desperately to maintain his balance using the banana bundle as leverage. Then they watched in horror as he twisted and fell forward into the river. The splash of James's large frame, together with the heavy fruit, released a thunderous clap resounding loudly through the camp. The boys on the riverbank stood frozen. Des and Ron looked at each other in horror, expecting an angry group of guards to show up. None appeared. The young boys leaped into the water splashing noisily to cover up the sound of James' thrashing, and he safely floated the bananas down river.

Ron was visibly shaken. "I thought that was the end of us," he complained.

When James was safely inside the camp, the boys bombarded him with anxious questions.

"Why did you let yourself go like that? You shouldn't have been carrying such a heavy load."

"I didn't!" James retorted. "It had nothing to do with the load! I was managing fine. I only just about was eaten by a giant monitor lizard, that's all. You should have seen it. I'd like to see you try and keep your balance with one foot just inches away from the back of one of those."

"Probably was stalking its prey in the grass," volunteered Des. "You're lucky you saw it first."

"Luckier still that the bloody guards didn't hear it," Ron grumbled.

James adjusted his wet headcovering back over his dripping locks. "Come on men," he said, motioning to the younger boys, "let's have another splash, shall we? We've still got three others out there waiting to come back in."

Des and Ron returned to their post by the perimeter and waited for the next returning harvester to signal his readiness to enter. Kenny was the last to come in. He dipped noiselessly under the river current outside the fence, re-emerging a few yards downstream within the prison. Three jackfruits, their yellow coats gleaming faintly in the early evening dimness, floated just ahead of him into the waiting arms of the younger boys. Kenny slid out of the river and sat by the bank, scanning the area for any sign of the guards. All seemed normal.

"Another successful mission, gentlemen," he commented to the group. "Let's just get this food put away. James's accident was close, but no one saw us and that's all that matters."

In the ensuing weeks, the boys gained experience as they streamlined their hunt. Little by little they raided the *ladang* and other neighbouring farms, relieving them of fruits, vegetables and even some chicken and goat meat when they could be found. They even came to know which guards were friendly and which were to be avoided. The Indonesians were never to be trusted. Their hatred for their former Dutch masters extended to every fair-skinned inhabitant of the island.

One afternoon, the breeze picked up, bringing a welcome freshness to the stagnant air. It lifted leaves and rustled the dense foliage of the plants outside. Des listened to their whispers, forgetting his earlier fear of the casuarinas' menacing murmurs. For a moment, he imagined he could hear the sound of singing amid the soft windy tones. The voices were soon followed by the sound of brass horns and gongs which grew louder as they approached. The boys began to chuckle to themselves as the familiar lyrics resounded through the forest. As they watched, a parade of rag-tag Chinese emerged.

'Wish me luck as you wave me good-bye' they sang in heavily accented English.

Kenny nodded knowingly as he listened to the din. "I think there must be a Chinese cemetery nearby," he said. "I think this bunch must be headed there.".

As the mourners disappeared down the path, horns and gongs fading as they marched along singing the strange English words, they seemed like an illusion, an unreal scene from a dream or a nightmare.

36. THE WRATH OF THE EARTH

Des and Sonny sipped hot water flavoured with some edible grasses Sonny had brought back from one of his forays. Rations had been cut for some reason that Des no longer cared to know about. The Japs didn't really need a reason to withhold food from the captives. Of course they would always claim it was due to one imagined transgression or another, but the prisoners believed that their captors just wanted them to disappear.

"We've got to get something of substance to eat," Sonny said, downing the last few drops of his drink.

"Kenny and James have been scouting an exit point," observed Des. "We could get out and be back before the guards caught on.

Sonny shook his head. The furrows on his face deepened as he fixed his eyes on his son. "Now Des, you know we don't want you boys outside taking risks with your lives. Some of the *ladangs* aren't entirely abandoned and may be watched by the farmers or by the Japanese. If you were caught, the Indonesians wouldn't hesitate to hack you into bits."

"But we've done it before. We never get caught."

"Yes. You've been lucky, and have done well to find food, but I've told you each time not to go out again."

Des nodded. "I know. But we can do it Dad."

"No," Sonny said more firmly.

The tone of his father's voice told Des it was futile to argue. He sipped his water, fixing his eyes on the inside bottom of the cup to avoid displaying his disappointment.

"Besides," Sonny continued more gently, "we've already organized a group to go out tomorrow morning. One of the scouts has located a small paw-paw orchard. It appears to have been totally abandoned."

Des didn't answer. He continued to stare into his drink, taking miniscule sips. Finally, his father left. Des watched him cross the yard and pass two other men standing nearby. His pace did not falter as he passed them, but Des could see his father's face turn slightly toward them as he passed. One of the other men gave a barely perceptible nod while the other's lips moved momentarily in a gesture Des could not read.

Later, Des met up with Kenny and his onetime nemesis James. In a few minutes they were joined by another boy named Hans. Three years older than Des, his taller stature had been an asset on other forays. Des told them of his father's plans with the other men and how he had been forbidden to take part. Kenny smirked slyly.

"So they think they have an advantage because they are older? If you ask me, it's a disadvantage. We are younger and stronger, more agile too."

"But maybe we're not so smart as they are," interjected Hans.

"Speak for yourself," quipped James.

"Look," Des said decisively, "we can just follow them tomorrow."

"But how," asked Hans. "They'll see us."

"No they won't. If we keep a good distance, they won't see or hear us. We can hide in the tall grasses, the *lalang*. They won't catch us. They'll be too busy with their hunt."

After some more discussion of time and logistics, the boys had a perfectly mapped out plan. Despite their appalling condition, their youth made them feel invincible. Whatever the older men thought they would find, the boys were certain they would find more.

The next morning Des arose early. As expected, Sonny had already departed. Des headed out immediately, clad in his only article of clothing—a pair of shorts. He found his friends waiting for him in the dimness. As planned, they silently slipped past the guard and over to the perimeter fence where they quickly clawed out a new hole large enough for them to squeeze under. Once through, they scooped the dirt back into its place. Instead of taking a direct route, the boys wordlessly circled around a hill and approached the *ladang* from the opposite direction of the camp. Des had learned this technique from the Barding brothers who believed this to be the best way to thwart any villagers or Japanese guards who might be on the lookout for captives. On their way, they discovered some tapioca root, a welcome find after almost two days without rations.

Soon they arrived at an elevated spot about 600 feet from the abandoned farm where they secured themselves well hidden within the grassy *lalang*. The sun had still not risen high enough to sear the landscape, and Des and his friends rested contentedly, munching on the tapioca root as they scanned the foreground for their elders.

"I see them," Kenny enthused.

"Where," asked Hans.

"Over by the paw paws. I see one, two, three…"

"Four," Des said spying his father.

"But where's the fifth?" asked Kenny.

"Are you sure there were five?" asked James.

"Of course I am," Kenny snapped. "What do you take me for? He's probably hidden away on the lookout for Japs."

"Do you suppose he's spotted us, then?" Des wondered aloud.

"I don't know," answered Kenny. "Let's keep low a while longer."

They hunkered down into the deep, heavy grass, staring out between its spiky blades. The paw paws appeared to be too high to reach. Des saw his father approach a tree heavily laden with fruit. He expected Sonny to scour the ground for a fallen branch with which to knock the papayas down. Instead, to his horror, Sonny took the machete that he always kept hidden outside the camp and gave the narrow trunk five or six heavy whacks. As the tree fell, fruit tumbled to the ground, rolling in all directions. Sonny's comrades scrambled to find the best ones. Des was shocked to see his father waste an entire source of food like that. He thought of his daily pains from hunger and the sight of people wasting away and dying on the other side of the prison fence. This was one tree that would never again produce food—nourishment that was so badly needed. Des resolved to talk to Sonny about it that evening during their usual bedtime chat. He would have to find a way of bringing the subject up without letting on he had been there. He might even have to confess.

Having picked all they wanted from the first tree, the adults moved toward the second. Des shook his head in disdain at the men's obvious intent to kill yet another tree. He saw Sonny raise his machete. The feelings within him seem to grow stronger. All of a sudden they became physical. His insides trembled, weakly at first then stronger as the shaking spread to his face, his brain and finally his limbs. The very landscape quivered before his eyes. Now he looked to his friends. Their faces bore the same confused expressions as they stared, dumbfounded, at one another, growing more frightened by the second. Des believed he was going mad. The trees began to sway back and forth. Each thrust in one direction gave rise to an even more turbulent push to the opposite side. The trees rocked violently to and fro, ejecting paw paws in every direction. Sonny, along with another of his friends stood frozen, while the rest of the men scurried in panic toward the camp.

Up on the hill, Des began to feel sick to his stomach. Some of the other boys were retching. To maintain his balance, Des planted his fists on the ground, clutching handfuls of the vibrating grasses as he tried to steady his gaze on just one spot. About ten feet away, the place he picked to focus on rumbled and rose. In an instant, a trench about three feet wide and eight feet deep opened, exposing dark gray clay. The walls of the trench were dotted with steamy holes. Near the surface, fine ivory-coloured roots exposed their naked tendrils. It was as if an unseen knife had sliced into the earth as though it were a cooked sausage, exposing its roiling insides. Only here, instead of the tantalizing odour of a sizzling meal, there was now the putrid stench of something dead and rotten as the bowels of the earth expelled their gasses, fouling the sweetness of the fruity landscape.

Des thought he was seeing the end of the world. This was no madness of the mind. The earthquake was the wrath of the earth, over which he had no control. Its might was absolute.

He wanted his father. As he prepared to run down the hill towards him, he felt Kenny's hand on his arm.

"We've got to get out of here," Kenny said urgently.

The shaking had subsided leaving only a quivering fear inside Des's heart. "I know. I was just…"

"It's this way," he said. "We have to take a different route back. They may be on the watch for us."

The silence was deathly frightening as they began the long walk back to the camp. No insect or bird uttered a sound. Grasses and leaves stood still and unrustling. The boys too walked wordlessly, about fifteen feet apart. If their bare feet made a sound at all, they were oblivious; their traumatized minds were fixed on their fear.

Once they were back at the prison fence, the normal chatter of wildlife had resumed. Surprisingly, no one in camp had felt the earthquake. Almost the entire day had passed and Sonny was upset to find his son had been missing most of the day.

"You shouldn't have followed us," he scolded Des.

"I know." Des answered. He could think of nothing else to say.

By evening, both father and son had calmed down enough from the events of the day to have their usual good-natured chat as they settled down to sleep.

"How long before the earthquake did you arrive?" asked Sonny.

"Long enough to get a laugh from that group of yours," Des quipped.

"Why? What was so amusing?"

"It was not so much funny, actually," Des answered, "as queer."

"Queer?"

"Yes queer. The way you went about getting the paw paws. I would have knocked the paw paws down with a long stick. Instead, you killed you whole tree."

"You care so much about one tree?" Sonny asked.

"It's not merely one tree," Des countered. "It is a source of food. We get so little to eat, I just thought you wouldn't want to waste so much. Besides, you could have gone back again. With a broken tree in the orchard, the Japs might find out we were there, and keep it guarded."

Sonny was quiet for a few moments. Then he changed the subject. "Still Des," he said, "I don't want you or your gang to go out on your own anymore. Do you know what would happen if you were caught?"

"Probably nothing. The Japs know we're just kids. The worse they will do is give us a thrashing."

"I'm not talking about what the Japs will do—although you shouldn't assume you're safe with them. It's the Indonesians I worry about. We've found others of our group who weren't as lucky. They'll cut you into a hundred pieces if they catch you stealing their food."

Des slept badly that night, interrupted by nightmares that seemed to come one after another. He relived the earthquake over and over, only his nocturnal mind saw him falling into gaping slices in the earth and being swallowed up. The blackness would cut off his air, holding him fast like a clay statue within the earth. He would wake up in relief to find himself still alive, only to fall again into a tortured slumber where more trenches waited to take him again in varied and different ways—some with fire to split his skin from his flesh, making deep cuts like the wounds in the earth. Again and again, Des awoke trembling. He'd try to remain awake, feeling the sweat run coldly down his cheeks and forehead, only to be summoned back to his slumber where another ugly gash in the earth waited to swallow him again.

37. THE DOORWAY TO DEATH

All their efforts foraging, even the bounty of the eels, only gave a brief respite from the agony of hunger and something worse that gnawed at Des's insides. He tried to stand up as straight as he could with the ragged prisoners lined up for assembly while the Commandant, Captain Tenabe paced restlessly under the cloud-blanketed sky. Rain threatened to break at any second. The captain barked orders to his soldiers to hurry with the counting. The numbers were dwindling, but somehow, the counting seemed to stretch the minutes into interminable intervals, mocking the passage of time as it crawled through the weary day. For Des, time did not pass at all. The effort of remaining upright, drained him utterly. He wanted to clutch at his abdomen and fall to the ground, writhing in agony. But he dare not. No one must know how sick he really was, or they would send him to *that place*.

He wanted to use the small amount of energy he derived from the filthy scraps of roots and rice to scream out in pain. Instead, he stared straight ahead, beyond the rows of prisoners ahead of him—beyond the captain and his counting cronies, to the hospital. It stood in the distance, menacing, its muddy front doors unpainted and barren. Few who entered there ever came out again alive. In this terrible reality of prison life, it was less a hospital than a waiting room for an appointment with death.

Finally, they were finished and the prisoners given permission to fall out. Des ran past the hospital to the far end of the compound where the latrine stood. His insides burned with every step. He felt as though he would faint from the searing pain in his intestines, but kept running, willing his legs to move. He ran for his life. Falling would be fatal, earning him a trip to the hospital if he could not get up. As it was, the prison doctor, one of the inmates, had already noticed him and appeared to watch Des whenever he was in view. He was certain the doctor had seen the blood in the latrine when he had gone in one day immediately after him. If they suspected he had dysentery or any contagious disease, he would be put in the hospital to protect the others.

This time to his relief, no one else was there when he reached the latrine. He sat down and expelled the only thing he had consumed that day—tea brewed with some herbs and grasses scavenged by one of the other boys during the night. His bowels cramped as razor sharp pains sliced at his insides. Each movement of his bowel released more liquid than he recalled drinking and he knew that his life was slowly dripping away in crimson and black droplets into the latrine. When he was finished he sat for a while, trying to will himself to rise again. He needed to drink, but he knew that another sip too soon would only be drained away with more blood.

Fifteen minutes later, he lay on the floor of his space in the jail and dozed. Sleep was a mercy that let him forget his need for water. The soft padding of bare-footed steps jostled him from his rest and he opened his eyes. Sonny knelt down beside his son, offering a bowl to Des's view.

"Here son," he said, holding the bowl out to Des. "It's only rice and water. You must eat something."

"I can't. I'm too tired," Des said, dreading the rush to the latrine he knew would follow. He found himself suddenly scooped up to a sitting position, his father's hand supporting him by the base of his neck. His head spun.

"In this place, there is no such thing as too tired," his father said, holding the bowl in front of Des's face.

A musty odour wafted from the bowl, failing to stir his appetite. Only his fear reacted. The rice would move his bowels again, sapping his body of blood and energy. It would be discovered and he would be sent to *that building,* with only one visible door from which Des had never seen anyone emerge. Those who entered were eventually carried through another door on the other side of the hospital that led to the crematorium. Des knew if he went there, he would never see his father again.

"Eat this," Sonny continued. "I'll speak to the Barding brothers. Maybe I can get something else."

Des knew what 'something else' was. In the camp, protein was gold. He had seen the stark truth of this when he saved his father by sacrificing Koefer and Bluey. Meat was almost impossible to get but sometimes their nightly foraging missions would yield a few large beans or perhaps an egg. Even the vermin in the forest, if caught, could be skinned and boiled to supplement their shrinking rations. Trades with the local villagers were risky. Des recalled once again the poor Chinese trader he had seen murdered in the women's camp. They usually came at night, but on this occasion, the sun had not yet disappeared completely from view. Its aura cast enough light to illuminate the villager, exposing him to the sentry on duty. Des saw the sentry observe the man, who, knowing he was discovered began to run. The sentry calmly raised his rifle, took aim and fired at the back of the running man. The guard then lowered his rifle, with eyes still on his fallen target. Des stood frozen, stunned by how quickly it had happened. The sentry's head turned toward Des and he realized the peril he was in. The last thing he wanted was for the guard to believe that he was connected to this transaction. Before he was noticed, Des slipped out of sight, his heart beating so hard he felt his ribs would break.

In the men's camp, such risks were common. He continued to go out, often alone into the night, searching for food, and bringing it back—always hiding from the guards and stealing from the fruit trees of the surrounding land. When found out, the perpetrators were brutally punished and the already paltry rations of the entire camp further cut.

He stared at the mucky rice, its glutinous texture promising nothing more than further depletion of his energy in the latrine. But if he could get 'something else', if he could keep protein and rice together inside him for long enough, he could live. He could find the strength to get through another day, and another, until the Allies came. He could stay out of the hospital, avoiding its front door, *and its back.* Des turned his head away from the watery gruel. Sonny said nothing but merely placed the bowl on the floor and stroked his son's head until he slept.

38. BAGBY

A windless, starry night rested peacefully over the camp. Kenny and Des sat alone together in the compound listening to night insects as they hummed at the crescent moon. Des scanned the sky, drinking in the milky sight of the southern constellation.

"You know Kenny," he said, "in spite of everything we put up with here, it's a night like this that makes me want to cry the most."

Kenny looked at Des and saw his eyes, glossy with moisture. He too raised his face upward and bathed in the night light. "Yeah, it's pretty spectacular," he said. "I don't know about crying though. I guess it takes all kinds, doesn't it?"

Des jabbed his friend playfully with his elbow. "Shut up," he countered, smiling.

From the edge of the fence, a faint rustling broke the quiet. The two boys looked at the sentry on duty who had plainly heard it too. The sentry hardened his grip on his rifle, but did not raise it, listening harder instead, with his ear cocked toward the fence. It sounded again and the boys held their breath. A moment later, Kenny coughed several times, diverting the guard's attention from the fence. In the instant it took for the guard's head to turn, a shadow flashed, blackening the perimeter before disappearing. The guard looked back at the fence, only the see the tall grasses behind it settle into motionless ease, marked by a silence so serene as to make him wonder if the rustling had been real. Des and Kenny rose and ambled back to their quarters speaking innocently of their desire to get some rest.

In the morning, they lined up for roll call. Des stood with his father near the middle of the crowd. Some of the Australian jockeys assembled in front of him. These feisty horsemen were liked by everyone, with their good-natured humour, and their high spirits undampened by the ordeal they all suffered together. Des had never forgotten how Wally Bagby and Jimmy Martin and the Donnelly brothers had protected him from the wrath of the horrible banker in Muntok. Often Des sat with them while they passed the time with his father, and now of course, he figured they too were part of some of the resistance efforts.

One of them in the lineup however, was unfamiliar to Des. He thought he knew the wiry horsemen well enough, but although this one reminded him of someone he could not identify, he was fairly certain he hadn't seen him before.

"Who's that?" Des whispered to his father.

"Shhh," Sonny hissed sharply.

Des looked at the inmate's profile each time the man turned his head sideways, which was often. Although the sun was already well into the morning sky, the day was still fresh. He thought it odd that sweat should be dripping so freely down over the nape of the man's neck. When the guards passed his row, counting quietly under their breath, the man stood still as a statue, eliciting no interest from the guard as he passed. When the counting was done, it began again. Over and over they counted, from back to front, and front to back. The captives were rearranged and then counted again. The Japanese Commandant became more frustrated as the guards reported their tallies over and over.

Des studied those around him. His father stared straight ahead also, giving no sign of concern. Sonny's trusted friend Trevor also showed no interest in the proceedings. The jockeys, usually an active bunch, did not flinch. Finally, as Des himself began to sweat from his exhaustion and hunger, the Commandant summoned two of the captives' representatives to accompany him, under guard, to his office for interrogation.

The inmates were disbanded and at last Des felt free to question his father.

"What's going on?" he asked.

"It was Bagby," Sonny answered.

"What do you mean, Bagby?"

"The chap in front was Wally Bagby. He shaved his beard."

Des gasped. "Really? I didn't recognize him. He doesn't look like his old self with that big face of whiskers gone. Why did he do it? It mustn't have been easy with only a knife and some water."

"He had to," he Sonny answered.

"Why?" Des was growing frustrated at his father's stinginess with words.

Finally, when they reached their place, Sonny sat his son down on the ground while he made a fire to boil some water for a hot tea of potato skins and edible grasses. He handed a metal bowl of the brew to Des and sat down beside him with a cup for himself.

"This is what happened." He said. "Last night Wally went out to liaise with the Chinese resistance. He was supposed to pick up some information in addition to some food. It didn't go well for him… met some Japs on the way. He was able to conceal himself and thought they'd all passed. But when he tried to move, another Jap was trailing quite a ways behind and saw him."

Des felt his heart jump but stayed quiet, not wanting anything to slow down his father's recanting.

"In any event, you can imagine what he thought. If he allowed himself to be taken, they would have tortured him until he gave up all the information he had about the resistance. All our work would have been for nothing. The Chinese would be killed and many of us too."

"So what did he do?"

"Well, he says he did what any true-blooded Aussie would have done."

"Ossie?"

"Yes, an Australian. He gave the fellow a thrashing, relieved him of his weapon and left him tied to a tree with his own rope. When he was done, he stood the man's gun right by his side up against the tree. It must have been pretty impressive. Wally Bagby's such a small chap. He can't weigh more than a hundred pounds, if that. But he's a wiry sort; he can hold his own in any match."

"But why did he leave the Jap alive?"

"Why indeed? It's simple really. Killing a Jap would be a very serious offence. They'd starve us until they were sure we didn't know anything about it. Wally's smart; and he's careful. He knows the Jap would lose a great deal of honour by letting himself be beaten by a short little inmate from the camp. They'll come looking for him of course, but they'll be trying to find a jockey with a woolly face, not some young man with the face and body of a boy."

"Whew," whistled Des, impressed.

"So you see now, they were counting us to see if we were missing anyone. They may assume the attacker was from this camp and that they have an escapee."

"But we were all present and accounted for," Des finished.

"Yes, of course. Now we'll just have to wait for our men to get back from the Commandant's office and see what is to happen."

Des's stomach knotted at the thought of what the Japs would do. Rations would be cut almost certainly. But what if they found out it was Bagby? He shuddered at the prospect.

Later, when the captives had been released from the commandant's office, there was much whispering among the men. Des noticed that the Australians, usually an upbeat group, were sombre. The general mood made him edgy. In the distance, a shy and groaning thundercloud threatened rain. Military vehicles arrived in the camp and drew up at the Commandant's office, spilling out dour

Kempeitai. Harsh words which Des did not understand flew back and forth among them.

Finally, he heard the sound of the gong summoning him to line up again with the others. Several minutes elapsed as everyone assembled to await their punishment. Instead, a young Japanese soldier was brought forward, eliciting a few snickers from behind Des. The man was a fright, with welts and bruises clearly visible beneath a speckled array of mosquito bites and other insect stings. His face was frozen into a sullen mask barely concealing his humiliation and discomfort. He scoured the rows of prisoners, slowing his pace as he passed the Australian jockeys. He paused for a moment in front of one man with a small growth of whiskers before returning to have a few words with the commandant in front.

A flurry of words flew from the angry commandant's lips. Des only needed to hear two.

"Five days," his father whispered. "So many won't live."

Three days without food was not easily tolerated. Five days was almost impossible.

Dinner that evening consisted of half of a hoarded potato, stewed in a broth of edible grasses and water which Des shared with his father and Trevor. It was the first food Des had tasted that day.

Sonny and Trevor sat together as usual while Des perched on the veranda step. Trevor poured some tepid water from a can into his steel cup and swished it around the sides, gathering up every last trace of soup from the sides, before swallowing it down in one gulp. He sat still for a moment, his head bent over the empty vessel as if waiting for it to miraculously fill again. At last he looked up.

"I think Wally Bagby wants to confess," he said.

Sonny's head snapped around to face his friend. "What's that you say? How do you know this?"

"I saw him talking to our British camp Commander."

"What, Berkley?"

"Yes. Wally had two of his mates, as he calls them, with him."

"They'll execute him, for sure," Sonny mused. "We have to get him out."

"That's what I thought at first but you've seen the way the *Kempeitai* are passing through in droves. Our scouts have seen them all over the place outside searching the forests. It'll be impossible to get any of our men outside for days."

"They may be looking for advance paratroopers from our side. Our scouts say there's word the Allies have penetrated Indonesia."

"Exactly. So you see why Bagby might want to stand up. With no extra food coming in from our men, so many more will die, when maybe rescue is at hand. There's a chance the Japs could be so relieved the Allies aren't actually here, they may be willing to go easier on him. Maybe it'll be possible to negotiate something."

"And if he has no intention of confessing?" Sonny asked.

"Then heaven help him if someone snitches."

Des hardly slept. Worry overshadowed his hunger as Trevor's words ran through his head. '*Please let Mr. Bagby confess,*' he thought. By morning, he was a nervous wreck. Looming clouds that had hovered in the distance the day before, were now moving in, covering the camp with an oppressive pall. Boiled water had to sustain him throughout the day. By mid afternoon, his bowels were churning, and his own stomach acids burned inside him.

By the time he saw Bagby enter the Commandant's building along with Berkley, Des was too sick to run and tell his father. He waited and watched as the small group of jockeys stood off in the distance whispering among themselves.

A short time later, Berkley emerged, and quickly crossed the common area to confer with the Dutch Commander. By now much of the camp was poised to find out what had transpired in the Commandant's office. Seeing his father nearby, Des found the strength to approach him.

"What's happened?" he asked.

"Wally Bagby has confessed," his father announced, with relief in his voice.

"Will they kill him?"

"They didn't believe him."

"What? Why not?"

"The victim would not identify him."

"Why not?"

"Who knows why?' his father quipped. "Wally's a runt of a fellow. Did you see the size of the Jap he subdued? His pride is probably in ruins. They made Wally prove it."

"How?"

"He told them exactly how he did it and how he left the Jap tied to a tree with his sword propped up beside him."

"And did they believe him then?"

"I don't know. I suppose they had to."

Relief fell across Des like warm water. The rations would be restored. "What will they do to him?"

"That remains to be seen. They're probably so relieved it wasn't advance commandos for an impending Allied invasion, they might want to thank him."

"Really?" asked Des.

"Sonny looked down at his son. "Of course not, I was just…oh never mind. We'll have to wait and see what they have in store for him."

"I'd like to give him a medal," said Des.

39. THE HERO

No one could walk past the drab wooden boards that made up the Commandant's office building without feeling a pang of fear for Wally Bagby. Des kept close to his father and Trevor for most of the afternoon, trying to pick up useful tidbits of information that he could relay to his own group. The silence from behind the Commandant's closed door fuelled his imagination. Bagby could be dead already. Perhaps the Japs would now come for the others who knew of Bagby's whereabouts that night. Worse still, what if they were torturing him to get the names of the men in the Resistance? Des's father could be in danger too. His mind bombarded him with endless scenarios, all of which increased his anxiety.

When a shiny vehicle belonging to the officers of the *Kempeitai* showed up, he knew they were for Bagby. Their splendid, deadly swords hung ominously from their sashes, frightfully beautiful. Des pictured the courageous jockey's headless body on the Commandant's polished floor. A shiver ran through him.

Sonny was no help to Des. "We can only wait and see," he told Des. "The Dutch camp commander is with him. There's nothing you or I can do. Run along and catch up with your friends—and stay away from the *Kempeitai*."

Des did as he was told and soon found Kenny and Ron. They seemed to be less agitated about the situation, preferring to hang around the food preparation area in hopes of being asked to help with the rations, the first they had seen in two days. To Ron and Kenny's dismay, only Des was called in to assist with the evening meal. The sacks and bins of food seemed plentiful and made his empty stomach groan, but he knew that for him now, any of it would increase the pain and the bleeding from his insides. There was not nearly enough to provide the entire camp with a proper meal. After a couple of days of starvation, many had already died, far beyond the usual daily numbers, and there would be more.

Today, the cooks did not give any extra peanuts or pieces of jackfruit to Des. When the food was cooked and the inmates showed up to collect their portions, he was given a full ladle of the watery stew, pulled up from the bottom of the large cooking vat where a few extra beans tended to settle. He started to eat, promising himself to save some for the morning, and hope it would nourish him inspite of the pain. But as he devoured the first solid food he had eaten for two days, he could not stop himself from greedily swallowing every last morsel, even though he knew most of it would end up in a bloody pool in the latrine.

He stayed behind to clean the vats, which were already almost spotless from being rinsed with extra water to make a tea-like broth for some of the sicker inmates. When he finally headed back through the fenced walkway and past the common area to his quarters, the moon was shining weakly through the night haze. The Commandant's building was now in darkness and the *Kempeitai's* car was gone. Now that Des had eaten something, he could keep his nerves in check. He no longer felt sick at the sight of Bagby's hell. Whatever happened was done now and the feisty Aussie was most likely dead.

When Des arrived back at his quarters, his father and Trevor were whispering on the moonlit veranda where they always slept. Sonny moved a few inches, making room for his son.

"Bagby's alive," Sonny blurted, without waiting for Des to ask.

Des's eyes opened wide in shocked disbelief. "What? They let him live? But the *Kempeitai* were here for him."

"Yes, I know. But there were negotiations. The Dutch commander was able to convince the Japs that he wasn't running away… only looking for food. They were so relieved that it wasn't Allied reconnaissance soldiers preparing for an invasion, they decided to spare his life. It also went well for him that he voluntarily confessed. I think the Japs respected that."

Des nodded. "Sure," he said, "they'd take it as an honourable act, wouldn't they?"

"It would seem so," Sonny said.

"But they didn't let him off scot-free," Trevor interjected.

"What do you mean?" Des asked.

"They gave him quite a beating."

Des asked for no details. Instead, he lay down just as he was, in the humid darkness, and fell asleep.

Des did not see Wally Bagby for two days. On the third morning, he emerged, flanked by two of the other jockeys. Shuffling stiffly, he kept his eyes to the ground, carefully placing each foot in front of him as if anticipating the pain of his movements. Des walked by him at a fair distance so as not to seem impertinent. He was dying to catch a glimpse of the tiny titan who had single-handedly subdued a large, armed Japanese soldier and then was prepared to face his own death rather than see his fellow prisoners punished for his deed.

With his stooped gait, the jockey seemed smaller than ever. His fluffy beard that once set him apart from his fellow Australians was gone, making him appear almost childlike. As Des approached as close as he dared, he could see the heroic jockey slowly raise his head upward. Swollen to nearly twice its size, his face was almost entirely purple. His lips sported a brown crust of dried blood, and his jaw and chin seemed to join his neck directly in one ugly mass of bruised flesh. One of his eyes was completely shut, swollen black and blue. The other eye scanned the area, squinting briefly as its gaze passed the eastern sun, before taking note of Des. Des tried to turn away. This pain was private and Des felt unworthy to intrude. Bagby's one eye locked on Des's two. Years of coaching from both Rosie and Ah Mah told him not to stare—to turn away. In the instant before Des forced himself to look elsewhere, Wally Bagby winked at him.

40. THE HOSPITAL

"I'm sorry, Des." Sonny choked out his words as he gently rubbed his son's hand. "They insist you have to go to the hospital."

"No! Dad I'll be fine!" Des was frantic with fear, but so weak from starvation and bloody diarrhoea he hardly had enough energy to protest. He was now haemorrhaging huge amounts of blood in his stool.

"It was just the jungle berries I ate, Dad!" he argued.

Sonny was torn in two by the awful dilemma. He was terrified for his son. But the camp leaders were sure he had dysentery, and since it was highly contagious, and potentially fatal, anyone afflicted had to be quarantined in the hospital. Sonny could not go against the camp rules, even for his own son.

Des lay still, weak and sweating from the exertion of his latest run to the latrine. He had tried to drink sips of water and eat the bits of dirt mingled with rice. He had suffered the slicing agony in his intestines, watched his life bleeding away in the latrine, stood for as many headcounts as he could, knowing that time was his enemy. The Allies were not coming, at least not in time for him. Sonny lifted him to his feet, guiding him toward the door.

"No, please, I'm fine," Des whispered, twisting feebly away from his father's arm. He wanted to scream out with all his remaining strength—tell them he wasn't ready to go there, that he would find the energy somehow to stand up. He would eat more, get stronger. But it would be useless. He had to be separated from the others for their own good, not for his, to prevent contagion, they would say. His months of suffering had bought him a one-way ticket through the hospital's door.

His father escorted him to the front of the dingy single story building.

"I can't take you any further," he said, putting his arm around Des's shoulders. "Maybe with some rest you'll be better. You work so hard foraging with the others. Nikko and Trevor and I will find what we can for you."

Sonny's agonized expression belied his reassuring words, just as Rosie's had when he was torn away from her so long ago. Kneeling, Sonny embraced his son fiercely, as if willing his own remaining strength into the small tortured body.

Sonny was prepared to break any ordinary rules of their old normal life and any dictates of their captors, for survival. But he could not break the inmates' own rules of mutual dependency. Finally, as the doctor came to the door, he released Des, tears streaming silently down his face as he watched his small son disappear into the dreaded building.

Inside, Des was shocked out of his pain by the stench and sight of the human misery around him. He was shown to a cot in the back of the open area where a sea of wizened men, shrunken to dryness, waited for their last breath to carry them out of their prison. Their expressions were mostly peaceful, as if their minds had already left their physical surroundings and could see ahead to where they would spend eternity.

Lying down, Des began to think of his mother, whose face he could no longer picture. He remembered though, her pain the day he was taken from her, and he longed to be able to tell her that he understood why she let him go to the men's camp, that she had been right and he was sorry for acting the way he did.

He looked around. His fear at what he saw seemed to spark something new in him. He was unable to picture himself lying down like the others, passively waiting for death. He wasn't like them. He was Des Woodford. He was just a boy; his life was just beginning. He couldn't die—not if he didn't want it. Hadn't he survived the sinking of the Giang Bee, the days on the island, the capture of the Tappah? Hadn't he fought for and won the durian? Had he not avoided capture countless nights as he crawled under the fence through the mud and dirt, searching for whatever morsels he could find to keep starvation at bay?

Here though, he had no chance to add to the hospital fare that was the only food for the patients. There was an unspoken understanding that more would be a waste of rations. He was given a bitter, pungent tea made from boiled guava leaves, which was supposed to lessen the excretions of his bowels.

"Horrible stuff never works," one ravaged patient told him.

There was no medication; supplies from the Red Cross were always stolen by the Japanese for their own men. The tea was the best the British and Dutch doctors who ran the hospital could do for their patients – they were prisoners themselves. Sometimes the sick were given a glue-like broth made from tapioca. Occasionally Des saw that there were actually patients who recovered before succumbing to this utter starvation, and they could leave and return to the main prison compound. Strangely, after a short time on the awful tea and tapioca broth, Des discovered he did, in fact, feel less pain in his insides. Now he began to see how he could get out of the hospital – by the front door, not the back.

He knew he could have avoided the trip to hospital in the first place if he could have shown his stool was free of blood for three consecutive days, to prove to the doctor that he did not have dysentery or any of the other dangerous illnesses that threatened others in the camp. Perhaps he could earn a reprieve from his sentence here if he could find a way to fool him.

He spoke to the Dutch doctor, who was kindly, in spite of the brutality of his own situation, a hopeless and overwhelming effort to stem the tide of dying.

"What if you could see that I'm not bleeding, or only a little bit?" Des asked innocently. "That would mean I don't need to be here, wouldn't it?"

"I suppose it is possible," he said. "You don't seem to have the truly severe stomach pains that go with dysentery. Yours are lower. If you could go three days, maybe…." He trailed off, leaving Des hopeful.

Des went to sleep that first night, his decreasing pains dulled as well by his preoccupation with the details of his plan.

Under Des's cot was a small pot for excrement. Each morning, the pots were emptied. He drank what liquid was provided and used his metal pot during the night. In the early hours of the morning, before the doctors came in, he slipped from his cot and carried his pot over to where an unconscious older man lay. The dying man's breath rasped quietly amid the sounds of the other sleeping inmates. He did not stir as Des emptied half the contents of his own pot into the man's own metal container. Next Des made his way along the floor so as not to be noticed, and checked the contents of several other pots until he found a couple of firm bloodless stools. He added these to the now slightly less bloody contents of his own pot and returned to his cot.

When the doctor passed by later, Des showed him the pot. The doctor examined the contents sternly.

"This is your pot?" he asked in his thick Dutch accent.

"Yes, I'm feeling a little better," Des replied, careful not to claim too miraculous a cure.

He received a doubtful look. "There's still much blood here." He shook his head and walked away. Des stared at the doctor's back as he passed through the other patients. Some were dead and so were moved swiftly to their final destination out the back door.

The next couple of days saw Des engaged in a race for time. Without even the gritty rations provided in the camp, he knew he could not cling to life for very long. On the other hand, if he rushed his recovery, he risked being discovered. Oddly though, his stomach pains still abated. He still felt the stinging cuts of frequent bowel movements, but found enough relief to concentrate on his plan.

Then a small miracle appeared in the form of Nikko Barding.

"I have something for you, young man. Here, take it slowly, suck it a little at a time."

Like a precious jewel, an egg sat in his palm. Des looked at it, then at Nikko, with wordless gratitude. Doing as Nikko said, he sucked the raw yolk and eggwhite, feeling it flow down his throat, knowing it had the power to save his life.

He no longer even wondered how Nikko produced these feats of magic. He was Nikko. He was better than any magician, making life possible over and over again, where death seemed about to snuff it out.

Nikko brought him an egg whenever he could. At night, Des continued his desperate subterfuge. Bit by bit he replaced the bloody contents of his pot with the earthen coloured excrement of the dying inmates. After three days he presented a bloodless sample to the doctor. Two days after that, he dared to ask if he could be let out. The doctor seemed unconvinced, but Des stood up straight. His limbs were thinner than ever and he felt dizzy from lack of food. Still, Des clung to hope, willing himself back to the living with all the strength he could muster. Finally, the doctor nodded his head.

Des should have felt elated. He merely padded weakly from the building and back to his barracks. His life was not yet saved; he needed food. He found his father sitting on the floor of their bunk area and fell into his arms. Sonny clasped him to his chest with all his own remaining strength, a father whose son had come back alive from the grave.

"It`s like a miracle," he breathed into Des`s shoulder, believing his son was cured.

Over the next several days, Des eagerly accepted the additional rations that appeared as if by a miracle. His father regularly provided bits of nuts and fruit that helped him feel better. He was still plagued by bouts of bloody diarrhoea, but now he was more careful than ever to keep his poor health a secret, especially from Sonny. From now on, he would tell no one of the pain and bleeding. To disguise the truth, whenever he went to the latrine, he dropped a brick in, to disperse the telltale blood. Sometimes he allowed himself to believe he could survive long enough to see liberation.

41. JAPAN SURRENDERS

Des walked across the yard of his prison one morning in early August. His fair skin was weathered brown from the elements and his hair was like straw from the sun's bleaching rays. Three and a half years of captivity had seen him grow, in spite of the daily starvation that withered his body. He was fourteen now and finally stood nearly as tall as his father, but his hips and chest remained the same size they had been when he was a small child, his ribs clearly etched against his skin. He watched his feet plod slowly through the jail yard. Every bone in his limbs was clearly visible. His emaciated legs reached upward into the faded shorts he had worn as long as he could remember. The only change was that he could now see the skeletal outline of what he would look like as a corpse. His fear of returning to the hospital had vanished. The hospital was gone and with it the prisoners with medical experience who staffed it. The dead were now cleared out from where they fell.

Des moved slowly these days. If he felt the least bit of energy, he saved it for specific tasks relating to the incessant search for food. Des thought the latest ration cut would finish him, but to his surprise, he woke up each morning to the persistent sounds of the other inmates. He wanted to live, but wondered how he could go on much longer eating occasional morsels that his bowels too soon ejected, losing what little nutrition there was, whatever he consumed. Sonny and Trevor encouraged him to eat slowly, but this was impossible.

Their captors seemed edgy lately, even more nervous and temperamental than usual, often perceiving and punishing subterfuge when there was none. Then suddenly they increased the rations, and even released Red Cross supplies to the camp committee. Rumours abounded: that the Germans had capitulated in Europe; that the Allies had taken Indonesia. The camp bristled with an almost electric atmosphere.

One afternoon low-flying planes were sighted in the distance, but the prisoners had no way of knowing for certain if they were Japanese or Allied, or what turn the war might have taken. As they neared, Des quaked inside. Now he knew his years of suffering had been wasted, certain they were enemy aircraft approaching. They had all heard rumours of an enormous explosion in an attack by the Allies against Japan. Was this now payback? Were the Japs now coming to finish them off?

As the warplanes drew closer, their engines throbbing, Des felt the urge to run but he could not move his feet. He was aware of others around him. Some were running.

Others, like him, stood still and watched as the planes flew overhead. Suddenly Des felt his heart lift with a hope he hardly dared to feel. These were not Japanese planes homing in to finish off the prisoners! These were the Allies, coming to save them!

"They've come at last," Sonny said breathlessly, as the aircraft swooped off on their mission. "Those are American planes. We'll be safe now."

The next morning, Des woke and felt immediately that something had changed. Emerging from his shelter into the prison grounds, he looked around warily, trying to pinpoint the difference.

"The guards are gone!" Kenny called to him. "They've just up and left! Only the Commandant and a few officers are still here. All the Indonesian guards have run away too."

"Does that mean it's all over?" Des said, his eyes wide.

"Just about, I guess."

Sonny came up to them." The Commandant is meeting with our own commanders today," he told them. "And he's going to address the rest of us."

"What now Dad?" Des said at last. "Will the Allies come and get us?"

"Eventually. Right now, our own people are in charge of the camp. Captain Tenabe and some of the other guards will stay here, in their quarters, but we're in charge."

"Are they our prisoners now?"

"Well, sort of, I suppose you could say that."

Japanese soldiers who considered themselves innocent of war crimes had decided to stay to face whatever justice they might have from the Allies. The rest scattered.

"What about Mom?" Des said. "Can we find her?"

"I think they're letting the women come here," Sonny said. "We'll know for sure soon."

Captain Tenabe assembled the inmates. His demeanour was changed. He seemed nervous. Des noted that his heels no longer cut the dirt in sharp confident steps. Instead he scraped his feet in shuffling movements that were more suitable to someone twice his age. He stood before the group on his soapbox, his face maintaining a formal rigidity around eyes that could not conceal his sorrow.

Was he sorry, Des wondered? He looked it. Yes, they all looked very sorry indeed. But he could not believe the sorrow was for the skeletal group of hapless souls that stood before him. He must be sorry for his family, or perhaps the unbearable shame of defeat. No, they had never been sorry for the prisoners they had gathered up from the seas like so much flotsam. Nor had they been sorry as they herded them like livestock from camp to camp, deliberately starving them, allowing them to drop from illness and exhaustion.

Des decided Tanabe's wretchedness stemmed from his own plight: the shame of defeat. No more promotions would come his way. Tanabe had dreamt for years of a conqueror's existence. A new Japan, victorious under the sun banner, would see him prosper, rewarded and respected for his efforts for the betterment of the empire. Had he dared to picture life in any other way? Perhaps in the dark comfort of his furnished quarters, he had allowed himself a glimpse of another possibility. Des hoped Tanabe could see it all now: see Japan on its knees, and know true defeat.

Tanabe cleared his throat. His words were unembellished. "The war is over. It has ended in favour of The Allies. I am sorry for all the suffering that has been experienced. I have done the best I could for you under these circumstances, within my capacity."

Was this already a plea for mercy from Allied courts? Des sneered at this belated regret.

"You are now under the command of your own leaders. Allied officers will be arriving to arrange your repatriation. The women with family here will visit tomorrow at ten a.m.," the Captain said.

There was complete silence. Des blinked unbelievingly from his place in the assembly. Tanabe bowed and turned on his heel, returning at a faster pace back to his quarters. Sonny, who stood next to Des, stretched out his hand, briefly touching his son's shoulder. This small gesture communicated countless thoughts that evaded words. Des knew all that his father felt. Joy and dread commingled. Would she be alive? Would she be a feeble, skeletal creature, too ill to know them? He had thought of his mother so often and had grown accustomed to selecting random memories of her, dusting them off, then casually replacing them safely back into his farthest thoughts. Now he would finally see what these terrible years had done to her.

In just a few moments, years of struggling for survival and waiting for rescue had ended. Des stood with his father, hardly able to take it in. They were safe. They would live. Wordlessly, quiet tears falling from their eyes, they held each other close.

That night was long and sleepless for Des, as his mind was suddenly filled with a whole new set of worrisome thoughts. Could he catch up with more than three years of lost time at school? Would he be healthy enough to keep on living normally, or at all? Where would they go now, back to Singapore, Australia or even England? How could his father find work? But his worst worry overshadowed all of these: had his mother survived? This last agonizing question was almost too much for him, as his brain bombarded him with fragments of fears.

The next day, hardly daring to think of whether or not he would be once again with his mother, Des went off again to find his friends. Ron's voice breezed through the air. "Ho there, Des. Where are you going?"

Des stopped and waited for Ron to catch up. "I thought I'd head off to the cricket pitch for a lovely picnic of tea and crumpets. Care to join me?"

"Ow, stop it," Ron groaned. "I was trying not to think of food today."

"Good luck with that," Des retorted.

The two boys walked in silence together, grateful for the dry August air that kept the torturing mosquitoes at bay. Still a faint buzz intruded into Des's thoughts. The sound annoyed him, and he shook his head to chase it away. The noise increased. Des knew this was no insect.

"Shhh," he said.

"What do you mean 'shhh', I didn't say any…"

Des grabbed Ron's arm. "Shhh!" he said again more urgently.

The boys listened as the sound grew louder. Des could now make out its direction.

"A plane," he whispered. "A lot of planes!"

They arrived noisily, as the initial buzz became first a steady hum, then a low pitched groan, as the aircraft slowly skirted the prison. Some flew low. Others stayed aloft, supervising the lower planes as they swung around over the camp again, dropping torpedo-shaped bundles of life-saving food and medicines just outside the perimeter of the camp. Clearly they were making sure they didn't hit the prisoners by mistake, and as they flew over, they were so low that Des could see the grinning faces of the pilots. He felt strong, suddenly, full of renewed life, and a powerful sense of triumph over the Japanese enemy.

"We've made it!" Sonny cried, grabbing and Des in a rib-crushing hug.

We've really made it son!!"

Energy and elation pulsed through them both. The noise from the aircraft engines was deafening. As they swooped over, dropping their precious cargo, jubilation broke out in the camp, some prisoners weeping with joy, others speechless with emotion.

As soon as the drop was finished, men vaulted over the fence and dashed with joy to the packages, partly fearful that local Indonesians would try to claim possession. The big bundles, brought to a secure place in the camp, contained chocolate, high protein biscuits, powdered milk, medicines, and of course cigarettes, and soon the camp committee was organizing distribution of food and medicine to the most needy. Des and Sonny put much of their share aside for Rosie.

"We don't know if they have anything yet at their camp," Sonny said, determined not to even think that she might not be there at all.

"I can't eat much of it anyway. And Mom will need it. She'll still be looking after lots of other people," Des said, forcing himself to believe his own words.

Later, another miracle occurred. Allied officers, who had parachuted into the area out of sight of the camp, arrived at last to begin the rescue of the prisoners. After all these years, Des thought in awe, could it really be true? Were the friends of the British Empire really here to save him, just as he had been promised when he was a schoolboy?

"Hullo mates," said one of the men who approached Des and Kenny. "Sorry it took us so long." He spoke gently, his eyes reflecting the horror of starvation and desperation he was seeing all around him.

Hearing these words, hearing the familiar lilt of Australian that he knew from the jockeys, and further over, the voices of British officers who had parachuted in, Des felt surrounded by wonderful music. There were only about a half dozen of them, medics and communications officers and intelligence people, Sonny told him, but along with the food packages they made the liberation real, something you could see and touch.

"Hey, maybe we can turn those container things they dropped into canoes," Kenny said, his face now full of hope and optimism.

"Great idea," Des agreed, and they both laughed with the first true, deep joy either had felt in years.

As they planned this exploit, Des felt relief flow through his sick and withered form, calming the initial energy he had felt. Later, as Des folded himself into a crouch and lay down in his quarters, he let go of the last bit of strength he had tenuously clung to in order to survive. Someone else would save him. Now he could surrender.

42. WAITING FOR ROSIE

They waited. Sonny, Kenny and Des huddled inside the camp's perimeter, never allowing their glances to waver from the long straight road leading into the camp. As always, blades of pain cut through Des's stomach, but now an added jolt of dread honed their edge. What if his mother did not come? No, she had to come. She had to be alive. He had to have the chance to tell her he was sorry for that last day, when he ignored her heartbreak as he was taken away, to tell her she had been right, and he loved her.

How would they cope if she hadn't survived? Des worried more for his father than for himself. Though he was the child, he felt that after these terrible years, he could cope with absolutely anything life threw at him from then on. Losing his mother would be the ultimate pain, but he would survive, he knew. He was not as sure of his father, and feared that Sonny would be completely devastated. Young as he was, he did not see the piercing irony in this reversal of their positions.

Nausea joined his pain, making him even weaker. The sun dangled in the sky motionless, making the seconds pass too slowly to bear. As it drew closer to ten o'clock, Des became more fidgety and anxious.

At last the first woman emerged from around a distant bend in the road. The second, then a third appeared and finally a cluster of forms manifested like a miraculous apparition, or perhaps a mirage. Des scanned their faces, withered and unrecognizable. Their bodies exhausted, they plodded closer. The men were silent with shock. It dawned on Des as he watched that the women were in such dreadful condition that he may not recognize his mother. The trickle of women ceased and no more forms emerged from the shadow of the bend.

Sonny sat on the ground, stone-faced, never once looking away, even when the women stopped coming. It was clear that his Rosie was not among the group. A couple of the men had already recognized their family members and were on their feet straining their last bit of energy to reach them. The others waited silently, sick with dread that their loved ones had perished. Then another group of women appeared, gaunt and exhausted from the two mile walk. Their clothes were colourless rags bleached by the Sumatran sun. Their legs were skeletal. Bare feet scraped the dust.

Des couldn't stand the wait. He got up and hurried to the first group who were by now coming through the gates.

"Do you know my mother?" he asked. "Her name is Rosie Woodford."

The women stared into the distance, presumably looking for their men. Their eyes were hollow and haunted. No one paid any heed to the bony adolescent with the sandy hair.

"Please," he implored, "she's an English woman. Rosie Woodford. Is she alive? Is she coming?"

At last, a young woman, rail thin with straggly brown hair, answered. "No, she said, "I know of no one with that name."

Des was frantic now. He stopped the second group, asking them the same questions.

"No, no, she's not with us," someone answered.

Now Des was overcome with despair. Although he had not seen his mother for two years, he couldn't imagine life without her. She was always present, at least as an idea. All this time he had pictured her surviving conditions behind the Japanese barbed wire, so he could face his own plight too. He pushed away his thoughts. How could he even think about a life after liberation that did not include her? He ran to a third group, mechanically repeating his questions.

"Rosie Woodford. Does anyone know her?"

One woman emerged from the group, stunning Des with a sudden hug. She breathlessly panted as she drew in closer, wrapping him in her rail-like arms. He could feel her exhausted heart mightily beating against his chest. His memory of her embrace was old. They fit differently into each others' arms then. She had been softer, like a silk-covered pillow, lavender-scented and warm. His head had rested neatly into cushiony shoulders as his arms comfortably circled her waist. Now she was smaller, it seemed. Her body was like a fragile twig he dared not risk breaking. He placed his arms around her gently. Her body trembled then shook as breathless heaving turned to sobs.

"Oh Des," Rosie gasped. "Thank God." She squeezed him tighter, her weakness barely causing him to notice. "Is Dad…where is he? Is he alive?"

Rosie released Des abruptly as Sonny arrived. Des watched them embrace each other, drawing delight from their reunion. His stomach pains were forgotten; happiness spread through his blood like an elixir, resuscitating him. He felt too lucky for words. He had finally come through the war to see both of his parents survive and be re-united.

As he sat by his parents, content in their joy, he looked around and took in the changes to those he had left behind in the women's camp two and a half years earlier. One woman, a striking beauty when she first entered the camp was now unrecognizable. It was only when he heard his mother call her by name that Des realized that the frail old stick of a human, with tattered clothes and straggled hair bleached straw-like by the sun, was the same youthful beauty of his memory.

Those like Rosie who had stayed busy tending to others for the betterment of the camp, often stayed healthier than others who cared less for the wellbeing of their fellow prisoners. But she too had been depleted to the limits of human endurance, and the suffering and deprivation were written on her face and her emaciated body.

A major difference, he decided, between those who survived and those who perished, was hope. He had watched so many die when they simply lost hope, and let go. He had seen women and men perfectly healthy in the first months of internment, who seemed to just wither and die. He and his parents had always kept their flame of hope alive, and had acted as though they had a life to look forward to, always planning, working to survive, whatever it took.

Liberation should have been a continuous joyous event. The first wonderful realization of rescue brought on a general euphoria as the prisoners looked into the blueness above and saw Allied planes passing over. But Des was now brutalized by his own emotions as he was wrenched back and forth first by happy reunions, and then by the sight of strong-willed men reduced to sheer despair as they collapsed upon confirmation that their loved ones in the women's camp had perished.

His own elation was brought low by the sight of Kenny, who slumped in grief when his mother did not appear. But then, like a miracle, his eldest sister appeared. His mother was too ill to move, but the liberation had come for her just in time. Kenny wept with relief. Three of his sisters were in the nearby women's camp. Other children learned that none of their family members had survived. Des sat with his friends, sharing their joy and grief in silence, overwhelmed at the end of this war that had been cruelly waged upon helpless civilians. While he watched his parents talking quietly together, Des reflected how lucky he was, and how easily he, too could have been orphaned.

Rosie stayed for two hours. The women had to return to their own camp, because the supplies dropped were not enough for all, and there was no room for them. They had provisions now in their own camp, and they had to get back while it was still light. Darkness increased the threat of wild animals and hostile Indonesians on the route between the camps. It turned out that they had not been far apart all this time, both men and women within the huge Belalau plantation area, not far from the nearest town of Lubbuek Linggau. For healthy people, it was perhaps a thirty-minute walk; for people in their pathetic condition, it was an exhausting marathon. When it was time for her to go back, Sonny gave Rosie two hard-boiled eggs that he had saved just for her, and some of the other provisions from the airdrop. They stared at each other constantly and Des in turn stared at them both.

"We'll be back tomorrow," she said.

"Or we'll come to you," Sonny replied, worried for her. "Our own Commanders will work it out with the Allied officers here."

Soon it was time to go. Des worried about his mother's ability to endure the long walk twice in one day. But he saw that when she left, her steps were lighter. He was certain now of the energizing power of happiness. The hope of rescue had helped them endure the hardships of prison life; but real gladness, the kind that was seeded and grew from the heart, could enliven their existence.

43. A SURPRISE THREAT

The next day the men rose and walked. They set out together at first, on the two mile journey down the clay road through the jungle to the women's camp. After the last move of the men's camp, they had been so close, and still had no idea their wives and sisters and daughters were near. They trudged doggedly on. For the most part, the bottoms of their feet were hardened and leathery from shoeless years of trudging over nature's debris. The few elderly still remaining somehow found the strength to get to their feet, compelled by the power of hope. Even those who were the most frail and sick, who had for months been prostrate and immobile in their suffering, somehow were able to summon a personal miracle, rising from where they lay, to walk once more.

Des was awestruck by their courage. Worn and close to death, it seemed impossible that they could even move. Now their faces belied their bodies' desperate conditions, exuding happiness, even though they knew they might not live to see the day's end.

Eventually, they spread out in a rag-tag assortment of small groups as the weak lagged behind the strong. The mass exodus to the women's camp became a trickle of humanity dribbling through the tropical bush. The road was clay, baked hard by the relentless sun. At times the route almost disappeared under dense growth, and on either side rose jungle that harboured wild animals.

Des first ventured out with Ron, letting his father lag behind with some of the men. They had secured a machete and a club-shaped stick before embarking. The trek through such difficult terrain was arduous and fraught with ample opportunity to lose one's footing, making two miles seem like twenty.

"Do you think we're half way there yet?" queried Ron.

Des paused in his tracks a few feet ahead, holding the machete at his side. He looked back at his mate in disbelief.

"How would I know that?" he answered impatiently. "It's hard enough to tell how much ground we've covered."

"Well I suppose we must be," Ron continued. "I'm getting tired enough."

Des scowled. His heart raced from the effort of walking along with the ever-present pains in his intestines. Eating still only invited a renewed onslaught of cramps and bloody diarrhoea.

Every footstep caused grasses and shrubs to rustle and whisper. The two boys became inured to the sounds as they plodded wearily onward. It was Ron who first noticed the change in the rustling.

"Shhh," he ordered, quickly sprinting to span the few feet between them.

"What?" Des asked, stopping in his tracks.

The crunching and rustling sound of something moving through the foliage continued, drawing closer to them. Ron held firmly onto the handle of his club, balancing the heavier end in his other hand. Des too stood alert with his machete. Stomach pains were forgotten. The noise grew louder, adding the click of snapping twigs beneath alien-sounding feet. To their right they watched, horrified, as two black heads emerged into view about thirty feet away. Seconds later more rustling heralded the arrival of several more black faces.

"God save us, we're for it" Ron hissed in a whisper audible only to Des.

They were staring at a group of apes who stood hunched over in the thick bush along the fringes of the jungle, keeping their distance momentarily as they assessed the boys, their teeth slightly bared.

While Ron regarded them with horror, Des found himself counting them: ten, eleven, twelve - an even dozen. About three feet tall, the apes' diminutive size was more than compensated for by their aggression. They stared at the boys, snarling and grunting now to each other. Some of them moved about posturing threateningly while Des and Ron stood statue-like within the open swath of the narrow roadway, perspiring with fear. Des could feel the soft, tropical breeze of the late afternoon blow upon his sweat making him shiver, a tremor that became an uncontrollable quake. He held fast to the handle of the machete, lest his sweat and trembling cause him to drop it. He swallowed a lump in his throat.

"Ron," he whispered, "we have to attack them."

Ron groaned. "We can't," he breathed. "There's too many."

"It's our only chance. You're right we can't take them if they attack. We have to do it first. If we're loud and fierce enough, they might run away."

"And if they don't?"

"They will. They must." Des tried to sound convincing. "Hurry, when I say 'go'."

"No, wait…"

"Goooaaaaahhhh!!" Des shouted raising his voice into a screaming roar. He lifted his machete high into the air and was joined by Ron as he ran full tilt toward the crowd of apes. Together, they brandished their weapons, chopping furiously at the air in front of them, thrashing through the bush.

At first, the apes appeared confused. For a couple of seconds, which seemed like an eternity to Des, they held their ground. Then, two of them moved back several steps. Their retreat spread a persuasive message to the rest of the band, scattering them back into the dense growth. Ron and Des continued shouting even after they lowered their weapons. Finally, they stopped, exhausted and ran back to the road.

"Let's keep going," Des said. "There's no time to stop now. They could come back."

To Des's utter astonishment, Ron was sporting an open-mouthed grin. He looked so pleased with himself that the remains of Des's fear quickly dissipated into the same self-satisfaction he saw in Ron.

"Did you see them? They ran like rabbits," Ron beamed. "Hard to believe it was so easy, isn't it?"

"It may not be so easy next time," countered Des. "We'd better tell our camp commander. I'd hate to think what'd happen if some of the sicker men ran into them, or even the women."

The boys were elated after their narrow escape. The feeling buoyed them for the rest of the walk, allowing Des to forget his tortured stomach as he enjoyed their victory.

When they arrived at the women's camp, his elation gave way to the grimness of their situation again, as he took in the sight of the once beautiful women and girls. They looked like wraiths, so insubstantial they might suddenly float away, or simply drop to the ground. Then he realized he and the men must look the same. They had become accustomed to their own daily deterioration, but seeing the women suddenly, with the full impact of three years of deprivation and suffering, was still a shock. As was also the case in the men's camp, some of the small boys who had stayed with their mothers had grown taller while others had remained stunted by lack of nourishment. His teenaged eye now noticed that some of the younger girls had developed into young women, although quite thin. The adult women were mostly skin and bones.

He soon found Rosie and watched happily as she and his father embraced again. Sonny tenderly offered her the provisions they had saved for her and her patients. Rosie's smile was weak but full of deep gratitude and love.

Sitting on the ground beside them, Des watched the bustling activity of families exchanging stories of conditions in both camps. He watched them exchange precious gifts—a cob of corn, a couple of bananas, an egg or two. He learned from some of the other women that his mother had continued to be a godsend around the camp, always thinking of others and nursing those who needed care. He was told that this had helped her survive to see her son and husband again. One feeling Des found surprising was a tendency to still keep an eye out for the Japanese and Indonesian Guards. Although they had scurried out a few days earlier, and the rest were in their quarters as prisoners now of the Allied troops, it was hard to get used to their absence after so much time worrying about their presence.

Then he saw Betty. She hadn't come to the men's camp as she had no relations there, but now he went up to her. She was taller, and terribly thin, but seemed to have survived better than most. Perhaps her inner calm had kept her intact. She greeted him shyly, but with evident relief and affection.

Des boasted to Betty and his mother about how he and Ron had routed the apes. She immediately told him to inform the Dutch camp commander who soon had the women moving about in groups of no fewer than half a dozen.

Sonny agreed. "Your mother's right," he said. "We must inform the others here too, and in the men's camp. We've not come this far just to be ruined by other dangers now. I'll tell our commander to give orders."

Des nodded. "I had hoped the noise we made would attract some help, if not from some of the walkers, then at least from some villagers."

Sonny's eyes narrowed. His expression changed kind concern to one of stern rebuke. "Des," he blurted sharply, "you are avoid any contact whatsoever with the locals. Is that clear?"

Des was taken aback. "But why? The war is over."

"Exactly. There will be a lot of settling of accounts. Revenge and just plain killing." he added as Des looked puzzled. "They won't care who you are, Dutch or British, remember. Just stay away from them. Please," he added, "just to be on the safe side."

Nominally, the British were in control of both Sumatra and Java, at least of the main towns, but they had yet to extend their reach to the villages and jungles. The men were all aware of the murderous chaos outside their prison camp, which was now, ironically, a safe haven. Some of the Indonesians were taking out their anger on any Japanese they could waylay; others were concentrating on revenge against the Dutch; some were happy to kill Japanese, Dutch, or anyone else who was not Indonesian.

But they weren't the only ones who wanted rough justice. Sometime after they returned to the men's camp again, after the trek back along the baked path, Des noticed Jan and Nikko had disappeared.

"Have you seen the Barding brothers around?" he asked Kenny.

"Not for a couple of days. No." Kenny scanned the area of the camp visible from where he and Des sat, half-reclining against the floorboards of the outside veranda of one of the buildings. He leaned in closer to Des, lowering his voice as he spoke. "I'm sure they're busy organizing things as they usually do."

"Organizing things," Des echoed. "What things? Our soldiers have things under control. What could they be organizing?"

Kenny shrugged. His bony shoulders almost touched his ears. "Do you remember what they used to say? They'd talk about it sometimes when the camp was quiet. Not to everyone, and never to us. But I'd overhear them sometimes when my Dad was alive."

Des was instantly reminded of Kenny's loss the year before. He'd been through so much that Des sometimes couldn't understand how Kenny had found the strength to help him and so many other boys all these years.

"Overhear what?" Des asked.

"Nikko and Jan said that when the war was over, they would go out and find the guards – the bad ones at least – and set things right."

Des didn't react. He knew the Barding brothers would get the job done. He had seen them operate from their earliest days on Bangka Island after the seizure of the Tappah. He wondered if they would track down The Dog. There was nothing Jan and Nikko couldn't do. He remembered back the way they had found him work in the tinwinning, then teaching the boys how to catch eels, and when they had brought him Bluey and Koefer. Their help and praise when he had to do what was necessary to save his father's life would stay in his mind forever. He would never forget the magic of Nikko appearing in the horrible hospital with eggs for him. It was dazzling to watch them get things into the camp, always eluding the watchful eyes of the sentries, or explaining their way out of blatantly impossible situations. Des believed they would be back. They would do whatever they set out to do. And they would return.

Back in the men's camp, word eventually came that the sickest prisoners were to be flown out to Singapore for medical attention. Des felt if he could just hang on a bit longer, he was sure to have a chance to live. He was still tormented by the deep sharp pains in his abdomen, and his stool was still bright red with blood. But nobody knew that. Should he tell his father now? He fretted and agonized over whether or not to tell his secret, until finally he decided to tell his father and the camp doctor that the problem had just started again.

"He must be taken out as soon as possible," the doctor decreed.

Sonny nodded, swallowing back this new worry, holding Des by the shoulders to help him make his way back to their bunks to lie down. In the meantime, they waited. As the others ate their fill from the supplies dropped by the Americans, Des was restricted to spoonfuls of egg-whites.

"You must give your system a chance to clean itself and rest," he was told by an Australian medical officer, one of those who had parachuted in near the camp.

Des rested, quelled by the sweet security of knowing there was nothing more he need do or say to ensure their survival. Within the same barbed wire that wrapped around his prison for the past three and a half years of his life, nothing was physically different. But inside his weary and frail body, his brain soared over the limitless space created when the burden of keeping himself alive was lifted. He gladly sipped spoonfuls of what was offered.

44. LIBERATION

The stars appeared extra brilliant that night. Never before had Des seen them glow so brightly. They cut a swathe of light against the blackness of beyond, so thick that the sky took on a milky texture.

"*Twinkle, twinkle little star*," Des mumbled under his breath, taking in the meaning of the childhood rhyme he used to recite by rote. His bowels were mercifully at rest for the time being as he lay in his space under the sheltering cover of the veranda. His body was weak, but his mind flooded with activity. For hours he had watched the stars grow stronger. He knew daylight would come soon, and with it his final release from prison. He would stay awake to savour the day's arrival.

"Des," His father's voice jarred him. "How do you feel?"

His wandering mind was pulled into the light of morning. Des wondered at what point his starry vision had drifted into a dream, missing the sun's ascent.

"Can you walk?" Sonny asked.

Des nodded.

His father held a cup out to him. He sat up. Taking it in both hands, he tasted it. The same warm sugary water the Dutch doctor had given him the day before, soothed the walls of his dry throat, deepening the elation he already felt.

Sonny was oblivious to his son's joy, registering only grave concern at Des's terrible condition. "Today we go, son. They'll take us to pick up Mum first, and then we'll finally be out of this place."

Des merely nodded. Because he had finally at least partially revealed how ill he was, it had been arranged that the Woodfords would be among the first group evacuated. Des had said goodbye to most of his friends, and Kenny and Trevor came to see the Woodfords off, everyone full of hope and relief. There were no tearful goodbyes, as everyone expected to be together again at the holding centre in Singapore they had been told about, where they would all have medical checkups and treatment. Instead, it was a quiet farewell, for now.

A truck arrived within the hour. Des struggled onto the back, assisted by Sonny. He noticed the Indonesian driver, wondering how people could so casually flip from playing the role of brutal guards to now working for the Allied occupation.

"Does he know we're English, not Dutch?" Des asked his father.

"I don't think he cares," answered Sonny, which made Des worry even more.

It soon became clear that the comfort of his passengers was not at the forefront of their driver's mind. He careened through the narrow jungle roads at breakneck speed, first picking up Rosie and some others at the women's camp before barreling out to an Allied airfield.

"This chap's a lunatic," pronounced Rosie as they bounced and swayed, knocking themselves repeatedly against the hard wooden planks of the floor.

Des worried whether he had survived his years of imprisonment only to perish in a crumpled truck crashed on a dusty jungle road at the hands of a maniac hired by his rescuers. After an hour and a half they arrived at a field of the tall *lalang* grass. The Woodfords lowered themselves awkwardly from the truck with the others and were met by several military personnel. Stationed to the side was a jeep complete with radio communications equipment, which fascinated Des, despite all his pains. One of the troopers approached him, reaching into his pocket and extracting a bar of chocolate.

"Here y'go mate," he said. "Y'may want this for the ride."

"Thank you," Des said weakly.

The man then pulled an open packet of cigarettes from his breast pocket and offered them to Sonny. Sonny gratefully took one from its wrinkled container.

"Take a few for later," he added, thrusting the pack closer.

Des loved the man's Australian accent. Its melodic inflections were soothing and friendly. An unaccustomed feeling wrapped itself briefly around him. He had felt it before as a young child in Singapore without realizing it. Only now, after so many years of daily suffering, did he acknowledge this familiar feeling that seemed more like a soft caress. He felt safe.

In the distance, Des could hear the approaching hum of an airplane. The Australian troopers used their radio equipment to communicate with its pilot. Des looked sceptically at the tall thick *lalang* covering the field.

"How can he land without a runway?" he asked his father. "There could be anything under it. Rocks or water…anything."

"We've checked every inch of this area, mate," replied the trooper, obviously overhearing. "Don't you worry. It's completely safe for the operation."

As the plane neared, Des saw it enlarge into view. It was bigger than any plane he had ever seen. It soared into the field, skimming the tall grass and making a perfect landing. After it had almost stopped, it pivoted and headed back to where it had first touched down a short distance away from the troopers and their jeep. The wretched group of sickly passengers applauded and cheered as loudly as their limited strength allowed. Somehow they were energized by the sight of the famous twin-engine Dakota DC3. With the insignia of the Royal Australian Air Force on its fuselage, its wings stretched out across the grasses, and the deafening roar of the running engines, it looked invincible. It also looked enormous, and now Des began to wonder how it could ever take off again through the heavy grass. The truck ride hadn`t killed them, but maybe the airlift would. Once more, he feared life would be snatched away at the last minute.

The liberated prisoners were gently escorted on board where they were greeted by two army nurses. Des and his parents were shown a place to sit on some metal benches along the walls of the Dakota's interior. With a clang that was audible over the sound of the noisy engines, the door closed and almost immediately the plane began to move, the engines vibrating as it roared bumpily down the field. Des trembled in fear. Then, in one whoosh, their movement became smooth and Des realized he was in the air.

The excitement of his first plane ride was overshadowed by nervousness at being so high above the ground without any support. The hard bench pressed uncomfortably against his bony frame. Communication was nearly impossible above the thunderous engines. Some of the passengers tried to use hand signals but mostly everyone was silent, numbed by the shock of their survival. Now, it was real. They were finally returning to life as normal civilians.

After a while, one of the nurses offered Des some warm milk. Des looked up gratefully and saw a young Australian woman in a military nurse's uniform, with dark hair framing her pale, pretty, smiling face. She indicated that he was to sip it slowly, miming with her hands at first, as he seemed so fragile. Des, who still held the chocolate bar in his right hand, transferred it to his left in order to take the cup. Seeing the candy, the nurse bent lower toward his ear, touching her fingertips to his left wrist.

"Do not eat this," she commanded gently, tapping his left wrist twice. "Your stomach won't be able to digest any rich foods. Just sip on the milk for now and eat nothing until you're in hospital in Singapore. We'll be there in an hour and a half. The doctors will decide then what you should eat."

The milk soothed his fiery bowels. Des hoped they would stay calm enough throughout the flight. The young nurse regularly took his pulse and fed him glucose through a tube.

"He'll be taken to a British military hospital as soon as we land in Singapore," she told Rosie. "I'll visit him there if I can."

Des heard this with relief, but spent most of the flight in an exhausted sleep.

The absence of his captor's gritty rations along with a limited diet of raw eggs and sugar water seemed to stabilize his intestines, providing some respite from the bouts of gushing blood that fled his system often several times a day. He hoped he would not be left an invalid from his years of sickness; for now it was enough that he no longer had to hide his bloody stool by dispersing it in the latrine with a carefully dropped brick. He could welcome going into hospital, knowing that there would be a safe and promising way out, into a new life.

45. FREEDOM

Aboard the Dakota, Des thought about his freedom. Above all else, his mind was freed from the daily burden of survival. Food was available, as would be medicine and shelter. Although he still faced the possibility that he might not recover from the damage to his health, his fate was no longer in the hands of his enemies.

His free thoughts tortured him as well. He worried about his friends back in the camps who would soon be scattered into uncertain futures. He thought of Ron and Kenny and Trevor and Nikko and Jan and wondered what their lives would be like. He thought of James and other children whose parents would never go home with them. Des looked at his own parents and wondered guiltily why he was so lucky. They were all he had, yet they were everything he could want.

The past three and a half years had seen him gradually stripped of everything he had known and possessed. Even his very childhood had been ripped away and replaced by a kind of limbo, where all activity was in furtherance of a nebulous cause—that of waiting. He waited to be counted. He waited for the guards to avert their attention so he could leave the camp and search for food. He waited for opportunities to eat; for night to fall, for sleep to come and provide even a brief respite from his pain, for the war to end, for rescue by the Aliies, and for a single durian to fall. Each one was a step toward living again.

Feeling overwhelmed, Des blocked these thoughts and took refuge behind the same shocked expression worn by his companions. A short time later, they were all signaled by the nurse to look outside. Des found a view through one of the windows and looked out at the most awesome sight he had ever seen. Stretching below them into the horizon, the sea was dotted with countless warships, troop ships and support vessels. They appeared tiny and frozen in their positions.

"*Peaceful,*" Des thought as a comforting tingle climbed his back, making him shudder.

"That's the Allied fleet," he heard someone's voice shout behind him. "They were ready to invade if the Bomb failed to bring on an unconditional surrender."

Des turned and saw one of the Australian military men. He had heard of a couple of large bombs that had exploded on Japanese soil, but was sceptical of the news that two single explosions could bring on such a complete capitulation. He knew the Japanese. They would never surrender. He had heard that national honour required them to fight to the last man.

At last the Dakota soared in over Singapore, touching down at a military airfield. Sonny helped Des disembark first, handing him over to a soldier in a military vehicle, before being joined by Rosie.

"Where are you taking him?" Sonny asked.

"Alexandra Military Hospital," was the reply.

"Aren't you coming?" Des frantically asked his parents as he was guided onto a padded seat. To lose them would kill him. He tried to scramble off, but was firmly deterred by one of the attendants.

Both Sonny and Rosie looked with pleading eyes at the officer. "Sorry," he said, "They can visit you later. There's a good lad."

Once in hospital, Des was fed half a boiled egg, served with a slice of toast and some warm milk. Later, he was given oatmeal and steamed fish and chicken. Many of the patients on the ward as well as their visitors marveled at a new medicine which was prescribed for many of them, saving several lives. Penicillin was the wonder drug which promised to eradicate infection.

Rosie and Sonny came daily to see him. One afternoon, Sonny had news which bolstered Des's spirits.

"I've been offered a position," his father told him. "The British military stationed in Singapore requires a store for the officers and their wives to purchase imported wares. I'm to set it up and run it as soon as I'm recovered enough."

Des beamed, relieved that his parents had found a living so soon. Both of them were already looking healthier on a regular regimen of healthy food, small quantities at first, but now enough to start putting real muscle and flesh back on their bones. They had a long way to go to regain full health, but they were sustained by their joy that they had survived, and new life could begin.

"There's more," Rosie added. "We've arranged to buy a house too."

"Oh," said Des, disappointed that he would not be moving back into his old house. "I had hoped we might go home again," he said.

"That's not possible. It wasn't ours. We only rented. Now someone else is in there. But our new place is just two houses away."

"And we've found Ah Mah, Ah Wah and Cookie. They're coming back with us."

Des was elated. "And Sami too?" he asked.

Sonny's face dropped and he shook his head. "No son. I'm sorry. No one has seen him since the invasion."

"Have you checked with the Indian army?" Des pleaded. "He was going to join up with them when they got here. We could leave word where we are."

Sonny shook his head more emphatically now. "We are on the list. He could have found us if he was looking. I'm sorry, but it will serve no good to dwell on the past. We must look to the future now. What's done is done."

Des tried to see things his father's way. As the weeks passed, his body grew stronger and his stomach healed. His doctors said that camp rations heavily laden with sandy grit and dust had shredded his already delicate insides until they were bleeding wounds. The more he ate, the worse he bled. Only times of sheer starvation allowed his intestines to improve, but then gave way to the agony of hunger. The prison food he ate to ward off death, in time would have been the very thing that killed him.

He had been snatched back from the brink of death by gentle nourishment and wondrous penicillin and would now live. He spent his days doing just that. He chatted with nurses and the other patients. He listened to his parents' plans for the future. He congratulated those who had joyful stories of miraculous reunions. But his nights did not allow him to let go of his three and a half years away from Singapore. Now, more so than at any time during his captivity, his dreams were plagued by horrible images of the Giang Bee. Drowning faces called to him from the water, some pleading for rescue, others praying for God to help them transcend easily into death. Hospitalized prisoners smiled at him with hollow eyes, begging him to remember the cruel irony of the building's name—a 'hospital' where cures were impossible. And on the island of his nightmares, casuarinas whispered to him in their eerie voices to remember those who had waited in vain, in the afternoon breezes of Indonesia.

Epilogue: After the War

Des Woodford continued his recovery in a British military hospital in Singapore. He rested there for several weeks where he was treated for severe lacerations in his stomach and intestines. Many years later, he would discover through modern diagnostic techniques that he was an early childhood sufferer of celiac disease, a debilitating affliction that damages the small intestine and inhibits the absorption of vital nutrients. That Des survived the horrendous camp conditions at all is a particular testament to his strong will to live, especially in light of the chronic and severe pain that constantly plagued him. He believes that his Japanese captors' frequent habit of cutting rations may have given him short respites from the gritty, filth that made his condition worse, allowing a day or even a few days for is stomach to occasionally heal, as it did on the tea and gruel in the camp hospital he feared so much.

It was only after their liberation that he told his parents of his desperate subterfuges in the camp hospital to deceive the doctor, and later his father, into thinking he was not seriously ill, and how he had continued to hide his true condition throughout his internment. When he heard this, Sonny broke down and wept for his young son.

After his release from the military hospital, he spent several more weeks recuperating at home with his parents, who had also been given restorative care. When they were well enough, they had both been given jobs with the British Military Administration in Singapore and Malaya, which also provided a penthouse apartment. The Woodfords wanted a home and garden though, and used their prewar savings and a bank loan to buy a new home on Florence Street, in Singapore—the very same street they had lived on before the Japanese invasion in 1942. Ah Mah, Ah Wah and Cookie were with them, after a joyful reunion. Ah Wah grew to be a lovely young woman, unusually tall at five feet eight inches, and became a successful accountant.

For the remainder of 1945, Des attended school at St. Joseph's Institution. Unlike schools of today, where programs exist to assist children like Des through trauma counseling and special classes, St. Joseph's expected the child prisoners of war to pull up their bootstraps and get on with their studies.

Des tried to do just this, but he had a difficult time adjusting to normal reality. At home, he discussed his experiences with Rosie and Sonny for awhile, but eventually Sonny declared the matter to be in the past and that it was no use to dwell on such unpleasant times. In 1946, Des was sent to boarding school at Aquinas College in Perth, Australia where he eventually settled. That same year, Sonny and Rosie at long last had a baby daughter, whom they called Anne. She was joined by another brother, Llewellyn, in 1952.

Sonny and Rosie declined an offer from British post war administration to relocate in either of England or Australia, choosing instead to stay behind in Singapore to manage the ROAC Officers' Shop, established to cater for the needs of the British army officers stationed there. When the establishment closed in the late 1960's, Des's parents retired and moved to Perth to be close to family and friends.

In 1954, at the age of twenty-three, Des joined the Far East Oxygen and Acetylene Company and was stationed in Malaya (now Malaysia) as a gas manufacturing production foreman. Upon arriving in Malaya, he located fellow prisoner Betty (Edith) Kenneison who had been interned with his mother in the women's camp. Des met Betty's younger sister Gillian in 1955 and was instantly smitten. They married in 1956 and raised three children together, Wendy, Wayne and Dale. Des and Gillian both love durian fruit.

One of the more shocking outcomes of liberation was the fate of Trevor, Sonny Woodford's closest confidante in the men's prisons. After liberation, evacuation of the inmates took nearly two weeks, with the sickest and most injured being flown out first. The remaining liberated prisoners were dropped supplies of food and medicines and left free to do as they pleased. They were cautioned not to venture too far from the grounds, for fear of indiscriminate killing of whites by local Indonesians. Trevor was among a few brave men of compassion who ventured out to other camps to help rescue some Dutch civilians who were stranded in an isolated area. It was on a second such mission that he and his group were ambushed by Indonesians who hacked them all to death with machetes.

Sonny Woodford found this terrible news extremely difficult to bear, that the friend he regarded like an older son had survived so much, only to be killed so savagely when his evacuation was only a few days away. Des was also deeply affected by Trevor's death but worried more about his father who took the news very badly. It was only small comfort that the perpetrators were actually caught and brought to justice, because one Dutchman survived the massacre and was able to identify them.

As would be expected of two such intrepid heroes, the Barding brothers, Jan and Nikko survived the war and were believed to have moved to The Netherlands. To this day, Des does not know what became of them after the war, but they have always lived on in his memory as heroes, and pivotal influences that helped him and so many others survive the war.

Des met up with Kenny in Singapore a few months after the war, but they lost touch when Des went to Perth Australia to study. They did re-connect years later, in 1958, when both were working in Kuala Lumpur, Malaya. He stayed in touch with some of Kenny's family after his wonderful friend passed away. Recently, Des reconnected with his old friend Ron as well.

The amazing Australian jockeys returned to Singapore and Malaya and resumed horse racing. The Woodfords frequently saw Wally Bagby, the two Donnelly brothers, and Jimmy Martin and their families. Mickey Donnelly died in an accident in Singapore, but the rest, like the Woodfords, retired to Perth.

Many other former prisoners in both camps have published memoirs and personal accounts of their time as prisoners of the Japanese. In this memoir I have tried to give readers a view of this terrible experience in history from a child's eyes, and from his heart and soul. Despite all the horrors, Des Woodford emerged from this ordeal without bitterness, but instead with a profound joy of living, and an enduring appreciation of every single day of normal life.

Des remained devoted to his parents the rest of their lives, never forgetting their extraordinary bravery and resourcefulness, and the love and devotion that they had for each other and for their son in the dreadful prison camps. Rosie passed away of brain cancer in 1995 at the age of 84, and Sonny survived to be 92, until taken by a heart attack not even a year after his beloved wife, in 1996.

The British negotiated with the Japanese for compensation to be paid to civilian prisoners of war. Japan paid this in a timely manner to the British Government, which held the money for several decades before even informing the former prisoners about it. By that time, most of them, including Rosie and Sonny Woodford, had died, and next of kin were not given the compensation. Des is scathing in his assessment of this "arrogance and ignorance by the British establishment...who saw no disgrace from profiting from our sufferings". Eventually, he received what he calculated to be a paltry $2.80 for every day of his own internment and abuse.

One friend who read this manuscript, and is acquainted with Des, said she marveled that he had grown up to be so joyful and positive in his enjoyment of life after his dreadful experiences.

He replied jokingly, "Well there are some who say I never really have grown up."

This is typical of the remarkable spirit of the man I met, his resiliency, his warmth and good humour, and his quiet courage. His character, as much as his experience, inspired me to write his story. Des and I both hope it will be an inspiration, as well as a valuable personal and historical record of a child of war.

Susan McCabe
February 2010

The Woodford Family (circa 1948) with a teenaged Des and his long-awaited sister Anne, born after liberation.

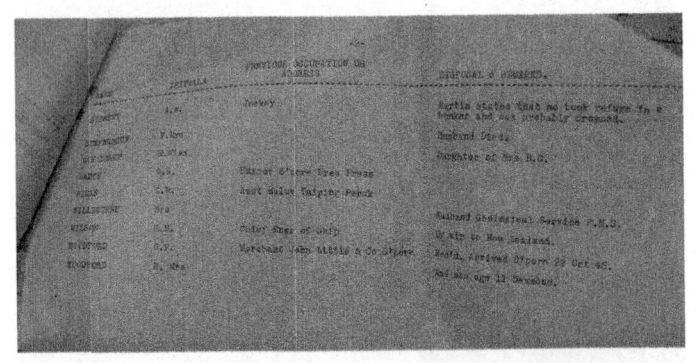

A page from a list of passengers on the Giang Bee's fateful voyage. The Woodfords' names are shown along with the fate (if known) of some others on board. It was estimated that of the 300 people on board, 230 perished.

Des and his beautiful wife Gillian, whose late sister Betty was also held captive along with Rosie and Des in the women's internment camps of Indonesia.